The Romantic Tradition in American Literature

The Romantic Tradition in American Literature

Advisory Editor

HAROLD BLOOM
Professor of English, Yale University

POETRY

LYRICAL, NARRATIVE, AND SATIRICAL

OF

THE CIVIL WAR

SELECTED AND EDITED

BY RICHARD GRANT WHITE

ARNO PRESS
A NEW YORK TIMES COMPANY
New York • 1972

Reprint Edition 1972 by Arno Press Inc.

Reprinted from a copy in The University
of Illinois Library

The Romantic Tradition in American Literature
ISBN for complete set: 0-405-04620-0
See last pages of this volume for titles.

Manufactured in the United States of America

ᖇᖇᖇᖇᖇᖇᖇᖇᖇ

Library of Congress Cataloging in Publication Data

White, Richard Grant, 1821-1885, comp.
    Poetry, lyrical, narrative, and satirical, of the
Civil War.

    (The Romantic tradition in American literature)
    Reprint of the 1866 ed.
    1.   United States--History--Civil War--Poetry.
I. Title. II. Series.
E647.W58 1972   811'.4'0803   72-4981
ISBN 0-405-04650-2

POETRY

LYRICAL, NARRATIVE, AND SATIRICAL

OF

THE CIVIL WAR

SELECTED AND EDITED

By RICHARD GRANT WHITE

NEW YORK
THE AMERICAN NEWS COMPANY
119 & 121 NASSAU STREET
1866

PREFACE.

———♦———

IT is generally true that great events do not inspire great poems. Upon the Reformation, the Cromwellian Rebellion, the French Revolution, our own War of Independence, nothing important and enduring has been written in verse. Barlow's " Columbiad " is a fair type of the poetry produced upon such subjects. There is little hope for a poem, if the poet trusts for the interest of his work to the dignity of his theme. To the poet pertains the power of elevating his subject ; nay, the very essence of his poetry is in that elevation, — in his adding himself to his subject. The choice of a great event as the theme for a poem is unwise, because the poet can hardly fail to fall short of the mental elevation produced by the relation of such an event in simple prose. He will find himself compelled to assume the position of a decorator rather than that of a creator ; and his decorations will only call attention to their littleness and the grandeur of the reality to which they have been appended. The " Iliad," and the " Gerusalemme Liberata," are not exceptions to this rule ; and the " Paradise Lost " may be one only in seeming. It was no mere poetical formula, that prayer of Milton's that he might have strength to rise to the height of his great argument; and with all the beauty and nobility of thought and sustained power in his chief epic, another generation must pass ere it can be safely said that the fame which he owes to the criticism of the Queen Anne school of literature will endure in its present proportions, and that he did indeed soar high enough to be above his theme. And unless he did so, the chief merit of his poem is not in its poetry, which is his, but in the facts narrated in it, which he derived from others. " The Iliad " is a marked instance of the power of a poet's genius to aggrandize the subject of his song. The bloody strife between the chiefs of a few petty semi-barbarous tribes about a wanton woman have been made by the genius of Homer to assume such dignity and proportion that for centuries they have filled the minds of men as the ideal of great and martial enterprise ; and two little streams that would hardly more than turn a village mill, and which are associated with no event or function so important to mankind, (unlike the Jordan or the Rubicon, for instance,) have a place in the world's memory unequalled by that of rivers that have fertilized half a continent, and have been for centuries the highways of commerce and the channels of civilization.

But although great poems are rarely inspired by great events, in modern days the feelings of civilized people in periods of national peril or great political excitement have generally found expression in verse, which has not only an historical value as a contemporary record, but a peculiar and sometimes a very high value as poetical literature. The ballads and lyrical pieces that were written during the civil wars of our forefathers in England, during the Scotch civil wars, the British Revolution of 1688, in France during the war of the Fronde, and during the great Revolution and its successors, not only tell us of the actors in those scenes, what they did, and how their souls were stirred by the events which passed before them, but they have an intrinsic poetical charm which pertains to every elevated and skilful rhythmical expression of human experience or emotion. The struggle which has just decided that the Anglo-American commonwealths lying between the Great Lakes and the Gulf of Mexico form one republic and not thirty-six, or even two, and which, beginning in a determination on one side that slavery should be, and on the other that it should not be propagated, ended in the utter demolition of the original bone of contention, has been remarkably fruitful of what in the last generation was well styled occasional poetry. It was inevitable that it should be so, from the education of the people who were the actors in the strife, from their general ability, not only to write and read, but to express themselves with readiness, and from their acquaintance with the rich poetical literature of their

mother tongue. And as in no other war that ever
was fought were there among the actual combatants,
the rank and file, and among their mothers, wives,
and daughters, so many persons capable of writing,
so of no other war are there such voluminous con-
temporary records, in verse as well as in prose, writ-
ten by those who could say, with Virgil's hero, that,
either in action or in suffering, they were part of
what they told.

From as much of the mass thus produced as I
could gather for examination, I have selected for this
volume all that appeared worthy of preservation on
any account. In the making of this selection poet-
ical merit has not been the only consideration.
Verses which celebrated at all worthily, or with spirit,
any important event in the war, — which expressed
truthfully any mood of popular feeling, or which em-
bodied any type of character, whether enduring or the
transitory creation of the circumstances of the day, —
have been deemed peculiarly fit for this collection, al-
though merely for their intrinsic excellence they might
not be worthy of permanent preservation. No poem of
conspicuous worth elicited by the war will be found
lacking in these pages ; but some of moderate merit
have been omitted in favor of others of no greater po-
etical value, because from their subject, or from their
embodiment of character or revelation of feeling, the
latter presented claims not found in the former. Nor
have I been at all fastidious as to the quarter in which

I looked for this poetry, or as to the subjects of the verses. In the formation of a volume which aims to be a poetical reflex of the mind of a whole people under the excitement of a war lasting four years, fastidiousness in these respects would be much out of place. I have looked through the street ballads as well as the monthly magazines, and have taken as readily what was printed upon a broadside, or written for negro minstrels, as what came from Bryant, Longfellow, Lowell, or Boker. Consequently there may be found among these poems pieces which some readers will pronounce decidedly vulgar, and others which will be thought objectionable by other readers because of the views they express on public affairs, or of their estimates of public characters. As to the question of vulgarity, that I shall leave to be settled by the genteel people who may be offended; as to the other point, I will only say that this collection would not have been worthy of the attention which I hope it may receive, if it did not contain somewhat of which I cannot approve myself. For example, I have read all that I could discover of the war-poetry written by the confederated enemies of my government, and have preserved here all that in the most catholic spirit I deemed of any intrinsic merit or incidental interest. It was my original purpose to embody this with the substance of the volume, giving each piece its place in the order of time; but finding so little of this poetry which possessed any kind of interest, instead of scattering it sparsely through the collection, I have put it by itself in an appendix. The secessionists fought much better than they wrote ; and it is worthy of remark that the best poem on their side, " The Confederate Flag," was published in a New York newspaper, " The Freeman's Journal." When they next fight, — may it be long ere then, and may we stand together ! — they will fight as well, and write better, and in a better cause. Aside, moreover, from the sentiment which they express or their poetical merits, there is undoubtedly a quality in certain songs which insures popularity, and which seems to be a certain rhythm, or *lilt*, which seizes upon the memory and bewitches without always pleasing the ear ; and I have not passed over compositions of which this was the only merit. It may be that some people complacently thought, as they listened to that nonsensical farrago, " Old John Brown," that here was proof that " the great popular heart of this country beat in unison the impulses of humanity toward universal freedom." But the truth was that the alternate jig and swing of the air caused it to stick in the uneducated ear as burrs stick to a blackberry girl. Evidence of this appears in the fact that the song, already unheard and passing rapidly into oblivion with us, is now just as popular in London as it ever was here. The " Pall Mall Gazette " of October 14th, 1865, tells us that " the street boys of London," not, it may perhaps be safely assumed, from views of broad philanthropy

have decided in its favor against " My Maryland," and
" The Bonnie Blue Flag." The " Gazette " goes on to
say that " the great Federal war-song [meaning ' Old
" John Brown '] is the favorite of the *people*, — of
" those who sing in the highways. The somewhat
" lugubrious refrain — ' Glory, glory, hallelujah ! ' —
" has excited their admiration to a wonderful degree,
" and almost threatens to extinguish that hard-worked,
" exquisite effort of modern minstrelsy, — ' Slap Bang.'
" The slight flavor of blasphemy which ' Old John
" Brown ' contains does not apparently give any offence
" to the popular appetite, — rather the contrary effect
" is observable." When neither patriotic nor party
feeling is involved, and the question is between Glory
Hallelujah ! and Slap Bang ! and the doxology carries
the day, we need be in no doubt as to the reason for
the preference.

The poetry elicited by any civil war is found either
to relate the events of the war or the acts of person-
ages more or less distinguished in it, and so to be in
the nature of the ballad, — to describe or celebrate
some character or type individual brought by the war
into prominence, — to express the feelings of the par-
tisans, — or to attack one side or the other with ridi-
cule and satire. Our civil war did not fail to produce
poetical compositions having all these motives, although
it was inevitable that in our case, as in others, many
of them partook in such a marked degree of the
characteristics of two classes that they could not with

propriety be assigned to either. Such is the first
piece in this volume, " Brother Jonathan's Lament
for Sister Caroline," in which Dr. Holmes gave ex-
pression to the feeling throughout the North on the
passage of the so-called secession ordinance by South
Carolina, and with certain foreknowledge told, not
only the consequences of that act to our " wayward
sister," but the spirit in which she would be received
in her time of suffering and her sorrow, if not her re-
pentance, — such are " The Flag," by Mr. Woodman,
" The Present' Crisis," by Mr. Lowell, and " On the
Hill before Centreville," which not only tells vividly
the story of the battle of Bull Run, but puts in living
lines the shame and the anguish which overwhelmed
us upon hearing of the senseless panic which closed
that battle ; although now, understanding the vicissi-
tudes of that day and knowing the fortunes of war
better, we can hold up our heads while we talk of the
behavior of our raw, peacefully-bred soldiers, even on
that disastrous occasion. Such also is Mr. Stedman's
" Wanted — A Man," which embodies the mingled
sickness of heart and suppressed wrath which, justly
or unjustly, filled people's souls at the events of the
battle summer of 1862. The poems by Mr. Long-
fellow and Mr. Boker upon the unflinching contest
of the *Cumberland* with her invulnerable assailant,
and Lieutenant Brownell's " River Fight," and " Bay
Fight," Mr. Whittier's " Barbara Fritchie," with many
others in the collection, are almost purely narrative in

character, and may be regarded as ballads. In some
of them the simplicity of the narration and the men-
tion of the names of the actors give great vitality to
the composition. This is particularly the case with
" Barbara Fritchie," which is interesting no less for its
portrait of Stonewall Jackson than for its celebration
of its heroine, and its description of the stirring inci-
dent to which, as it has been told by Mr. Whittier,
she will owe an enduring fame. The rebel " Stone-
wall Jackson's Way " is a very spirited, and, it would
seem, faithful piece of figure-painting somewhat of the
same kind. And what an air of truth, and a pres-
ence of real flesh and blood, is given to Mr. Brownell's
descriptions by his telling, with their deeds, the names
of Admiral Farragut's subordinates, — Craven and
Drayton, Bell and Bailey, Kimberly, Marchand, and
Strong, and Jouett, the mate of the flag-ship. In Mr.
Bayard Taylor's " Chicago Surrender," written imme-
diately upon the adjournment of the Chicago Conven-
tion, we have a reflex of the feeling which the pro-
ceedings of that assembly excited throughout the Free
States; a feeling which, enduring in spite of all the
claims of party interests, and the effect of party dis-
cipline, manifested itself in a manner unprecedented
in the election which this convention assembled to
carry. Therefore the presence of that poem in such
a collection is insured in spite of a palpable plagia-
rism in the first stanza from Mr. Dickens, speaking in
the person of his own creature, Elijah Pogram ; — a

slip the more surprising, even in this fugitive compo-
sition, as Mr. Taylor shows us his best points, sim-
plicity and manliness of style, when he is writing
verse.   In such pieces as Lieutenant De Forest's
" In Louisiana, " we get clear glimpses of the country
over which this great struggle raged for four long
years ; and appearing in Mr. Whittier's " At Port
Royal," and Mrs. Gray's " Fisherman of Beaufort,"
and one or two other pieces of lighter character, the
negro, " *causa teterrima hujus belli,*" occupies his
subordinate, though important place, upon the scene
which his inherited captivity has deluged with frater-
nal blood.

Of the pictures of life and character in these poems
a striking specimen is " The Brier-Wood Pipe," in
which that singular worthy, the New York volunteer
fireman, appears drawn to the life.   This sketch is
the more valuable because the subject of it has now
vanished into the past ; his life having ended with,
although not because of, the war, his behavior in which,
in his collective capacity, did not justify all the expec-
tations of his friends.   Other compositions of this kind
are " Uncle Sam," and " The Bounty Jumper," both
of which, even if the " Brier-Wood Pipe " escapes,
will be voted exceedingly low by certain people.

It would have been strange, indeed, if the position
taken by the British Government and the bulk of the
British governing classes toward our republic, as soon
as it seemed to them that there was a fair chance, if

the rebellion were nursed, that we might be destroyed,* being, as it was, the mere supplement of two defeated attempts at oppression, and sixty years of continued insult, had not produced a feeling which sought expression in satire and invective. And here again Mr. Whittier and Mr. Lowell speak for their countrymen just as we would have them speak. The spirit which produced " Punch's Run from Manassas Junction " meets its proper rebuke in the address " To Englishmen," and gets a Roland for its Oliver in Mr. Lowell's " Jonathan to John." But the " New Song to an Old Tune " tells the whole truth upon this subject. Our British cousins who continually speak as if the feeling which their conduct has awakened in this country

* This is no supposition based upon a mere concurrence of events which might have been fortuitous. Half this volume might be filled with extracts from British newspapers, vituperating " the slaveholders " without measure, when it was thought that their rebellion was only strong enough to derange trade and hinder the export of cotton, and the pages of *Punch* (Britannia's rose-tinted mirror) will be found full at this period of savage ridicule of the secessionists. But when it appeared that there really was a chance for the destruction of the great republic, how sudden and how shameless was the change! One candid Briton, who has since seen the error of his ways, said to me, frankly, " There's no use lying about it and denying that we all felt a secret satisfaction at the possible destruction of a successful rebel against the British government, and a great commercial and manufacturing rival." And Mr. Rosetti, a British painter and writer of repute, writing in the *Atlantic* magazine upon British feeling in regard to our war, says: " The first of the four motives in question . . . and by far the most powerful of all: The English as a nation dislike the Americans as a nation. . . . The second is a natural, though assuredly not a laudable feeling, — the residual soreness left by our defeat in the old American War of Independence."

were a new one, or at least had its source in the
events of the present day, and as if what they call
the Trent outrage were without a precedent, and also
as if we were always eager for a quarrel with them,
would do well to read the unpretending production
of this anonymous parodist, and then take the little
trouble that will be needful to discover, if they do not
know already, the facts about this matter.

Perhaps the most interesting of these little poems
are those which express the feelings and emotions of
the actors and sufferers in the struggle, and portray
the various phases of our social and political life
during those four years of eventful memory. The
variety of these is very great, and their general faith-
fulness to fact very noteworthy. From Mr. Cutler's
" Lullaby," so simple, so tender, and so true, that it
seems hardly more than a literal record of what must
have been sung in twilight hours by thousands of sad-
hearted women in farmsteads and cities the country
over, to Lieutenant Realf's " Io Triumphe ! " in
which the whole nation's faith and hope, repentance
and rejoicing, struggle into words that, in their alternate
pause and rush, reflect the turbulence of the time, —
from the cry, in " The Potomac, 1861," of the girl
bereaved of her lover, to the " Horatian Ode," in
which Mr. Stoddard tells, in prolonged but well-sus-
tained quatrains, the style of which smacks rather of
England in the first quarter of the seventeenth cen-
tury than of Rome in the first, a people's sober, deco-

rous grief at the violent death of Abraham Lincoln,
the gradation is full and perfect.   No man, no woman,
lacks a representative voice, and it would seem that
no passing emotion, more than any abiding sentiment,
fails of expression.   How unexaggerated in all their
strength most of these poems now are seen to be by
us !   The writers seem to have found in their imagi-
nations the real facts, and in their fancies the words
that most truthfully expressed them.   Even the ter-
rible threat which closes General Lander's " Rhode
Island to the South," and which might have been not
without reason looked upon by a mere spectator of the
struggle as a poetical hyperbole pushed to the verge
of extravagance, proved to be hardly more than a
literal announcement of what was to happen.   And
yet, striking as are such utterances (and there are
others like this) of a determination to maintain the
republic at whatever cost of life, there is throughout
these compositions a notable absence of sanguinary or
revengeful feeling, or even of hatred, — a negative
trait rendered the more remarkable by the single
manifestation of that feeling among the many loyal
pieces, and its frequent recurrence among the few
written by rebel pens.   Coming under this class, and
yet having characteristic traits of their own, are the
poems which paint the home life and the daily trials
of the people that furnished the volunteer soldiers
who did the fighting of this war.   Such are " Driv-
ing Home the Cows," " A Woman's Waiting," " The

Song of the Camps," " After All," and " The Heart
of the War." No painted picture, no long-drawn de-
scription, could give a more faithful and vivid por-
traiture of rural life in the Free States during the
war than these compositions, and some others like
them, scattered through this volume, — most of them
anonymous, and written for the columns of a news-
paper or a magazine by people who lived among the
scenes which they describe. " Driving Home the
Cows " might be called as faithful as a photograph,
were it not that in addition to its faithfulness it tells
a tale that can only be told by human lips, and em-
bodies a feeling that will only take form under the
touch of human hands. It is noteworthy that the
rebel poetry furnishes no corresponding pictures of
life and character in whatever class. I have looked
for them in vain.

Whether we have reason to be proud or ashamed
of the poetry produced by our civil war, — most of it
written by unpractised hands,— it will be for each reader
to decide for himself after perusal of this volume ; but
this I may venture to say from knowledge, that these
poems being arranged in the order of time, the book
tells the story of the war like a rhymed chronicle.

My thanks are due to the authors of many of the
following poems for permission that they should ap-
pear in these pages. Some are printed without such
permission, because I knew not where or how to
address their authors, and others because they had

been already so often quoted as to be almost common property. My acknowledgments are also due to the proprietors of " Harpers' Magazine," " Harpers' Weekly Journal," and the " Atlantic Monthly " magazine, for permission to make selections from their pages ; and to those useful collections, Mr. Frank Moore's " Rebellion Record," and Littell's " Living Age," I am also indebted. Many of the compositions — of those owned by their authors as well as of those which have remained anonymous — I have been unable to trace to papers in which they first appeared.

R. G. W.

CONTENTS.

CONTENTS.

APPENDIX.

BROTHER JONATHAN'S LAMENT FOR SISTER CAROLINE.*

BY OLIVER WENDELL HOLMES.

SHE has gone, — she has left us in passion and pride,—
Our stormy-browed sister, so long at our side !
She has torn her own star from our firmament's glow,
And turned on her brother the face of a foe !

O Caroline, Caroline, child of the sun,
We can never forget that our hearts have been one, —
Our foreheads both sprinkled in Liberty's name,
From the fountain of blood with the finger of flame !

You were always too ready to fire at a touch ;
But we said, " She is hasty, — she does not mean much."
We have scowled, when you uttered some turbulent threat ;
But Friendship still whispered, " Forgive and forget ! "

Has our love all died out ?   Have its altars grown cold ?
Has the curse come at last which the fathers foretold ?
Then Nature must teach us the strength of the chain
That her petulant children would sever in vain.

They may fight till the buzzards are gorged with their spoil.
Till the harvest grows black as it rots in the soil,

---

* Written upon the announcement of the passage of the " Ordi-
nance of Secession," on the 20th of December, 1860, by the Con-
vention of South Carolina, the first State which attempted to secede

1

Till the wolves and the catamounts troop from their caves,
And the shark tracks the pirate, the lord of the waves:

In vain is the strife!   When its fury is past,
Their fortunes must flow in one channel at last,
As the torrents that rush from the mountains of snow
Roll mingled in peace through the valleys below.

Our Union is river, lake, ocean, and sky:
Man breaks not the medal, when God cuts the die!
Though darkened with sulphur, though cloven with steel,
The blue arch will brighten, the waters will heal!

O Caroline, Caroline, child of the sun,
There are battles with Fate that can never be won!
The star-flowering banner must never be furled,
For its blossoms of light are the hope of the world!

Go, then, our rash sister! afar and aloof, —
Run wild in the sunshine, away from our roof;
But when your heart aches and your feet have grown sore,
Remember the pathway that leads to our door!

Atlantic Monthly.

———◆———

A PSALM OF THE UNION.

I.

GOD of the Free! upon thy breath
   Our flag is for the Right unrolled;
Still broad and brave as when its stars
   First crowned the hallowed time of old:
For Honor still its folds shall fly,
   For Duty still their glories burn,

Where Truth, Religion, Freedom guard
  The patriot's sword and martyr's urn.
    Then shout beside thine oak, O North!
      O South! wave answer with thy palm;
    And in our Union's heritage
      Together lift the Nation's psalm!

II.

How glorious is our mission here!
  Heirs of a virgin world are we;
The chartered lords whose lightnings tame
  The rocky mount and roaring sea:
We march, and Nature's giants own
  The fetters of our mighty cars;
We look, and lo! a continent
  Is crouched beneath the Stripes and Stars!
    Then shout beside thine oak, O North!
      O South! wave answer with thy palm;
    And in our Union's heritage
      Together lift the Nation's psalm!

III.

No tyrant's impious step is ours;
  No lust of power on nations rolled:
Our Flag — for friends a starry sky,
  For foes a tempest every fold!
Oh! thus we'll keep our nation's life,
  Nor fear the bolt by despots hurled:
The blood of all the world is here,
  And they who strike us, strike the world.
    Then shout beside thine oak, O North!
      O South! wave answer with thy palm;
    And in our Union's heritage
      Together lift the Nation's psalm!

IV.

God of the Free! our Nation bless
  In its strong manhood as its birth;

And make its life a Star of Hope
  For all the struggling of the Earth :
Thou gav'st the glorious Past to us ;
  Oh ! let our Present burn as bright,
And o'er the mighty Future cast
  Truth's, Honor's, Freedom's holy light!
    Then shout beside thine oak, O North !
      O South ! wave answer with thy palm ;
    And in our Union's heritage
      Together lift the Nation's psalm !

        Harpers' Monthly, December, 1861.

GOD FOR OUR NATIVE LAND.

BY REV. G. W. BETHUNE, D. D.

God's blessing be upon
  Our own, our native land !
The land our fathers won
  By the strong heart and hand,
  The keen axe and the brand,
When they felled the forest's pride,
And the tyrant foe defied,
The free, the rich, the wide :
  God for our native land !

Up with the starry sign,
  The red stripes and the white !
Where'er its glories shine,
  In peace, or in the fight,
  We own its high command ;
For the flag our fathers gave,
O'er our children's heads shall wave,
And their children's children's grave !
  God for our native land !

Who doth that flag defy,
  We challenge as our foe ;
Who will not for it die,
  Out from us he must go !
    So let them understand.
Who that dear flag disclaim,
Which won their fathers' fame,
We brand with endless shame!
    God for our native land !

Our native land ! to thee,
  In one united vow,
To keep thee strong and free,
  And glorious as now —
    We pledge each heart and hand ;
By the blood our fathers shed,
By the ashes of our dead,
By the sacred soil we tread !
    God for our native land !

—◆—

THE FLAG.*

BY HORATIO WOODMAN.

WHY flashed that flag on Monday morn
  Across the startled sky ?
Why leapt the blood to every cheek,
  The tears to every eye ?

* Fort Sumter, after being occupied by Major Anderson four months with ninety men, was evacuated after bombardment on Saturday, April 14th, 1861. On the following Monday, as if by one consent, the flag of the Republic was raised throughout the Free States, so that wherever the eye turned the national colors were in sight; and the demand for flags was so great that the price of bunting quadrupled in a few days.

The hero in our four months' woe,
  The symbol of our might,
Together sunk for one brief hour,
  To rise forever bright.

The mind of Cromwell claimed his own,
  The blood of Naseby streamed
Through hearts unconscious of the fire
  Till that torn banner gleamed.
The seeds of Milton's lofty thoughts,
  All hopeless of the spring,
Broke forth in joy, as through them glowed
  The life great poets sing.

Old Greece was young, and Homer true,
  And Dante's burning page
Flamed in the red along our flag,
  And kindled holy rage.
God's Gospel cheered the sacred cause,
  In stern, prophetic strain,
Which makes His Right our covenant,
  His Psalms our deep refrain.

Oh, sad for him whose light went out
  Before this glory came,
Who could not live to feel his kin
  To every noble name;
And sadder still to miss the joy
  That twenty millions know,
In Human Nature's Holiday,
  From all that makes life low.

Boston Transcript, April, 1861.

APOCALYPSE.*

BY CLARENCE BUTLER.

STRAIGHT to his heart the bullet crushed,
Down from his breast the red blood gushed,
And o'er his face a glory rushed.

A sudden spasm rent his frame,
And in his ears there went and came
A sound as of devouring flame.

Which in a moment ceased, and then
The great light clasped his brows again,
So that they shone like Stephen's, when

Saul stood apart a little space,
And shook with shuddering awe to trace
God's splendor settling o'er his face.

Thus, like a king, erect in pride,
Raising his hands to heaven, he cried,
" All hail the Stars and Stripes !" and died.

Died grandly; but, before he fell,
(O blessedness ineffable !)
Vision apocalyptical

Was granted to him, and his eyes,
All radiant with glad surprise,
Looked forward through the centuries,

---

* After the bombardment and evacuation of Fort Sumter, the
6th Regiment of Massachusetts militia was the first that moved to
the defence of Washington. It was attacked on the 19th of April
by a mob in the streets of Baltimore, and two of its members
killed and eight wounded; one of the former, Luther C. Ladd,
cheered the flag with his dying breath.

And saw the seeds that sages cast
In the world's soil in cycles past,
Spring up and blossom at the last:

Saw how the souls of men had grown,
And where the scythes of Truth had mown,
Clear space for Liberty's white throne ;

Saw how, by sorrow tried and proved,
The last dark stains had been removed
Forever from the land he loved.

Saw Treason crushed, and Freedom crowned,
And clamorous faction gagged and bound,
Gasping its life out on the ground ;

While over all his country's slopes
Walked swarming troops of cheerful hopes,
Which evermore to broader scopes

Increased, with power that comprehends
The world's weal in its own, and bends
Self-needs to large, unselfish ends.

Saw how, throughout the vast extents
Of earth's most populous continents,
She dropped such rare heart-affluence,

That, from beyond the farthest seas,
The wondering peoples thronged to seize
Her proffered pure benignities ;

And how, of all her trebled host
Of widening empires, none could boast
Whose strength or love was uppermost,

Because they grew so equal there
Beneath the flag, which, *debonnaire*,
Waved joyous in the golden air;

Wherefore the martyr, gazing clear
Beyond the gloomy atmosphere
Which shuts us in with doubt and fear, —

He, marking how her high increase
Ran greatening in perpetual lease
Through balmy years of odorous peace,

Greeted, in one transcendent cry
Of intense, passionate ecstacy,
The sight that thrilled him utterly:

Saluting, with most proud disdain
Of murder and of mortal pain,
The vision which shall be again.

So, lifted with prophetic pride,
Raised conquering hands to heaven, and cried,
"All hail the Stars and Stripes!" and died.

THE MASSACHUSETTS LINE.

BY ROBERT LOWELL.

AIR: — " *Yankee Doodle.*"

I.

STILL first, as long and long ago,
  Let Massachusetts muster;
Give her the post right next the foe;
  Be sure that you may trust her.

She was the first to give her blood
    For freedom and for honor;
She trod her soil to crimson mud:
    God's blessing be upon her!

II.

She never faltered for the right,
    Nor ever will hereafter;
Fling up her name with all your might,
    Shake roof-tree and shake rafter.
But of old deeds she need not brag,
    How she broke sword and fetter;
Fling out again the old striped flag!
    She 'll do yet more and better.

III.

In peace her sails fleck all the seas,
    Her mills shake every river;
And where are scenes so fair as these
    God and her true hands give her?
Her claim in war who seek to rob?
    All others come in later; —
Hers first it is to front the Mob,
    The Tyrant and the Traitor.

IV.

God bless, God bless the glorious State!
    Let her have her way to battle!
She 'll go where batteries crash with fate,
    Or where thick rifles rattle.
Give her the Right, and let her try,
    And then, who can, may press her;
She 'll go straight on, or she will die;
    God bless her! and God bless her!

Duanesburgh, May 7, 1861.

OUR COUNTRY'S CALL.

BY WILLIAM CULLEN BRYANT.

LAY down the axe, fling by the spade :
　Leave in its track the toiling plough ;
The rifle and the bayonet-blade
　For arms like yours were fitter now ;
And let the hands that ply the pen
　Quit the light task, and learn to wield
The horseman's crooked brand, and rein
　The charger on the battle-field.

Our country calls ; away ! away !
　To where the blood-stream blots the green.
Strike to defend the gentlest sway
　That Time in all his course has seen.
See, from a thousand coverts — see
　Spring the armed foes that haunt her track ;
They rush to smite her down, and we
　Must beat the banded traitors back.

Ho ! sturdy as the oaks ye cleave,
　And moved as soon to fear and flight,
Men of the glade and forest ! leave
　Your woodcraft for the field of fight.
The arms that wield the axe must pour
　An iron tempest on the foe ;
His serried ranks shall reel before
　The arm that lays the panther low.

And ye who breast the mountain storm
　By grassy steep or highland lake,
Come, for the land ye love, to form
　A bulwark that no foe can break.

Stand, like your own gray cliffs that mock
  The whirlwind; stand in her defence:
The blast as soon shall move the rock,
  As rushing squadrons bear ye thence.

And ye, whose homes are by her grand
  Swift rivers, rising far away,
Come from the depth of her green land
  As mighty in your march as they;
As terrible as when the rains
  Have swelled them over bank and bourne,
With sudden floods to drown the plains
  And sweep along the woods uptorn.

And ye who throng beside the deep,
  Her ports and hamlets of the strand,
In number like the waves that leap
  On his long murmuring marge of sand,
Come, like that deep, when o'er his brim
  He rises, all his floods to pour,
And flings the proudest barks that swim
  A helpless wreck against his shore.

Few, few were they whose swords of old
  Won the fair land in which we dwell;
But we are many, we who hold
  The grim resolve to guard it well.
Strike for that broad and goodly land
  Blow after blow, till men shall see
That Might and Right move hand in hand,
  And glorious must their triumph be.

UNITED STATES NATIONAL ANTHEM.

BY WILLIAM ROSS WALLACE.

GOD of the Free! upon Thy breath
  Our Fag is for the Right unrolled
As broad and brave as when its Stars
  First lit the hallowed time of old.

For Duty still its folds shall fly,
  For Honor still its glories burn,
Where Truth, Religion, Valor, guard
  The patriot's sword and martyr's urn.

No tyrant's impious step is ours;
  No lust of power on nations rolled:
Our Flag — for *friends*, a starry sky;
  For *traitors*, storm in every fold.

O, thus we 'll keep our Nation's life,
  Nor fear the bolt by despots hurled;
The blood of all the world is here,
  And they who strike us strike the world!

God of the Free! our Nation bless
  In its strong manhood as its birth;
And make its life a Star of Hope
  For all the struggling of the earth.

Then shout beside thine Oak, O North!
  O South, wave answer with thy Palm!
And in our Union's heritage
  Together sing the Nation's Psalm!

THE SEVENTH.*

BY FITZJAMES O'BRIEN.

AIR — "*Gilla Machree.*"

I.

Och! we're the boys
That hearts desthroys
Wid making love and fighting;
We take a fort,
The girls we court,
But most the last delight in.
To fire a gun,
Or raise some fun,
To us is no endeavor;
So let us hear
One hearty cheer —
The Seventh's lads forever!
Chorus — For we're the boys
That hearts desthroys,
Wid making love and fighting;
We take a fort,
The girls we court,
But most the last delight in.

---

* The Seventh Regiment New York Militia left the city of New York, on its way to the defence of the National Capital, April 19th, 1861. The news of the attack upon the Sixth Massachusetts reached the city just before they left their armory. No one who was in the city at that time will ever forget the excitement, solemn, tender, and enthusiastic, in the midst of which this favorite regiment set out upon a march which it was supposed would be bloody, and which proved to be eventful. A prolonged cry, which seemed to be both cheer and wail, accompanied every step of its march down Broadway. War was new to us then. In the event this regiment never went into action as a body; but its highly disciplined ranks furnished more officers than came from any other to the national army. The above lines were written by a young Irishman, one of its members.

II.

There 's handsome Joe,
Whose constant flow
Of merriment unfailing,
Upon the tramp,
Or in the camp,
Will keep our hearts from ailing.
And B—— and Chat.,
Who might have sat
For Pythias and Damon,
Och! whin they get
Their heavy wet,
They get as high as Haman.
For we 're the boys
That hearts desthroys, &c.

III.

Like Jove above
We 're fond of love,
But fonder still of victuals;
Wid turtle-steaks
An' cod-fish cakes
We always fills our kittles.
To dhrown aich dish
We dhrinks like fish,
And mum 's the word we utther;
An' thin we swill
Our Léoville,
That oils our throats like butther.
For we 're the boys
That hearts desthroys, &c.

IV.

We make from hay
A splindid tay,
From beans a gorgeous coffee;
Our crame is prime,
Wid chalk and lime —

In fact, 't is quite a throphy.
  Our chickens roast,
  Wid butthered toast,
I 'm sure would timpt St. Payther;
  Now you 'll declare
  Our bill of fare
It could n't be complayther.
      For we 're the boys
      That hearts desthroys, &c.

                v.

  Now silence all,
  While I recall
A memory sweet and tender;
  The maids and wives
  That light our lives
With deep, enduring splendor —
  We 'll give no cheer
  For those so dear,
But in our hearts we 'll bless them,
  And pray to-night,
  That angels bright
May watch them and caress them.
      For we 're the boys
      That hearts desthroys,
        Wid making love and fighting;
      We take a fort,
      The girls we court,
But most the last delight in.

SOUTH CAROLINA GENTLEMAN.

Air: — " *The Fine Old English Gentleman.*"

Down in a small Palmetto State the curious ones may
    find,
A ripping, tearing gentleman, of an uncommon kind,
A staggering, swaggering sort of chap, who takes his
    whiskey straight,
And frequently condemns his eyes to that ultimate ven-
    geance which a clergyman of high standing has
    assured must be a sinner's fate :
This South Carolina gentleman, one of the present time.

You trace his genealogy, and not far back you 'll see,
A most undoubted octoroon, or mayhap a mustee,
And if you note the shaggy locks that cluster on his
    brow,
You 'll find that every other hair is varied with a kink
    that seldom denotes pure Caucasian blood, but on
    the contrary betrays an admixture with a race
    not particularly popular now :
This South Carolina gentleman, one of the present time.

He always wears a full-dress coat, pre-Adamite in cut,
With waistcoat of the loudest style, through which his
    ruffles jut,
Six breastpins deck his horrid front, and on his fingers
    shine
Whole invoices of diamond rings which would hardly
    pass muster with the Original Jacobs in Chatham-
    street for jewels gen-u-ine :
This South Carolina gentleman, one of the present time.

He chews tobacco by the pound and spits upon the floor
If there is not a box of sand behind the nearest door,
2

And when he takes his weekly spree he clears a mighty
    track,
Of everything that bears the shape of whiskey-skin, gin
    and sugar, brandy sour, peach and honey, irre-
    pressible cock-tail rum, and gum, and luscious
    apple-jack:
This South Carolina gentleman, one of the present time.

He takes to euchre kindly, too, and plays an awful hand,
Especially when those he tricks his style don't under-
    stand,
And if he wins, why then he stoops to pocket all the
    stakes,
But if he loses, then he says to the unfortunate stranger
    who had chanced to win: " It 's my opinion you
    are a cursed abolitionist, and if you don't leave
    South Carolina in one hour you will be hung
    like a dog." But no offer to pay his loss he
    makes:
This South Carolina gentleman, one of the present time.

Of course he 's all the time in debt to those who credit
    give,
Yet manages upon the best the market yields to live ;
But if a Northern creditor asks him his bill to heed,
This honorable gentleman instantly draws two bowie-
    knives and a pistol, dons a blue cockade, and
    declares that in consequence of the repeated
    aggressions of the North, and its gross violations
    of the Constitution, he feels that it would utterly
    degrade him to pay any debt whatever, and that
    in fact he has at last determined to SECEDE :
This South Carolina gentleman, one of the present time.

ARMY HYMN.

BY OLIVER WENDELL HOLMES.

" *Old Hundred.*"

O LORD of Hosts! Almighty King!
Behold the sacrifice we bring!
To every arm Thy strength impart,
Thy spirit shed through every heart!

Wake in our breasts the living fires,
The holy faith that warmed our sires;
Thy hand hath made our Nation free:
To die for her is serving Thee.

Be Thou a pillared flame to show
The midnight snare, the silent foe;
And when the battle thunders loud,
Still guide us in its moving cloud.

God of all nations! Sovereign Lord!
In Thy dread name we draw the sword,
We lift the starry flag on high
That fills with light our stormy sky.

From Treason's rent, from Murder's stain,
Guard Thou its folds till Peace shall reign, —
Till fort and field, till shore and sea
Join our loud anthem, PRAISE TO THEE!

THE STARS AND STRIPES.

BY JAMES T. FIELDS.

RALLY round the flag, boys, —
  Give it to the breeze !
That's the banner we love
  On the land and seas.

Brave hearts are under it ;
  Let the *traitors* brag ;
Gallant lads, fire away !
  And fight for the flag.

Their flag is but a rag —
  Ours is the true one ;
Up with the Stars and Stripes !
  Down with the new one !

Let our colors fly, boys, —
  Guard them day and night ;
For victory is liberty,
  And God will bless the right.

———◆———

THE PRESENT CRISIS.

BY JAMES RUSSELL LOWELL.

WHEN a deed is done for Freedom, through the broad
    earth's aching breast
Runs a thrill of joy prophetic, trembling on from east to
    west ;
And the slave, where'er he cowers, feels the soul within
    him climb

To the awful verge of manhood, as the energy sublime
Of a century bursts full-blossomed on the thorny stem of
    Time.

Through the walls of hut and palace shoots the instan-
    taneous throe,
When the travail of the Ages wrings earth's systems to
    and fro;
At the birth of each new Era, with a recognizing start,
Nation wildly looks on nation, standing with mute lips
    apart,
And glad Truth's yet mightier man-child leaps beneath
    the Future's heart.

For mankind are one in spirit, and an instinct bears
    along,
Round the earth's electric circle, the swift flash of right
    or wrong;
Whether conscious or unconscious, yet humanity's vast
    frame,
Through its ocean-sundered fibres, feels the gush of joy
    or shame;
In the gain or loss of one race, all the rest have equal
    claim.

Once, to every man and nation, comes the moment to
    decide,
In the strife of Truth with Falsehood, for the good or
    evil side;
Some great cause, God's *new* Messiah, offering each the
    bloom or blight,
Parts the goats upon the left hand, and the sheep upon
    the right,
And the choice goes by forever 'twixt that darkness and
    that light.

Hast thou chosen, O my people, on whose party thou
    shalt stand,
Ere the Doom from its worn sandals shakes the dust
    against our land?
Though the cause of Evil prosper, yet 't is Truth alone
    is strong;
And albeit she wander outcast now, I see around her
    throng
Troops of beautiful, tall angels, to enshield her from all
    wrong.

We see dimly, in the Present, what is small and what is
    great;
Slow of faith how weak an arm may turn the iron helm
    of Fate;
But the soul is still oracular — amid the market's din,
List the ominous stern whisper from the Delphic cave
    within:
"They enslave their children's children who make com-
    promise with Sin!"

Slavery, the earth-born Cyclops, fellest of the giant
    brood,
Sons of brutish Force and Darkness, who have drenched
    the earth with blood,
Famished in his self-made desert, blinded by our purer day,
Gropes in yet unblasted regions for his miserable prey;
Shall we guide his gory fingers where our helpless children
    play?

'T is as easy to be heroes, as to sit the idle slaves
Of a legendary virtue carved upon our fathers' graves;
Worshippers of light ancestral make the present light a
    crime.
Was the Mayflower launched by cowards? — steered by
    men behind *their* time?
Turn those tracks toward Past, or Future, that make
    Plymouth Rock sublime?

They were men of *present* valor — stalwart old icono-
     clasts ;
Unconvinced by axe or gibbet that all virtue was the
     Past's ;
But we make *their* truth *our* falsehood, thinking that has
     made *us* free,
Hoarding it in mouldy parchments, while our tender
     spirits flee
The rude grasp of that great Impulse which drove *them*
     across the sea.

New occasions teach new duties ! Time makes ancient
     good uncouth ;
They must upward still, and onward, who would keep
     abreast of Truth ;
Lo, before us gleam her camp-fires ! we *ourselves* must
     Pilgrims be,
Launch *our* Mayflower, and steer boldly through the des-
     perate winter sea,
Nor attempt the Future's portal with the Past's blood-
     rusted key.

———◆———

THE TWO FURROWS.

BY C. H. WEBB.

THE spring-time came, but not with mirth ; —
     The banner of our trust,
And, with it, the best hopes of earth
     Were trailing in the dust.

The farmer saw the shame from far,
     And stopped his plough a-field ;
" Not the blade of peace, but the brand of war,
     This arm of mine must wield.

" When traitor hands that flag would stain,
   Their homes let women keep ;
Until its stars burn bright again,
   Let others sow and reap."

The farmer sighed — " A lifetime long
   The plough has been my trust ;
In truth it were an arrant wrong
   To leave it now to rust."

With ready strength the farmer tore
   The iron from the wood,
And to the village smith he bore
   That ploughshare stout and good.

The blacksmith's arms were bare and brown,
   And loud the bellows roared ;
The farmer flung his ploughshare down —
   " Now forge me out a sword ! "

And then a merry, merry chime
   The sounding anvil rung ;
Good sooth, it was a nobler rhyme
   Than ever poet sung.

The blacksmith wrought with skill that day ;
   The blade was keen and bright ;
And now, where thickest is the fray,
   The farmer leads the fight.

Not as of old that blade he sways,
   To break the meadow's sleep,
But through the rebel ranks he lays
   A furrow broad and deep.

The farmer's face is burned and brown,
   But light is on his brow ;

Right well he wots what blessings crown
   The furrow of the Plough.

"But better is to-day's success,"
   Thus ran the farmer's word;
"For nations yet unborn shall bless
   This furrow of the Sword."

Harpers' Weekly.

"OUT IN THE COLD."*

BY LUCY LARCOM.

WHAT is the threat? "Leave her out in the cold!"
Loyal New England, too loyally bold:
Hater of treason, — ah! that is her crime!
Lover of Freedom, — too true for her time!

Out in the cold? Oh, she chooses the place,
Rather than share in a sheltered disgrace;
Rather than sit at a cannibal feast;
Rather than mate with the blood-reeking beast!

Leave out New England? And what will she do,
Stormy-browed sisters, forsaken by you?
Sit on her Rock, her desertion to weep?
Or, like a Sappho, plunge thence in the deep?

No; our New England can put on no airs, —
Nothing will change the calm look that she wears:

---

* Among the many propositions for compromise after the outbreak of the rebellion, perhaps none was more persistently urged by a certain class of politicians than the formation of a new "Union," from which New England was to be excluded, — left out in the cold, was the phrase. The proposers forgot that New England had stretched westward along the banks of the Ohio to the Mississippi.

Life 's a rough lesson she learned from the first,
Up into wisdom through poverty nursed.

Not more distinct on his tables of stone
Was the grand writing to Moses made known,
Than is engraven, in letters of light,
On her foundations the One Law of Right.

She is a Christian : she smothers her ire,
Trims up the candle, and stirs the home fire ;
Thinking and working and waiting the day
When her wild sisters shall leave their mad play.

Out in the cold, where the free winds are blowing ;
Out in the cold, where the strong oaks are growing ;
Guards she all growths that are living and great, —
Growths to rebuild every tottering State.

" Notions " worth heeding to shape she has wrought,
Lifted and fixed on the granite of thought :
What she has done may the wide world behold !
What she is doing, too, out in the cold !

Out in the cold ! she is glad to be there,
Breathing the north wind, the clear healthful air ;
Saved from the hurricane passions that rend
Hearts that once named her a sister and friend.

There she will stay, while they bluster and foam,
Planning their comfort when they shall come home ;
Building the Union an adamant wall,
Freedom-cemented, that never can fall.

Freedom, — dear-bought with the blood of her sons, —
See the red current ! right nobly it runs !
Life of her life is not too much to give
For the dear Nation she taught how to live.

Vainly they shout to you, sturdy Northwest !
'T is her own heart that beats warm in your breast ;
Sisters in nature as well as in name ;
Sisters in loyalty, true to that claim.

Freedom your breath is, O broad-shouldered North !
Turn from the subtle miasma gone forth
Out of the South land, from Slavery's fen,
Battening demons, but poisoning men !

Still on your Rock, my New England, sit sure,
Keeping the air for the great country pure !
There you the " wayward " ones yet shall enfold :
There they will come to you, out in the cold !

Taunton Gazette.

HO! SONS OF THE PURITAN.

The Cavaliers, Jacobites, and Huguenots, who settled the South, naturally hate, condemn, and despise the Puritans who settled the North. The former are master races; the latter, a slave race, descendants of the Saxon serfs. — *De Bow's Review.**

> ——— who through a cloud,
> *Not of war only but detractions rude,*
> Guided by faith and matchless fortitude,
> To peace and truth thy glorious way hast ploughed.
> Milton's Sonnet to Cromwell.

Ho ! sons of the Puritan ! sons of the Roundhead,
   Leave your fields fallow and fly to the war ;
The foe is advancing, the trumpet hath sounded, —

---

* This nonsense had been so long talked and written in the Slave States before the rebellion, that many of the people there actually believed it, although the population of those States is as purely Anglo-Saxon as that of the Free States, or of England. The Huguenot blood at the South is so small in quantity as to be

To the rescue of freedom, truth, justice, and law!
    Hear His voice bid ye on
    Who spake unto Gideon:
    " Rend the curtains of Midian
    From Heshbon to Dor!"

From green-covered Chalgrave, from Naseby and Marston,
    Rich with the blood of the Earnest and True,
The war-cry of Freedom, resounding hath passed on
    The wings of two centuries, and come down to you:
    " Forward! to glory ye,
    Though the road gory be!
    Strong of arm — let your story be —
    And swift to pursue!"

List! list! to the time-honored voices that loudly
    Speak from our Mother-land o'er the sad waves, —
From Hampden's dead lips, and from Cromwell's who
    proudly
    Called freemen to palaces, tyrants to graves:
    " Sons of the Good and Pure!
    Let not their blood endure
    The attaint of a brood impure
    Of cowards and slaves!"

And old Massachusetts' hills echo the burden:
    " Sons of the Pure-in-heart never give o'er!
Though blood flow in rivers, and death be the guerdon,
    All the sharper your swords be, — death welcome the
    more!

of no account; and if there ever were a master-race, it is the
Anglo-Saxon, as every other which has been brought into contact
with it knows. And what shall be said of the ignorance that
could be presumed not to know that the Cavaliers were utterly
overthrown by the Puritans, and that the party which overcame
the Jacobites, and brought in William of Orange, and maintained
the new dynasty, was composed in great measure of the noblest
families in England?

Swear ye to sheathe your swords
Not till the heathen hordes
On their craven knees breathe the words,
   ' The Lord's we restore ! ' "

Accursed be the land that shall give ye cold greeting, —
   Cursed in its coffers, and cursed in its fame !
And woe to the traitors, feigning friendship and meeting
   Your trust with assassins' dark weapons of shame.
      As did Penuel's high
      Parapets lowly lie,
      And the Princes of Succoth die,
        So fare these the same !

Though sharp be the throes of these last tribulations,
   Look ye ! a brighter dawn kindles the day !
O, children of Saints, and the hope of the Nation,
   Look aloft ! your deliverance cometh for aye !
      Soon, from those fairer skies,
      White-winged, the herald flies
      To the warders of Paradise,
        To call them away !

Then on to the battle-shock ! and if in anguish,
   Gasping, and feeble-pulsed, low on the field,
Struck down by the traitor's fell prowess ye languish,
   In Jehovah behold ye your Refuge and Shield !
      Or, if in victory,
      Doubts shall come thick to ye,
      Trust in Him, — He shall speak to ye
        The mystery revealed.

Ho ! sons of the Puritan ! sons of the Roundhead,
   Leave your fields fallow, your ships at the shore !
The foe is advancing, the trumpet hath sounded,
   And the jaws of their Moloch are dripping with gore

Raise the old pennon's staff!
Let the fierce cannons laugh,
Till the votaries of Ammon's calf
  Blaspheme ye no more!

THE UNIVERSAL COTTON-GIN.

BY THE AUTHOR OF " COTTON STATES."

HE journeyed all creation through,
  A pedlar's wagon trotting in;
A haggard man of sallow hue,
Upon his nose the goggles blue,
And in his cart a model U-
    niversal nigger-cotton-gin-
    niversal nigger-cotton-gin.

His seedy garb was sad to view —
  Hard seemed the strait he 'd gotten in;
He plainly could n't boast a *sou*,
And meanly fared on water-gru-
el, or had swallowed whole a U-
    niversal nigger-cotton-gin-
    niversal nigger-cotton-gin.

To all he met — Turk, Christian, Jew —
  He meekly said, " I 'm not in tin;
In fact, I 'm in a serious stew,
And therefore offer unto you,
At half its worth, my model U-
    niversal nigger-cotton-gin-
    niversal nigger-cotton-gin.

" As sure as four is two and two,
  It rules the world we 're plotting in;

It made and ruined Yankee Doo-
dle, stuck to him like Cooper's glue,
And so to you would stick this U-
    niversal nigger-cotton-gin-
    niversal nigger-cotton-gin."

Now Johnny Bull the pedlar knew,
    And thus replied with not a grin :
" Hi loves yer ' gin' like London brew-
ed ale, but loathes the hinstitu-
tion vitch propels your model U-
    niversal nigger-cotton-gin-
    niversal nigger-cotton-gin.

" Hi know such coves as you a few,
    And, zur, just now, hi 'm not in tin ;
Hi tells you vot, great Yankee Doo-
dle might hincline to put me through,
Hif hi should buy your model U-
    niversal nigger-cotton-gin-
    niversal nigger-cotton-gin."

Then spoke smooth Monsieur *Parlez-vous*,
    Whose gilded throne was got in sin —
(As was he, too, if tales are true :)
" I does not vant your model U-"
(He sounds a V for a W)
    " niversal nigger-cotton-gin-
    niversal nigger-cotton-gin."

" A negar in de fence I view,
    Your grand machine he 's rotting in ;
I smells him now ; he stinketh — *w-h-e-w !*
Give me a good tobacco chew,
And you may keeps your model U-
    niversal nigger-cotton-gin-
    niversal nigger-cotton-gin."

The pedlar then sloped quickly to
        The land he was begotten in;
With woeful visage, feelings blue,
He sadly questioned what to do,
When none would buy his model U-
        niversal nigger-cotton-gin-
        niversal nigger-cotton-gin.

From out his pocket then he drew
        A rag that *blood* was clotting in;
It had a field of heavenly blue,
Was flecked with stars — the very few
That glimmered on his model U-
        niversal nigger-cotton-gin-
        niversal nigger-cotton-gin.

He gazed long on its tarnished hue,
        And mourned the fix he'd gotten in;
Then filled his eyes with contrite dew,
As in its folds his nose he blew,
And thus addressed his model U-
        niversal nigger-cotton-gin-
        niversal nigger-cotton-gin.

" Then, crownless king, thy days are few;
        The world thou art forgotten in;
Ere thou dost die, thy life review, —
Repent thy crimes, thy wrongs undo,
Give freedom to the dusky crew
Whose blood now stains the model U-
        niversal nigger-cotton-gin-
        niversal nigger-cotton-gin."

UPON THE HILL BEFORE CENTREVILLE.

July 21, 1861.*

BY GEORGE H. BOKER.

I 'LL tell you what I heard that day:
I heard the great guns, far away,
Boom after boom.   Their sullen sound
Shook all the shuddering air around;
And shook, ah me! my shrinking ear,
And downward shook the hanging tear
That, in despite of manhood's pride,
Rolled o'er my face, a scalding tide.
And then I prayed.   O God! I prayed,
As never stricken saint, who laid
His hot cheek to the holy tomb
Of Jesus, in the midnight gloom.

"What saw I?"   Little.   Clouds of dust;
Great squares of men, with standards thrust
Against their course; dense columns crowned
With billowing steel.   Then, bound on bound,
The long black lines of cannon poured
Behind the horses, streaked and gored
With sweaty speed.   Anon shot by,
Like a lone meteor of the sky,
A single horseman; and he shone
His bright face on me, and was gone.
All these with rolling drums, with cheers,

---

* The day of the battle of Bull Run, in which the reserve of
the Union Army rested upon Centreville. In regard to the mere
time at which it was written, this poem is here out of place, as will
be seen by an allusion toward its close. But it paints so faithfully
that disastrous, shameful day, and so truthfully expresses the feel-
ings which it roused throughout the Free States, that this is its
proper position.

3

With songs familiar to my ears,
Passed under the far-hanging cloud,
And vanished, and my heart was proud!

For mile on mile the line of war
Extended; and a steady roar,
As of some distant stormy sea,
On the south-wind came up to me.
And high in air, and over all,
Grew, like a fog, that murky pall,
Beneath whose gloom of dusty smoke
The cannon flamed, the bombshell broke,
And the sharp rattling volley rang,
And shrapnel roared, and bullets sang,
And fierce-eyed men, with panting breath,
Toiled onward at the work of death.
I could not see, but knew too well,
That underneath that cloud of hell,
Which still grew more by great degrees,
Man strove with man in deeds like these.

But when the sun had passed his stand
At noon, behold! on every hand
The dark brown vapor backward bore,
And fainter came the dreadful roar
From the huge sea of striving men.
Thus spoke my rising spirit then:
" Take comfort from that dying sound,
Faint heart, the foe is giving ground!"
And one, who taxed his horse's powers,
Flung at me, "Ho! the day is ours!"
And scoured along.   So swift his pace,
I took no memory of his face.
Then turned I once again to Heaven;
All things appeared so just and even;
So clearly from the highest Cause
Traced I the downward-working laws —

Those moral springs, made evident,
In the grand, triumph-crowned event.
So half I shouted, and half sang,
Like Jephtha's daughter, to the clang
Of my spread, cymbal-striking palms,
Some fragments of thanksgiving psalms.

Meanwhile a solemn stillness fell
Upon the land.   O'er hill and dell
Failed every sound.   My heart stood still,
Waiting before some coming ill.
The silence was more sad and dread,
Under that canopy of lead,
Than the wild tumult of the war
That raged a little while before.
All Nature, in her work of death,
Paused for one last, despairing breath ;
And, cowering to the earth, I drew
From her strong breast my strength anew.
When I arose, I wondering saw
Another dusty vapor draw
From the far right, its sluggish way
Toward the main cloud, that frowning lay
Against the western-sloping sun ;
And all the war was re-begun,
Ere this fresh marvel of my sense
Caught from my mind significance.
And then — why ask me ?   O my God !
Would I had lain beneath the sod,
A patient clod, for many a day,
And from my bones and mouldering clay
The rank field grass and flowers had sprung,
Ere the base sight, that struck and stung
My very soul, confronted me,
Shamed at my own humanity.
O happy dead ! who early fell,
Ye have no wretched tale to tell

Of causeless fear and coward flight,
Of victory snatched beneath your sight,
Of martial strength and honor lost,
Of mere life bought at any cost,
Of the deep, lingering mark of shame,
Forever scorched on brow and name,
That no new deeds, however bright,
Shall banish from men's loathful sight!
Ye perished in your conscious pride,
Ere this vile scandal opened wide
A wound that cannot close or heal.
Ye perished steel to levelled steel,
Stern votaries of the god of war,
Filled with his godhead to the core!
Ye died to live, these lived to die,
Beneath the scorn of every eye!
How eloquent your voices sound
From the low chambers under ground!
How clear each separate title burns
From your high set and laurelled urns!
While these, who walk about the earth,
Are blushing at their very birth!
And, though they talk, and go, and come,
Their moving lips are worse than dumb.
Ye sleep beneath the valley's dew,
And all the nation mourns for you;
So sleep till God shall wake the lands!
For angels, armed with fiery brands,
Await to take you by the hands.

The right-hand vapor broader grew;
It rose, and joined itself unto
The main cloud with a sudden dash.
Loud and more near the cannon's crash
Came toward me, and I heard a sound
As if all hell had broken bound, —

A cry of agony and fear.
Still the dark vapor rolled more near,
Till at my very feet it tossed
The vanward fragments of our host.
Can man, Thy image, sink so low,
Thou, who hast bent Thy tinted bow
Across the storm and raging main ;
Whose laws both loosen and restrain
The powers of earth, without whose will
No sparrow's little life is still ?
Was fear of hell, or want of faith,
Or the brute's common dread of death
The passion that began a chase,
Whose goal was ruin and disgrace ?
What tongue the fearful sight may tell ?
What horrid nightmare ever fell
Upon the restless sleep of crime —
What history of another time —
What dismal vision, darkly seen
By the stern-featured Florentine,
Can give a hint to dimly draw
The likeness of the scene I saw ?
I saw, yet saw not.   In that sea,
That chaos of humanity,
No more the eye could catch and keep
A single point, than on the deep
The eye may mark a single wave,
Where hurrying myriads leap and rave.
Men of all arms, and all costumes,
Bare-headed, decked with broken plumes ;
Soldiers and officers, and those
Who wore but civil-suited clothes ;
On foot or mounted — some bestrode
Steeds severed from their harnessed load ;
Wild mobs of white-topped wagons, cars,
Of wounded, red with bleeding scars ;
The whole grim panoply of war

Surged on me with a deafening roar!
All shades of fear, disfiguring man,
Glared through their faces' brazen tan.
Not one a moment paused, or stood
To see what enemy pursued.
With shrieks of fear, and yells of pain,
With every muscle on the strain,
Onward the struggling masses bore.
O, had the foemen lain before,
They 'd trampled them to dust and gore,
And swept their lines and batteries
As autumn sweeps the windy trees!
Here one cast forth his wounded friend,
And with his sword or musket-end
Urged on the horses; there one trod
Upon the likeness of his God,
As if 't were dust; a coward here
Grew valiant with his very fear,
And struck his weaker comrade prone,
And struggled to the front alone.
All had one purpose, one sole aim,
That mocked the decency of shame,
To fly, by any means to fly;
They cared not how, they asked not why.
I found a voice. My burning blood
Flamed up. Upon a mound I stood;
I could no more restrain my voice
Than could the prophet of God's choice.
"Back, animated dirt!" I cried,
"Back, on your wretched lives, and hide
Your shame beneath your native clay!
Or if the foe affrights you, slay
Your own base selves; and, dying, leave
Your children's tearful cheeks to grieve,
Not quail and blush, when you shall come,
Alive, to their degraded home!
Your wives will look askance with scorn;

Your boys, and infants yet unborn,
Will curse you to God's holy face!
Heaven holds no pardon in its grace
For cowards.   Oh, are such as ye
The guardians of our liberty ?
Back, if one trace of manhood still
May nerve your arm and brace your will!
You stain your country in the eyes
Of Europe and her monarchies !
The despots laugh, the peoples groan ;
Man's cause is lost and overthrown!
I curse you, by the sacred blood
That freely poured its purple flood
Down Bunker's heights, on Monmouth's plain,
From Georgia to the rocks of Maine !
I curse you, by the patriot band
Whose bones are crumbling in the land !
By those who saved what these had won —
In the high name of Washington ! "
Then I remember little more.
As the tide's rising waves, that pour
Over some low and rounded rock,
The coming mass, with one great shock,
Flowed o'er the shelter of my mound,
And raised me helpless from the ground.
As the huge shouldering billows bear,
Half in the sea and half in air,
A swimmer on their foaming crest,
So the foul throng beneath me pressed,
Swept me along, with curse and blow,
And flung me — where, I ne'er shall know.

When I awoke, a steady rain
Made rivulets across the plain ;
And it was dark — oh! very dark.
I was so stunned as scarce to mark
The ghostly figures of the trees,

Or hear the sobbing of the breeze
That flung the wet leaves to and fro.
Upon me lay a dismal woe,
A boundless, superhuman grief,
That drew no promise of relief
From any hope.   Then I arose,
As one who struggles up from blows
By unseen hands; and as I stood
Alone, I thought that God was good,
To hide, in clouds and driving rain,
Our low world from the angel train,
Whose souls filled heroes when the earth
Was worthy of their noble birth.
By that dull instinct of the mind,
Which leads aright the helpless blind,
I struggled onward, till the dawn
Across the eastern clouds had drawn
A narrow line of watery gray;
And full before my vision lay
The great dome's gaunt and naked bones,
Beneath whose crown the nation thrones
Her queenly person.   On I stole,
With hanging head and abject soul,
Across the high embattled ridge,
And o'er the arches of the bridge.
So freshly pricked my sharp disgrace,
I feared to meet the human face,
Skulking, as any woman might,
Who 'd lost her virtue in the night,
And sees the dreadful glare of day
Prepare to light her homeward way,
Alone, heart-broken, shamed, undone,
I staggered into Washington !

Since then long sluggish days have passed,
And on the wings of every blast
Have come the distant nations' sneers

To tingle in our blushing ears.
In woe and ashes, as was meet,
We wore the penitential sheet.
But now I breathe a purer air,
And from the depths of my despair
Awaken to a cheering morn,
Just breaking through the night forlorn,
A morn of hopeful victory.
Awake, my countrymen, with me !
Redeem the honor which you lost,
With any blood, at any cost !
I ask not how the war began,
Nor how the quarrel branched and ran
To this dread height. The wrong or right
Stands clear before God's faultless sight.
I only feel the shameful blow,
I only see the scornful foe,
And vengeance burns in every vein
To die, or wipe away the stain.
The war-wise hero of the West,
Wearing his glories as a crest,
Of trophies gathered in your sight,
Is arming for the coming fight.
Full well his wisdom apprehends
The duty and its mighty ends ;
The great occasion of the hour,
That never lay in human power
Since over Yorktown's tented plain
The red cross fell, nor rose again.
My humble pledge of faith I lay,
Dear comrade of my school-boy day,
Before thee, in the nation's view,
And if thy prophet prove untrue,
And from our country's grasp be thrown
The sceptre and the starry crown,
And thou, and all thy marshalled host
Be baffled, and in ruin lost ;

Oh, let me not outlive the blow
That seals my country's overthrow!
And, lest this woeful end come true,
Men of the North, I turn to you.
Display your vaunted flag once more,
Southward your eager columns pour!
Sound trump, and fife, and rallying drum;
From every hill and valley come.
Old men, yield up your treasured gold!
Can liberty be priced and sold?
Fair matrons, maids, and tender brides,
Gird weapons to your lovers' sides;
And, though your hearts break at the deed,
Give them your blessing and God speed;
Then point them to the field of flame,
With words like those of Sparta's dame;
And when the ranks are full and strong,
And the whole army moves along,
A vast result of care and skill,
Obedient to the master will;
And your young hero draws the sword,
And gives the last commanding word
That hurls your strength upon the foe —
Oh, let them need no second blow!
Strike, as your fathers' struck of old,
Through summer's heat and winter's cold,
Through pain, disaster, and defeat;
Through marches tracked with bloody feet;
Through every ill that could befall
The holy cause that bound them all!
Strike as they struck for liberty!
Strike as they struck to make you free!
Strike for the crown of victory!

THE RUN FROM MANASSAS JUNCTION.

YANKEE DOODLE went to war,
  On his little pony,
What did he go fighting. for,
  Everlasting goney !
Yankee Doodle was a chap
  Who bragged and swore tarnation,
He stuck a feather in his cap,
  And called it Federation.
        Yankee Doodle, etc.

Yankee Doodle, he went forth
  To conquer the seceders,
All the journals of the North,
  In most ferocious leaders,
Breathing slaughter, fire and smoke,
  Especially the latter,
His rage and fury to provoke,
  And vanity to flatter.
        Yankee Doodle, etc.

Yankee Doodle, having floored
  His separated brothers,
He reckoned his victorious sword
  Would turn against us others,
Secession first he would put down,
  Wholly and forever ;
And afterward, from Britain's crown,
  He Canada would sever.
        Yankee Doodle, etc.

England offering neutral sauce
  To goose as well as gander,
Was what made Yankee Doodle cross,
  And did inflame his dander.

As though with choler drunk he fumed,
  And threatened vengeance martial,
Because Old England had presumed
  To steer a course impartial.
      Yankee Doodle, etc.

Yankee Doodle bore in mind,
  When warfare England harassed,
How he, unfriendly and unkind,
  Beset her and embarrassed;
He put himself in England's place,
  And thought this injured nation
Must view his trouble with a base
  Vindictive exultation.
      Yankee Doodle, etc.

We for North and South alike
  Entertain affection;
These for negro slavery strike;
  Those for forced protection.
Yankee Doodle is the pot,
  Southerner the kettle;
Equal morally, if not
  Men of equal mettle.*
      Yankee Doodle, etc.

Yankee Doodle, near Bull Run
  Met his adversary,
First he thought the fight he 'd won,

---

* And so slavery and a high tariff are now equal morally in John Bull's eyes! The admission of what the whole world more than suspected has come at last. Its candor, not to say effrontery, gives it some claim upon admiration. And is it thus that Britain stands confessed before us! Britain indeed; but, alas, how much changed from that Britain that decked herself in the spoils of slavery, and hurled the fires of consuming vengeance upon the inhuman fleets! — See Earl Russell's Dispatch to Lord Lyons upon the Proclamation of Emancipation.

Fact proved quite contrary.
Panic-struck he fled, with speed
    Of lightning glib with unction,
Of slippery grease, in full stampede,
    From famed Manassas Junction.
        Yankee Doodle, etc.

As he bolted, noways slow,
    Yankee Doodle hallooed,
" We are whipped ! " and fled, although
    No pursuer followed.
Sword and gun right slick he threw
    Both away together,
In his cap, to public view,
    Showing the white feather.
        Yankee Doodle, etc.

Yankee Doodle, Doodle, do,
    Whither are you flying ?
" A cocked hat we 've been licked into,
    And knocked to Hades," crying ?
Well, to Canada, sir-ree,
    Now that, by secession,
I am driven up a tree,
    To seize that there possession.
        Yankee Doodle, etc.

Yankee Doodle, be content,
    You 've had a lenient whipping ;
Court not further punishment
    By enterprise of stripping
Those neighbors, whom, if you assail,
    They 'll surely whip you hollow ;
Moreover, when you 've turned your tail,
    Won't hesitate to follow.
        Yankee Doodle, etc.
           London Punch.

THE BRIER-WOOD PIPE.

BY CHARLES DAWSON SHANLY.

HA! Bully for me * again, when my turn for picket is
    over;
And now for a smoke, as I lie, with the moonlight in the
    clover.

My pipe it is only a knot from the root of the brier-wood
    tree;
But it turns my heart to the northward: Harry, give it
    to me.

And I'm but a rough at best, bred up to the row and the
    riot,
But a softness comes o'er my heart when all are asleep
    and quiet.

For many a time in the night strange things appear to
    my eye,
As the breath from my brier-wood pipe sails up between
    me and the sky.

Last night a beautiful spirit arose with the wisping smoke;
O, I shook, for my heart felt good, as it spread out its
    hands and spoke,

Saying, "I am the soul of the brier: we grew at the
    root of a tree
Where lovers would come in the twilight, — two ever, for
    company.

* The use of "bully," as an expression of encouragement and
approval among our roughs and Bowery boys, and boys not Bow-
ery, is no novelty in the language. The word is found similarly
used in the dramatists of the Elizabethan period, and those of the
Restoration.

" Where lovers would come in the morning, — ever but
    two, together ;
When the flowers were full in their blow, the birds in
    their song and feather.

" Where lovers would come in the noontime loitering, —
    never but two,
Looking in each other's eyes, like the pigeons that kiss
    and coo.

" And O ! the honeyed words that came when the lips
    were parted,
And the passion that glowed in eyes, and the lightning
    looks that darted !

" Enough, — Love dwells in the pipe: so ever it glows
    with fire.
I am the soul of the bush, and the spirits call me Sweet-
    Brier."

That 's what the Brier-wood said, as nigh as my tongue
    can tell,
And the words went straight to my heart, like the stroke
    of the fire-bell.

To-night I lie in the clover, watching the blossomy
    smoke ;
I 'm glad the boys are asleep, for I 'm not in the humor
    to joke.

I lie in the hefty clover : * between me and the waning
    moon
The smoke from my pipe arises : my heart will be quiet
    soon.

   * I do not know what the author means by " hefty " clover.
Hardly, having " heft," or weight.

My thoughts are back in the city; I'm everything I've
    been;
I hear the bell from the tower; I run with the swift ma-
    chine.

I see the red-shirts crowding around the engine-house
    door;
The foreman's hail through the trumpet comes with a
    sullen roar.

The reel in the Bowery dance-house, the row in the beer
    saloon,
Where I put in my licks at Big Paul, — come between
    me and the moon.

I hear the drum and the bugle, the tramp of the cow-
    skin boots;
We are marching to the Capital, — the Fire-Zouave re-
    cruits.

White handkerchiefs wave before me. O! but the sight
    is pretty
On the white marble steps, as we march through the
    heart of the city.

Bright eyes and clasping arms, and lips that bring us
    good hap,
And the splendid lady that gave me the havelock for my
    cap.

O! up from my pipe-cloud rises, between me and the
    moon,
A beautiful white-robed lady: my heart will be quiet
    soon.

The lovely golden-haired lady ever in dreams I see,
Who gave me the snow-white havelock; but what does
    she care for me?

Look at my grimy features: mountains between us stand;
I with my sledge-hammer knuckles, she with her jewelled
hand.

What care I? The day that is dawning may see me
when all is over,
With the red stream of my life-blood staining the hefty
clover.

Hark! the reveille sounding out on the morning air!
Devils are we for the battle: — Will there be angels
there?

Kiss me again, Sweet-Brier; the touch of your lips to
mine
Brings back the white-robed lady, with hair like the
golden wine.

Vanity Fair, July 6, 1861.

———◆———

JONATHAN TO JOHN.

A YANKEE IDYL.

BY JAMES RUSSELL LOWELL.

IT don't seem hardly right, John,
 When both my hands was full,
To stump me to a fight, John —
 Your cousin, tu, John Bull!
 Ole Uncle S. sez he, "I guess
 We kno it now," sez he;
 "The lion's paw is all the law,
 Accordin' to J. B.,
 Thet's fit for you an' me!"

4

Blood an't so cool as ink, John :
    It 's likely you 'd ha' wrote,
An' stopped a spell to think, John,
    Arter they 'd cut your throat !
        Ole Uncle S. sez he, " I guess
          He 'd skurce ha' stopped," sez he,
        " To mind his p's and q's ef that weasan'
          Hed belonged to ole J. B.,
          Instid o' you an' me ! "

Ef *I* turned mad dogs loose, John,
    On *your* front-parlor stairs,
Would it jest meet your views, John,
    To wait an' sue their heirs ?
        Ole Uncle S. sez he, " I guess,
          I on'y guess," sez he,
        " Thet, ef Vattel on *his* toes fell,
          'T would kind o' rile J. B.,
          Ez wall ez you an' me ! "

Who made the law thet hurts, John,
    Heads I win — ditto, tails ?
"*J. B.*" was on his shirts, John,
    Onless my memory fails.*
        Ole Uncle S. sez he, " I guess,
          (I 'm good at thet,) " sez he,
        " Thet sauce for goose an't *jest* the juice

---

* Mr. Biglow's memory (for we suppose Hosea *loquitur*) did not fail, as may be seen by the following extract from the London *Times' first* article about the Trent affair, October 28th, 1861 : — " Unwelcome as the truth may be, it is nevertheless a truth that *we have ourselves established a system of international law which now tells against us.* In high-handed and almost despotic manner we have in former days claimed privileges over neutrals which have at different times banded all the maritime powers of the world against us. We have insisted upon stopping ships of war of neutral nations and taking British subjects out of them."

For ganders with J. B.,
No more than you or me ! ' "

When your rights was our wrong, John,
  You did n't stop for fuss :
Britanny's trident-prongs, John,
  Was good 'nough law for us.
    Ole Uncle S. sez he, " I guess,
      Though physic's good," sez he,
    " It does n't foller that he can swaller
      Prescriptions signed ' *J. B.*,'
      Put up by you and me ! "

We own the ocean, tu, John :
  You must n't take it hard
Ef we can't think with you, John,
  It 's jest your own back yard.
    Ole Uncle S. sez he, " I guess,
      Ef *thet*'s his claim," sez he,
    " The fencin'-stuff 'll cost enough
      To bust up friend J. B.,
      Ez wal ez you an' me ! "

Why talk so dreffle big, John,
  Of honor, when it meant
You did n't care a fig, John,
  But just for *ten per cent ?*
    Ole Uncle S. sez he, " I guess
      He 's like the rest," sez he :
    " When all is done, its number one
      Thet 's nearest to J. B.,
      Ez wal ez you an' me ! "

A NEW SONG TO AN OLD TUNE.

JOHN BULL, Esquire, my jo John,
  When we were first acquent,
You acted very much as now
  You act about the Trent.
You stole my bonny sailors, John,
  My bonny ships also,
You 're aye the same fierce beast to me,
  John Bull, Esquire, my jo!

John Bull, Esquire, my jo John,
  Since we were linked together,
Full many a jolly fight, John,
  We 've had with one another.
Now must we fight again, John?
  Then at it let us go!
And God will help the honest heart,
  John Bull, Esquire, my jo.

John Bull, Esquire, my jo John,
  A century has gone by,
Since you called me your slave, John,
  Since I at you let fly.
You want to fight it out again —
  That war of waste and woe;
You 'll find me much the same old coon,
  John Bull, Esquire, my jo.

John Bull, Esquire, my jo John,
  If lying loons have told
That I have lost my pluck, John,
  And fight not as of old;
You 'd better not believe it, John,
  Nor scorn your ancient foe;

For I've seen weaker days than this,
   John Bull, Esquire, my jo.

John Bull, Esquire, my jo John,
   Hear this my language plain :
I never smote you unprovoked,
   I never smote in vain.
If you want peace, peace let it be !
   If war, be pleased to know,
Shots in my locker yet remain,
   John Bull, Esquire, my jo !

———◆———

TO ENGLISHMEN.

BY JOHN GREENLEAF WHITTIER.

You flung your taunt across the wave,
   We bore it as became us,
Well knowing that the fettered slave
Left friendly lips no option, save
   To pity or to blame us.

You scoffed our plea. " Mere lack of will,
   Not lack of power," you told us ;
We showed our Free-State records ; still
You mocked, confounding good and ill,
   Slave haters and slave holders.

We struck at Slavery ; to the verge
   Of power and means we checked it ;
Lo ! — presto, change ! its claims you urge,
Send greetings to it o'er the surge,
   And comfort and protect it.

But yesterday you scarce could shake,
   In slave-abhorring rigor,
Our Northern palms. for conscience' sake :

To-day you clasp the hands that ache
    With " walloping the nigger ! "

O Englishmen ! — in hope and creed,
    In blood and tongue our brothers !
We too are heirs of Runnymede ;
And Shakspeare's fame and Cromwell's deed
    Are not alone our mother's.

" Thicker than water," in one rill
    Through centuries of story
Our Saxon blood has flowed, and still
We share with you its good and ill,
    The shadow and the glory.

Joint heirs and kinfolk, leagues of wave
    Nor length of years can part us ;
Your right is ours to shrine and grave
The common freehold of the brave,
    The gift of saints and martyrs.

Our very sins and follies teach
    Our kindred frail and human :
We carp at faults with bitter speech,
The while for one unshared by each
    We have a score in common.

We bow the heart, if not the knee,
    To England's Queen, God bless her !
We praised you when your slaves went free :
We seek to unchain ours.   Will ye
    Join hands with the oppressor ?

And is it Christian England cheers
    The bruiser, not the bruised ?
And must she run, despite the tears
And prayers of eighteen hundred years,
    A-muck in Slavery's crusade ?

O black disgrace! O shame and loss
　　Too deep for tongue to phrase on!
Tear from your flag its holy cross,
And in your van of battle toss
　　The pirate's skull-bone blazon!

———◆———

THE LONDON "TIMES" ON AMERICAN AFFAIRS.

JOHN BULL vos a-valkin' his parlor von day,
Ha-fixin' the vorld wery much 'is hown vay,
Ven igstrawnary news cum from hover the sea,
Habout the great country vot brags it is free.

Hand these vos the tidins this news it did tell,
That great Yankee Doodle vos going to — vell,
That ee vos a-volloped by Jefferson D.,
Hand no longer "some punkins" vos likely to be.

John Bull, slyly vinkin', then said hunto me:
"My dear *Times*, my hold covey, go pitch hinto ee;
Let us vollop great Doodle now ven 'e is down;
Hif ve vollops him vell, ve vill ' do 'im up brown.'

"'Is long-legged boots hat my 'ed 'e 'as 'urled,
I'd raither not see 'em a-trampin' the vorld;
Hand I howe him a grudge for 'is conduct so wile,
In himportin' shillalahs from Erin's green hile.

"I knows Jefferson D. is a rascally chap,
Who goes hin for cribbin' the Guvurnment pap;
That Hexeter 'All may be down upon me,
But as Jeff. 'as the cotton, I'll cotton to ee.

"I cares for the blacks not a drat more nor ee,
Though on principle I goes for settin' 'em free;

But hinterest, my cove, we must look hafter now,
Unless principle yields, it are poor anyhow."

So spoke Johnny Bull, so ee spake hunto me,
Hand I 'inted slyly to Jefferson D.,
Who, very much pleased, rubbed 'is 'ands in 'is joy,
Hand exclaimed: "You 're the man for my money,
    old boy.

" Go in, Johnny *Times !* I will feather your nest;
Never mind if you soil it, 'tis foul at the best;
Strange guests have been thar, but my cotton is clean,
And a cargo is yourn, if you manage it keen."

So I pitched hinto Doodle like a thousan' of brick, —
May'ap it warn't proper to do it — on tick,
But John Bull is almighty, he 'll see I am paid,
And my cargo of cotton will break the blockade.

PART SECOND.

So Bull ee vent hin the blockade for to bust;
The Christians they cried, and the sinners they cuss'd;
There vos blowin', and blusterin', and mighty parade,
And hall to get ready to break the blockade.

Ven hall hof a sudden it come in the 'ed
Hof a prudent hold covey, who up and 'e said:
" Hit 's bad to vant cotton, but worser by far,
His the sufferin' hand misery you 'll make by a war.

" There 'is cotton in Hingy, Peru, and Assam,
Guayaquil and Jamaica, Canton, Surinam ;
'Arf a loaf, or 'arf cotton, tight papers hi call,
But a 'ole var hentire his the devil and hall."

So he sent not 'is vessel hacross the broad sea,
Vich vos hawful 'ard lines for poor Jefferson D.,

Hand wrote hunto Doodle, " 'Old hon, and be true!"
And Jonathan hanswered Bull, " Bully for you!"

SEQUEL AFTER-TIMES.

Has Bull vos valking in London haround,
'E found the *Times* lyin' hupon the cold ground,
With a big bale hof cotton right hover 's side;
Says Bull, " Hi perceive 't was by cotton he died!"

———◆———

GOD SAVE JOHN BULL.*

GOD save me, great John Bull!
Long keep my pocket full!
   God save John Bull!
Ever victorious,
Haughty, vain-glorious,
Snobbish, censorious,
   God save John Bull

O Lords, our gods, arise!
Tax all our enemies,
   Make tariffs fall!
Confound French politics,
Frustrate all Russian tricks,
Get Yankees in a " fix,"
   God " bless " them all!   [*Sinistrâ manu*]

Thy choicest gifts in store,
On me, me only pour, —
   Me, great John Bull!

* It has been thought that should a time arrive when God save
the King cannot be sung in Great Britain, because, that peculiar
institution having been found superfluous and expensive, there
will be no king to be saved, the old national hymn will be altered
to something like the lines above given.

Maintain oppressive laws,
Frown down the poor man's cause!
So sing with heart and voice,
    I, great John Bull!

R. G. W.

THE POTOMAC — 1861.

THE light of stars shook through the trees,
    The large-eyed moon looked o'er the lawn,
    O day, I said, delay thy dawn!
A little whisper stirred the breeze.

A frightened bird thrilled through the place,
    A dead leaf fell at my still feet,
    And my wild heart, oh loud it beat!
He read my answer in my face.

All night across the moonlit land,
    Far southward, where the river runs,
    I heard the booming of their guns,
While in his own he held my hand.

Trust God, oh little heart! he said,
    And galloped forth into the light;
    That day he rode into the fight,
And there they shot my lover dead.

My stricken soul rose from the dust,
    And pushed rebellious hands toward God;
    I will not to the earth be trod,
Thou art nor wise, nor good, nor just!

And thus it was not sanctified —
    My sorrow — and when I did pray:

My end, O God ! no more delay,
Now take me to him, Lord, I cried.

One night I dreamed, and he stood by,
　　Clothed, angel-wise, in love and light.
　　I durst not touch his robes of white,
He chid me with his pitying eye.

Only that look, nor any word,
　　And I had learned, not all too late,
　　Had learned to live, and work, and wait,
And my dead faith to life was stirred.

Oh well I knew that not for me
　　Were robe of white, the palm, the crown,
　　Till I more worthy them had grown,
Had earned, like him, euthanasy !

Nor sitting still with folded palms,
　　To nurse my grief through the long years,
　　But reading through my bitter tears
Strange mockery in the eternal psalms ;

In some far circle from the throne
　　Content if I, at last, may stand,
　　He holding in his own my hand,
And our two voices making one —

One voice of praise, prevailing thence
　　Unto the Lamb upon the Hill —
　　The far-off memory of ill,
Crowning the long, long recompense.

Harpers' Weekly.

"EIN' FESTE BURG IST UNSER GOTT."

(*Luther's Hymn.*)

BY JOHN G. WHITTIER.

WE wait beneath the furnace blast
  The pangs of transformation;
Not painlessly doth God recast
  And mould anew the nation.
      Hot burns the fire
      Where wrongs expire;
      Nor spares the hand
      That from the land
  Uproots the ancient evil.

The hand-breadth cloud the sages feared,
  Its bloody rain is dropping;
The poison plant the fathers spared
  All else is overtopping.
      East, West, South, North,
      It curses the earth:
      All justice dies,
      And fraud and lies
  Live only in its shadow.

What gives the wheat-field blades of steel?
  What points the rebel cannon?
What sets the roaring rabble's heel
  On the old star-spangled pennon?
      What breaks the oath
      Of the men o' the South?
      What whets the knife
      For the Union's life? —
  Hark to the answer: SLAVERY!

Then waste no blows on lesser foes,
  In strife unworthy freemen;

God lifts to-day the veil, and shows
  The features of the demon!
    O North and South!
    Its victims both,
    Can ye not cry,
  "Let Slavery die!"
And Union find in freedom?

What though the cast-out spirit tear
  The nation in his going?
We who have shared the guilt must share
  The pang of his o'erthrowing!
    Whate'er the loss,
    Whate'er the cross,
    Shall they complain
    Of present pain,
Who trust in God's hereafter?

For who that leans on His right arm
  Was ever yet forsaken?
What righteous cause can suffer harm,
  If He its part has taken?
    Though wild and loud,
    And dark the cloud,
    Behind its folds
    His hand upholds
The calm sky of to-morrow!

Above the maddening cry for blood,
  Above the wild war-drumming,
Let Freedom's voice be heard, with good
  The evil overcoming.
    Give prayer and purse
    To stay The Curse,
    Whose wrong we share,
    Whose shame we bear,
Whose end shall gladden Heaven!

In vain the bells of war shall ring
        Of triumphs and revenges,
While still is spared the evil thing
        That severs and estranges.
                But, blest the ear
                That yet shall hear
                The jubilant bell
                That rings the knell
        Of Slavery forever!

Then let the selfish lip be dumb,
        And hushed the breath of sighing;
Before the joy of peace must come
        The pains of purifying.
                God give us grace,
                Each in his place
                To bear his lot,
                And, murmuring not,
        Endure, and wait, and labor!

———◆———

JEFF DAVIS,

ON HIS ELECTION AS PRESIDENT FOR SIX YEARS.*

BY " SIGMA".

SATAN was chained a thousand years,
        We learn from Revelation —
That he might not, as it appears,
        Longer "deceive the nation."
'T is hard to say, between the two,
        Which is the greater evil,
Six years of liberty, for you —
        A thousand for the devil!

* November 9, 1861.

'T is passing strange, if you 've no fears,
   Of being hanged within six years !

A hundred thousand rebels' ears
   Would not one half repay
The widows' and the orphans' tears,
   Shed for the slain to-day :
The blood of all those gallant braves,
   Whom Southern traitors slew,
Cries sternly, from their loyal graves,
   For vengeance upon you ;
And if you 're not prepared to die
The death of Haman, fly, Jeff, fly !

Fly, traitor, to some lonely niche,
   Far, far beyond the billow ;
Thy grave an ill-constructed ditch —
   Thy sexton General Pillow.
There may you turn to rottenness,
   By mortal unannoyed,
Your ashes undisturbed, unless
   Your grave is known by Floyd.
He 'll surely trouble your repose,
And come to steal your burial-clothes.

EPITAPH.

Pause for an instant, loyal reader.
Here lies Jeff, the great seceder.
Above, he always lied, you know,
And now the traitor lies below.
His bow was furnished with two strings,
He flattered crowds, and fawned on kings ;
Repaid his country's care with evil,
And prayed to God, and served the devil.
The South could whip the Yankee nation,
So he proposed humiliation !
Their blessings were so everlasting,

'T was just the time for prayer and fasting!
The record may be searched in vain,
From West-Point Benedict to Cain,
To find a more atrocious knave,
Unless in Cæsar Borgia's grave.

YANKEE PRIDE.

BY BRIG.-GENERAL LANDER.

On hearing that the Confederate troops had said that " Fewer
of the Massachusetts officers would have been killed if they had
not been too proud to surrender."

AY, deem us proud! for we are more
   Than proud of all our mighty dead;
Proud of the bleak and rock-bound shore
   A crowned oppressor cannot tread.

Proud of each rock and wood and glen,
   Of every river, lake, and plain;
Proud of the calm and earnest men
   Who claim the right and will to reign.

Proud of the men who gave us birth,
   Who battled with the stormy wave,
To sweep the red man from the earth,
   And build their homes upon his grave.

Proud of the holy summer morn,
   They traced in blood upon its sod;
The rights of freemen yet unborn,
   Proud of their language and their God.

Proud, that beneath our proudest dome,
   And round the cottage-cradled hearth,
There is a welcome and a home
   For every stricken race on earth.

Proud that yon slowly sinking sun
  Saw drowning lips grow white in prayer,
O'er such brief acts of duty done
  As honor gathers from despair.

Pride, — 't is our watchword, " Clear the boats ! "
  " Holmes, Putnam, Bartlett, Pierson — here ! "
And while this crazy wherry floats,
  " Let 's save our wounded ! " cries Revere.

Old State — some souls are rudely sped —
  This record for thy Twentieth corps,
Imprisoned, wounded, dying, dead,
  It only asks, " Has Sparta more ? "

Boston Post, Nov. 23, 1861.

PACIFIC MACARONICS.

Seward, qui est Rerum cantor
  Publicarum, atque Lincoln,
Vir excelsior, mitigantur —
  A delightful thing to think on.

Blatat Plebs Americana,
  Quite impossible to bridle.
Nihil refert ; navis cana
  Brings back Mason atque Slidell.

Scribit nunc amœne Russell ;
  Lætuslapis* claudit fiscum ;
Nunc finitur omnis bustle.
  Slidell — Mason — pax vobiscum !

London Press.

* The scholiast suggests — Gladstone.

5

JOHN BROWN'S SONG.*

John Brown's body lies a-mouldering in the grave ;
John Brown's body lies a-mouldering in the grave ;
John Brown's body lies a-mouldering in the grave ;
His soul is marching on !

CHORUS.

Glory, halle — hallelujah !   Glory, halle — hallelujah !
Glory, halle — hallelujah !
His soul is marching on !

He 's gone to be a soldier in the army of the Lord !
He 's gone to be a soldier in the army of the Lord !
He 's gone to be a soldier in the army of the Lord !
His soul is marching on !

CHORUS.

Glory, halle — hallelujah !   Glory, halle — hallelujah !
Glory, halle — hallelujah !
His soul is marching on !

John Brown's knapsack is strapped upon his back !
John Brown's knapsack is strapped upon his back !
John Brown's knapsack is strapped upon his back !
His soul is marching on !

* The origin of this senseless farrago — as senseless as the equally popular " Lillibulero " of the times of the great civil commotion in England — is, I believe, quite unknown. But sung to a degraded and jiggish form of a grand and simple old air, it was a great favorite in the early part of the war. It was heard everywhere in the streets; regiments marched to it, and the air had its place in the programme of every barrel-organ grinder. In fact no song was sung so much during the rebellion. Its popularity was doubtless due to its presentation of a single idea, and in great measure to the very marked rhythm of the air to which it was adapted, or rather, which had been adapted to it.

CHORUS.

Glory, halle — hallelujah !   Glory, halle — hallelujah !
Glory, halle — hallelujah !
His soul is marching on !

His pet lambs will meet him on the way ;
His pet lambs will meet him on the way ;
His pet lambs will meet him on the way ;
As they go marching on !

CHORUS.

Glory, halle — hallelujah !   Glory, halle — hallelujah !
Glory, halle — hallelujah !
As they go marching on !

They will hang Jeff. Davis to a tree !
They will hang Jeff. Davis to a tree !
They will hang Jeff. Davis to a tree !
As they march along !

CHORUS.

Glory, halle — hallelujah !   Glory, halle — hallelujah !
Glory, halle — hallelujah !
As they march along !

Now, three rousing cheers for the Union !
Now, three rousing cheers for the Union !
Now, three rousing cheers for the Union !
As we are marching on !

CHORUS.

Glory, halle — hallelujah !   Glory, halle — hallelujah !
Glory, halle — hallelujah !
Hip, hip, hip, hip, Hurrah !

BATTLE-HYMN OF THE REPUBLIC.

BY MRS. JULIA WARD HOWE.

MINE eyes have seen the glory of the coming of the
    Lord :
He is trampling out the vintage where the grapes of
    wrath are stored ;
He hath loosed the fateful lightning of His terrible swift
    sword :
        His truth is marching on.

I have seen Him in the watch-fires of a hundred circling
    camps ;
They have builded Him an altar in the evening dews and
    damps ;
I have read His righteous sentence by the dim and flaring
    lamps :
        His day is marching on.

I have read a fiery gospel writ in burnished rows of steel :
" As ye deal with my contemners, so with you my grace
    shall deal ;
Let the Hero, born of woman, crush the serpent with his
    heel,
        Since God is marching on."

He has sounded forth the trumpet that shall never call
    retreat ;
He is sifting out the hearts of men before His judgment-
    seat :
Oh ! be swift, my soul, to answer Him ! be jubilant, my feet !
        Our God is marching on.

In the beauty of the lilies Christ was borne across the sea,
With a glory in His bosom that transfigures you and me ;
As He died to make men holy, let us die to make men free,
        While God is marching on.

THE NATION'S HYMN.

OUR past is bright and grand
   In the purple tints of time;
And the present of our land,
   Points to glories more sublime.
For our destiny is won;
   And 't is ours to lead the van,
Of the nations marching on,
   Of the moving hosts of man!
      Yes, the Starry Flag alone,
        Shall wave above the van,
      Of the nations sweeping on,
        Of the moving hosts of man!

We are sprung from noble sires,
   As were ever sung in song;
We are bold with Freedom's fires,
   We are rich, and wise, and strong.
On us are freely showered
   The gifts of every clime,
And we 're the richest dowered
   Of all the heirs of Time!
      Brothers then, in Union, strong,
        We shall ever lead the van,
      As the nations sweep along,
        To fulfil the hopes of man!

We are brothers; and we know
   That our Union is a tower,
When the fiercest whirlwinds blow,
   And the darkest tempests lower!
We shall sweep the land and sea,
   While we march, in Union, great,

Thirty millions of the free
  With the steady step of fate!
      Brothers then, in Union, strong,
        Let us ever lead the van,
      As the nations sweep along,
        To fulfil the hopes of man!

See our prairies, sky-surrounded!
  See our sunlit mountain chains!
See our waving woods, unbounded,
  And our cities on the plains!
See the oceans kiss our strand,
  Oceans stretched from pole to pole!
See our mighty lakes expand,
  And our giant rivers roll!
      Such a land, and such alone,
        Should be leader of the van,
      As the nations sweep along
        To fulfil the hopes of man!

Yes, the spirit of our land,
  The young giant of the West,
With the waters in his hand,
  With the forests for his crest, —
To our hearts' quick, proud pulsations,
  To our shouts that still increase,
Shall yet lead on the nations,
  To their brotherhood of peace!
      Yes, Columbia, great and strong,
        Shall forever lead the van,
      As the nations sweep along,
        To fulfil the hopes of man!

"E PLURIBUS UNUM."

BY THE REV. JOHN PIERPONT.

AIR — *" The Star-Spangled Banner."*

I.

THE harp of the minstrel with melody rings,
  When the Muses have taught him to touch and to
      tune it;
And although it may have a full octave of strings,
  To both maker and minstrel the harp is a unit.
        So, the power that creates
        Our Republic of States,
  To harmony tunes them at different dates;
And, many or few, when the Union is done,
Be they thirteen or thirty, the nation is one.

II.

The science that measures and numbers the spheres,
  And has done so since first the Chaldean began it,
Now and then, as she counts them, and measures their
      years,
  Brings into our system and names a new planet.
        Yet the old and new stars,
        Venus, Neptune, and Mars,
  As they drive round the sun their invisible cars,
Whether faster or slower their races are run,
Are " E Pluribus Unum " — of many made one.

III.

Of those federate spheres, should but one fly the track,
  Or with others conspire for a general dispersion,
By the great central orb they would all be brought back,
  And held, each in its place, by a wholesome " coercion."

Were one daughter of light
Indulged in her flight,
They might all be engulfed by Old Chaos and Night;
So must none of our sisters be suffered to run,
For, " E Pluribus Unum," — We all go, if one.

IV.

Let the Demon of Discord our melody mar,
Or Treason's red hand rend our system asunder,
Break one string from our harp, or extinguish one star,
The whole system's ablaze with its lightning and
thunder.
Let that discord be hushed !
Let the traitors be crushed,
Though " Legion " their name, all with victory flushed ;
For aye must our motto stand, fronting the sun,
" E Pluribus Unum " — The many are one.

———◆———

UNITED STATES NATIONAL HYMN, L. M.*

Tune — *Yarmouth.*

BY JONATHAN ——— ———

I.

GOD bless United States ; each one
Has government, the people's own,
The people rule, their rulers are
Elected servants, to take care

---

* The above hymn, written to the old Long Metre Yarmouth,
was, like the four which precede it, among the twelve hundred
sent in to the committee appointed at the beginning of the civil
war, for the somewhat absurd purpose of obtaining a National
Hymn, — as if that could be written to order. The author's name

Of what is for the public good;
And the best men be chosen should;
And often changed, that surely we
May prosper, and be ever free.

II.

Foundation of our Union, find
On education, talent, mind;
God's Book, religion's only guide;
The supreme law, in all, reside;
Nor can majority oppress
Minority, but all confess
That each has Rights, which all must see
Respected in their purity.

III.

The Union and the Nation stand
A Government, o'er all the land;
Best, freest, strongest, wisest one,
Was, is, will be, beneath the sun;
The greatest numbers' greatest good;
And all protected, as we should;
Intelligence, ability,
For rulers, the best quality.

was really Jonathan, and he lived in one of the remotest and most primitive of the rural districts of Northern New England. His handwriting was plainly that of a man used rather to the plough than the pen, — one whose condition in life would in any other country than this limit his knowledge to what was necessary to the tilling of the few acres on which he lived. But rustic and unlettered as he was, what intelligent comprehension his rude verses exhibit of the structure and the principles of our government! In this respect he could manifestly put to school the smooth-mannered crowd of European statesmen and journalists who with an air of such profound wisdom discuss our politics, and who with such an assumption of judicial authority pronounced our doom in strict accordance with historical precedent. Viewed in this light, his quaint composition has an interest which makes it worthy of preservation.

IV.

Jehovah is our Head, and we
Acknowledge His supremacy;
He blesses us, year after year,
With all good things which do appear;
He is our Sovereign, only one;
We 'll have none else till Time is done;
Three times a year acknowledge Him:
Fast, July Fourth, Thanksgiving time.

V.

As we march down the stream of Time,
New States extend our happy clime;
Go on increasing, good and great;
One Union, formed of many States:
More States, the stronger shall we be
In union, peace, and liberty;
East, West, North, South, on sea and land,
Forever one, united stand.

VI.

Be every part to each most dear;
And law and order rule us here;
Our Constitutions good and great,
Amended for the good of State;
Our Statutes for the people's good;
And Science guide us as it should;
States within State; blest Freedom's land,
United States, forever stand!

VII.

Stand in thy strong integrity:
The North and South united be
With East and West: join heart and hand
By our good Union firm to stand.
Our President elected be,
By people's voice, plurality;

And the Vice-President the same ;
The highest offices of fame.

VIII.

Free governments o'er earth will go ;
The Bible, education too ;
The righteous wise shine as the sun ;
Knowledge and Arts o'er earth to run ;
All know the Lord, His service be
Extended over land and sea ;
His kingdom come o'er men to reign,
And earth be all the Lord's.   Amen.

———◆———

UNION.*

I.

INDIVIDUAL several, indisintegrative whole !
Corporeal nationality, national soul !
Matter indistinguishable, immaterial seen !
End of all means, of all ends mean !
    Chorus — Thus with eye unfilmed we see
        All the charms of unity ;
        Clearly thus have comprehended,
        What our forefathers intended.

II.

Of sempiternal potency, preëxistent power !
Sweet of our bitter, of our sweetness sour !

---

* Perhaps the writer of the above outrageous burlesque of some
of the traits which have been noticed in the style of the eminent
author of " Brahma " should be ashamed to have sent them to the
National Hymn Committee, of which he was a member. If bur-
lesque were all their purpose they would not be here preserved.
Mr. Emerson could well afford to forgive them, even if they did not
come from one of his warmest admirers.

Of Buncombe progenitor, issue of old Ops,
Live thou upon thy Buncombe, die he within thy chops !
  Chorus — Thus with eye unfilmed we see, &c.

III.

Infissiparous symbol of politic etern,
Securing Uncle Sam what's hisn and every State what's
  hern,
Of strength redintegrative, of pulchritude e'er fresh,
Secesh were not without thee, and with thee no secesh !
  Chorus — Thus with eye unfilmed we see, &c.

IV.

Thus, end of thy beginning, beginning of thy end,
Ample power to break bestowing, reserving power to
  mend,
Self-destroyer, self-producer, thou hast pluck and strength
  enough
To cuff well all thy enemies, were thy enemy not Cuff.
  Chorus — Thus with eye unfilmed we see
    All the charms of unity ;
    Clearly thus have comprehended,
    What our forefathers intended.

          R. G. W.

OVERTURES FROM RICHMOND.

A NEW LILLIBURLERO.

BY PROFESSOR F. J. CHILD.

" WELL, Uncle Sam," says Jefferson D.,
  Lilliburlero, old Uncle Sam,
" You 'll have to join my Confed'racy,"
  Lilliburlero, old Uncle Sam.

" Lero, lero, that don't appear O, that don't appear,"
     says old Uncle Sam.
" Lero, lero, fillibustero, that don't appear," says old
     Uncle Sam.

" So, Uncle Sam, just lay down your arms,"
        Lilliburlero, etc.,
" Then you shall hear my reas'nable terms,"
        Lilliburlero, etc.
" Lero, lero, I'd like to hear O, I'd like to hear," says
     old Uncle Sam.
" Lero, lero, fillibustero, I'd like to hear," says old Uncle
     Sam.

" First, you must own I've beat you in fight,"
        Lilliburlero, etc.,
" Then, that I always have been in the right,"
        Lilliburlero, etc.
" Lero, lero, rather severe O, rather severe," says old
     Uncle Sam.
" Lero, lero, fillibustero, rather severe," says old Uncle
     Sam.

" Then you must pay my national debts,"
        Lilliburlero, etc.,
" No questions asked about my assets,"
        Lilliburlero, etc.
" Lero, lero, that's very dear O, that's very dear," says
     old Uncle Sam.
" Lero, lero, fillibustero, that's very dear," says old Uncle
     Sam.

" Also, some few I.O.U's and bets," —
        Lilliburlero, etc.,
" Mine and Bob Toombs', and Slidell's and Rhett's,"
        Lilliburlero, etc.

" Lero, lero, that leaves me zero, that leaves me zero,"
   says Uncle Sam.
" Lero, lero, fillibustero, that leaves me zero," says Uncle
   Sam.

" And, by the way, one little thing more,"
      Lilliburlero, etc.,
" You 're to refund the cost of the war,"
      Lilliburlero, etc.
" Lero, lero, just what I fear O, just what I fear," says
   old Uncle Sam.
" Lero, lero, fillibustero, just what I fear, says old Uncle
   Sam.

" Next, you must own our cavalier blood ! "
      Lilliburlero, etc.,
" And that your Puritans sprang from the mud ! "
      Lilliburlero, etc.
" Lero, lero, that mud is clear O, that mud is clear," says
   old Uncle Sam.
" Lero, lero, fillibustero, that mud is clear," says old Uncle
   Sam.

" Slavery 's of course the chief corner-stone,"
      Lilliburlero, etc.
" Of our NEW CIV-IL-I-ZA-TI-ON ! "
      Lilliburlero, etc.
" Lero, lero, that 's quite sincere O, that 's quite sincere,"
   says old Uncle Sam.
" Lero, lero, fillibustero, that 's quite sincere," says old
   Uncle Sam.

" You 'll understand, my recreant tool,"
      Lilliburlero, etc.,
" You 're to submit, and we are to rule,"
      Lilliburlero, etc.

" Lero, lero, are n't you a hero! are n't you a hero!"
    says Uncle Sam.
" Lero, lero, fillibustero, are n't you a hero!" says Uncle
    Sam.

" If to these terms you fully consent,"
    Lilliburlero, etc.,
" I 'll be perpetual King-President,"
    Lilliburlero, etc.
" Lero, lero, take your sombrero, off to your swamps!"
    says old Uncle Sam.
" Lero, lero, fillibustero, cut, double-quick!" says old
    Uncle Sam.

"ALL WE ASK IS TO BE LET ALONE." *

BY H. H. BROWNELL.

As vonce I valked by a dismal svamp,
There sot an Old Cove in the dark and damp,
And at everybody as passed that road
A stick or a stone this Old Cove throwed.
And venever he flung his stick or his stone
He 'd set up a song of " Let me alone."

" Let me alone, for I loves to shy
These bits of things at the passers-by ;

---

* The humor and the point of these verses, based upon a well-
known declaration of Jefferson Davis, insured their popularity, and
demand their preservation. But it should not remain unnoticed
that the dialect in which they are written is one never heard in
this country, or in any other; it being an incongruous mixture of
that of the London cockney, as in " vonce," " valked," " ouse," and
" ome," and those of the rustic Yankee and the Southwestern man.

Let me alone, for I 've got your tin,
And lots of other traps snugly in;
Let me alone, I 'm riggin' a boat
To grab votever you 've got afloat —
In a veek or so I expects to come
And turn you out of your 'ouse and 'ome;
I 'm a quiet Old Cove," says he, with a groan:
"All I axes is — Let me alone."

Just then came along on the self-same vay,
Another Old Cove, and began for to say:
" Let you alone! that 's comin' it strong!
You 've *ben* let alone — a darned sight too long;
Of all the sarce that ever I heerd! —
Put down that stick! (You well may look skeered;)
Let go that stone! If you once show fight,
I 'll knock you higher than ary kite.
You must hev a lesson to stop your tricks,
And cure you of shying them stones and sticks;
And I 'll hev my hardware back, and my cash,
And knock your scow into tarnal smash;
And if ever I catches you 'round my ranch,
I 'll string you up to the nearest branch.
The best you can do is to go to bed,
And keep a decent tongue in your head;
For I reckon, before you and I are done,
You 'll wish you had let honest folks alone "

The Old Cove stopped, and the t' other Old Cove
He sot quite still in his cypress grove,
And he looked at his stick, revolvin' slow
Vether 't were safe to shy it or no;
And he grumbled on in an injured tone:
"All that I axed vos, *let me alone.*"

TARDY GEORGE.

WHAT are you waiting for, George, I pray ?
To scour your cross-belts with fresh pipe-clay ?
To burnish your buttons, to brighten your guns ;
Or wait you for May-day and warm-spring suns ?
Are you blowing your fingers because they are cold,
Or catching your breath ere you take a hold ?
Is the mud knee-deep in valley and gorge ?
What are you waiting for, tardy George ?

Want you a thousand more cannon made,
To add to the thousand now arrayed ?
Want you more men, more money to pay ?
Are not two millions enough per day ?
Wait you for gold and credit to go,
Before we shall see your martial show ;
Till Treasury Notes will not pay to forge ?
What are you waiting for, tardy George ?

Are you waiting for your hair to turn,
Your heart to soften, your bowels to yearn
A little more toward " our Southern friends,"
As at home and abroad they work their ends ?
" Our Southern friends ! " whom you hold so dear
That you do no harm and give no fear,
As you tenderly take them by the gorge, —
What are you waiting for, tardy George ?

Now that you 've marshalled your whole command,
Planned what you would, and changed what you planned ;
Practised with shot and practised with shell,
Know to a hair where every one fell,
Made signs by day and signals by night ;
Was it all done to keep out of a fight ?

6

Is the whole matter too heavy a charge ?
What are you waiting for, tardy George ?

Shall we have more speeches, more reviews ?
Or are you waiting to hear the news ;
To hold up your hands in mute surprise,
When France and England shall " recognize " ?
Are you too grand to fight traitors small ?
Must you have a nation to cope withal ?
Well, hammer the anvil and blow the forge, —
You 'll soon have a dozen, tardy George.

Suppose for a moment, George, my friend, —
Just for a moment, — you condescend
To use the means that are in your hands,
The eager muskets and guns and brands ;
Take one bold step on the Southern sod,
And leave the issue to watchful God !
For now the nation raises its gorge,
Waiting and watching you, tardy George.

I should not much wonder, George, my boy,
If Stanton get in his head a toy,
And some fine morning, ere you are out,
He send you all " to the right about," —
You and Jomini, and all the crew
Who think that war is nothing to do
But to drill and cipher, and hammer and forge, —
What are you waiting for, tardy George ?

January, 1862.

THE CUMBERLAND.*

BY HENRY W. LONGFELLOW.

AT anchor in Hampton Roads we lay,
  On board the Cumberland sloop-of-war,
And at times from the fortress across the bay
    The alarm of drums swept past,
      Or a bugle-blast
  From the camp on shore.

Then far away to the South uprose
  A little feather of snow-white smoke,
And we knew that the iron ship of our foes
    Was steadily steering its course
      To try the force
  Of our ribs of oak.

Down upon us heavily runs,
  Silent and sullen, the floating fort ;
Then comes a puff of smoke from her guns,
    And leaps the terrrible death,
      With fiery breath,
  From each open port.

We are not idle, but send her straight
  Defiance back in a full broadside !
As hail rebounds from a roof of slate,
    Rebounds our heavier hail
      From each iron scale
  Of the monster's hide.

---

* Sunk by the iron-clad ram Merrimac in Hampton Roads,
Saturday, March 8, 1862, going down with her colors flying, and
firing upon her impenetrable assailant as the water rose above her
own gun-deck.

" Strike your flag ! " the rebel cries,
    In his arrogant old plantation strain.
" Never ! " our gallant Morris replies ;
      " It is better to sink than to yield ! "
     And the whole air pealed
    With the cheers of our men.

Then, like a kraken huge and black,
    She crushed our ribs in her iron grasp !
Down went the Cumberland all a-wrack,
     With a sudden shudder of death,
     And the cannon's breath
    For her dying gasp.

Next morn, as the sun rose over the bay,
    Still floated our flag at the mainmast-head.
Lord, how beautiful was Thy day !
     Every waft of the air
     Was a whisper of prayer,
    Or a dirge for the dead.

Ho ! brave hearts that went down in the seas,
    Ye are at peace in the troubled stream.
Ho ! brave land ! with hearts like these,
     Thy flag, that is rent in twain,
     Shall be one again,
    And without a seam.

———◆———

ON BOARD THE CUMBERLAND.

March 8, 1862.

BY GEORGE H. BOKER.

" STAND to your guns, men ! " Morris cried.
    Small need to pass the word ;

Our men at quarters ranged themselves,
　Before the drum was heard.

And then began the sailors' jests:
　" What thing is that, I say ? "
" A long-shore meeting-house adrift
　Is standing down the bay ! "

A frown came over Morris's face;
　The strange, dark craft he knew;
" That is the iron Merrimac,
　Manned by a Rebel crew.

" So shot your guns, and point them straight;
　Before this day goes by,
We 'll try of what her metal 's made."
　A cheer was our reply.

" Remember, boys, this flag of ours
　Has seldom left its place;
And where it falls, the deck it strikes
　Is covered with disgrace.

" I ask but this : or sink or swim,
　Or live or nobly die,
My last sight upon earth may be
　To see that ensign fly ! "

Meanwhile the shapeless iron mass
　Came moving o'er the wave,
As gloomy as a passing hearse,
　As silent as the grave.

Her ports were closed, from stem to stern
　No sign of life appeared.
We wondered, questioned, strained our eyes,
　Joked, — everything but feared.

She reached our range.   Our broadside rang,
  Our heavy pivots roared;
And shot and shell, a fire of hell,
  Against her sides we poured.

God's mercy! from her sloping roof
  The iron tempest glanced,
As hail bounds from a cottage-thatch,
  And round her leaped and danced;

Or when against her dusky hull
  We struck a fair, full blow,
The mighty, solid iron globes
  Were crumbled up like snow.

On, on, with fast increasing speed,
  The silent monster came;
Though all our starboard battery
  Was one long line of flame.

She heeded not, no gun she fired,
  Straight on our bow she bore;
Through riving plank and crashing frame
  Her furious way she tore.

Alas! our beautiful, keen bow,
  That in the fiercest blast
So gently folded back the seas,
  They hardly felt we passed!

Alas! alas! my Cumberland,
  That ne'er knew grief before,
To be so gored, to feel so deep
  The tusk of that sea-boar!

Once more she backward drew a space,
  Once more our side she rent;

Then, in the wantonness of hate,
    Her broadside through us sent.

The dead and dying round us lay,
    But our foeman lay abeam;
Her open port-holes maddened us;
    We fired with shout and scream.

We felt our vessel settling fast,
    We knew our time was brief;
" The pumps, the pumps!" But they who pumped,
    And fought not, wept with grief.

" Oh, keep us but an hour afloat!
    Oh, give us only time
To be the instruments of Heaven
    Against the traitors' crime!"

From captain down to powder-boy,
    No hand was idle then;
Two soldiers, but by chance aboard,
    Fought on like sailor-men.

And when a gun's crew lost a hand,
    Some bold marine stepped out,
And jerked his braided jacket off,
    And hauled the gun about.

Our forward magazine was drowned;
    And up from the sick-bay
Crawled out the wounded, red with blood,
    And round us gasping lay.

Yes, cheering, calling us by name,
    Struggling with failing breath,
To keep their shipmates at the post
    Where glory strove with death.

With decks afloat, and powder gone,
  The last broadside we gave
From the guns' heated iron lips
  Burst out beneath the wave.

So sponges, rammers, and handspikes —
  As men-of-war's-men should —
We placed within their proper racks,
  And at our quarters stood.

" Up to the spar-deck ! save yourselves ! "
  Cried Selfridge. " Up, my men !
God grant that some of us may live
  To fight yon ship again ! "

We turned — we did not like to go;
  Yet staying seemed but vain,
Knee-deep in water; so we left ;
  Some swore, some groaned with pain.

We reached the deck.   There Randall stood :
  " Another turn, men — so ! "
Calmly he aimed his pivot-gun :
  " Now, Tenny, let her go ! "

It did our sore hearts good to hear
  The song our pivot sang,
As rushing on from wave to wave
  The whirring bomb-shell sprang.

Brave Randall leaped upon the gun,
  And waved his cap in sport ;
" Well done ! well aimed ! I saw that shell
  Go through an open port."

It was our last, our deadliest shot ;
  The deck was overflown ;

The poor ship staggered, lurched to port,
  And gave a living groan.

Down, down, as headlong through the waves
  Our gallant vessel rushed,
A thousand gurgling, watery sounds
  Around my senses gushed.

Then I remember little more;
  One look to heaven I gave,
Where, like an angel's wing, I saw
  Our spotless ensign wave.

I tried to cheer. I cannot say
  Whether I swam or sank;
A blue mist closed around my eyes,
  And everything was blank.

When I awoke, a soldier-lad,
  All dripping from the sea,
With two great tears upon his cheeks,
  Was bending over me.

I tried to speak. He understood
  The wish I could not speak.
He turned me. There, thank God! the flag
  Still fluttered at the peak!

And there, while thread shall hang to thread,
  Oh, let that ensign fly!
The noblest constellation set
  Against our northern sky.

A sign that we who live may claim
  The peerage of the brave;
A monument, that needs no scroll
  For those beneath the wave!

MARCHING ALONG.*

BY WILLIAM B. BRADBURY.

THE army is gathering from near and from far;
The trumpet is sounding the call for the war;
McClellan 's our leader, he 's gallant and strong;
We 'll gird on our armor and be marching along.

CHORUS.

Marching along, we are marching along,
Gird on the armor and be marching along;
McClellan 's our leader, he 's gallant and strong;
For God and our country we are marching along.

The foe is before us in battle array,
But let us not waver, or turn from the way;
The Lord is our strength, and the Union 's our song;
With courage and faith we are marching along.
Chorus — Marching along, &c.

Our wives and our children we leave in your care;
We feel you will help them with sorrow to bear;
'T is hard thus to part, but we hope 't won't be long;
We 'll keep up our hearts as we 're marching along.
Chorus — Marching along, &c.

We sigh for our country, we mourn for our dead;
For them now our last drop of blood we will shed;

---

* Few songs were more truly popular all through the war than this, which is here printed from a street broadside. It was sung in the streets and at the public schools, and by all sorts and conditions of men. The name McClellan, in the first stanza, was successively replaced by Hooker, Meade, and Grant, with " for," prefixed when necessary to eke out the measure. A vigorous and spirited melody, with a well-marked rhythm, which was particularly good in the chorus, contributed much to the universal favor in which this song was held.

Our cause is the right one — our foe's in the wrong ;
Then gladly we 'll sing as we 're marching along.
    Chorus — Marching along, &c.

The flag of our country is floating on high ;
We 'll stand by that flag till we conquer or die ;
McClellan 's our leader, he 's gallant and strong ;
We 'll gird on our armor and be marching along.
    Chorus — Marching along, &c.

——◆——

A YANKEE SOLDIER'S SONG.

I HEARKENED to the thund'ring noise,
  And wondered what 't was for, sir !
But when I heard 'em tell our boys,
  I started up and swore, sir !
      Yankee boys will fight it out !
      Yankees brave and handy !
      Freedom be our battle-shout !
      Yankee doodle dandy !

They said that traitors tore our flag,
  Down there in Dixie's land, sir ;
I always loved the striped rag,
  And swore by it to stand, sir.
      Yankee boys will fight it out ! &c.

I knew them Southern chaps, high-bred,
  Had called us "mudsills" here, sir :
If on these sills they try to tread,
  I guess 't will cost them dear, sir.
      Yankee boys will fight it out ! &c.

Down South I marched, rat-tat-a-plan,
  With heart brimful of pluck, sir;
I held my head up like a man;
  A righteous cause brings luck, sir.
        Yankee boys will fight it out! &c.

So proud was I of fatherland,
  Where humans all are free, sir,
I found it hard to understand
  Some things I lived to see, sir.
        Yankee boys will fight it out! &c.

To us one day a brown man came,
  In Dixie's land a slave, sir,
And pleaded hard, in Freedom's name,
  That him we 'd try to save, sir.
        Yankee boys will fight it out! &c.

" Of course we will," our men cried out;
  " All free beneath this flag, sir!"
Then he began, with hearty shout,
  To cheer the starry rag, sir.
        Yankee boys will fight it out! &c.

But, whip in hand, a master came,
  And drove that man away, sir;
We felt it was a burning shame,
  But could not have our say, sir.
        Yankee boys will fight it out! &c.

To us it seems a coward's shirk, —
  It makes us feel less brave, sir;
We call it mean and "mudsill" work,
  This sending back a slave, sir!
        Yankee boys will fight it out! &c.

We did not leave our homes to do
  Such dirty jobs as these, sir;

Our hearts within us, warm and true,
  It chills and makes 'em freeze, sir.
      Yankee boys will fight it out! &c.

The man who works with heart is strong,
  And right keeps up the pluck, sir;
We cannot feel so bold for wrong, —
  We cannot hope for luck, sir.
      Yankee boys will fight it out! &c.

We long to have our flag unfurled
  To make the *whole* land free, sir —
For we can proudly face the world
  When we that day shall see, sir.
      Yankee boys will fight it out! &c.

Oh, how we 'll hail our banner then!
  Its fame all clear and bright, sir;
When all can feel that they are men,
  And all have equal right, sir.
      Yankee boys will fight it out!
        Yankees brave and handy!
      Freedom be our battle-shout!
        Yankee doodle dandy!

THE IRISH PICKET.

BY " BARNEY."

AIR — " *I 'm sitting on the stile, Mary.*"

I 'M shtanding in the mud, Biddy,
  Wid not a spalpeen near,
And silence, spaichless as the grave,
  Is all the sound I hear.

Me goon is at a showlther-arms,
　　I 'm wetted to the bone,
And whin I 'm afther sphakin' out,
　　I find meself alone.

This Southern climate 's quare, Biddy,
　　A quare and bastely thing,
Wid winter absint all the year,
　　And summer in the spring.
Ye mind the hot place down below ?
　　And may ye never fear
I 'd dthraw comparisons — but thin
　　It 's awful warrum here.

The only moon I see, Biddy,
　　Is one shmall star, asthore,
And that 's fornint the very cloud
　　It was behind before ;
The watch-fires glame along the hill
　　That 's swellin' to the south,
And whin the sinthry passes them,
　　I see his oogly mouth.

It 's dead for shlape I am, Biddy,
　　And dramein' shwate I 'd be,
If them ould Rebels over there
　　Would only lave me free ;
But whin I lane against a shtump
　　And shtrive to get repose,
A musket ball be 's comin' shtraight
　　To hit me spacious nose.

It 's ye I 'd like to see, Biddy,
　　A shparkin here wid me ;
And then, avourneen, hear ye say,
　　" Acushla — Pat — machree ! "
" Och, Biddy, darlint," then says I ;
　　Says you, " Get out of that ;'

Says I, " Me arrum mates your waist ; "
　Says you, " Be daycent, Pat."

And how 's the pigs and doocks, Biddy ?
　It 's them I think of, shure,
That looked so innocent and shwate
　Upon the parlor-flure ;
I 'm shure ye 're aisy wid the pig,
　That 's fat as he can be,
And fade him wid the best, because
　I 'm towld he looks like me.

Whin I come home again, Biddy,
　A sargent tried and thrue,
It 's joost a daycent house I 'll build,
　And rint it chape to you.
We 'll have a parlor, bedroom, hall,
　A doock-pond nately done,
Wid kitchen, pig-pen, praty-patch,
　And garret — all in one.

But, murther ! there 's a baste, Biddy,
　That 's crapin' round a tree,
And well I know the crathur 's there
　To have a shot at me.
Now, Misther Rebel, say yer pray'rs,
　And howld yer dirty paw ;
Here goes ! — be jabers, Biddy, dear,
　I 've broke his oogly jaw !

WORDS THAT CAN BE SUNG TO THE " HALLELUJAH CHORUS."

BY HENRY H. BROWNELL, U. S. N.

If people *will* sing about Old John Brown, there is no reason why they should n't have words with a little meaning and rhythm in them.

OLD John Brown lies a-mouldering in the grave,
Old John Brown lies slumbering in his grave ;
But John Brown's soul is marching with the brave,
   His soul is marching on.
  Glory, glory, hallelujah !
  Glory, glory, hallelujah !
  Glory, glory, hallelujah !
   His soul is marching on.

He has gone to be a soldier in the army of the Lord,
He is sworn as a private in the ranks of the Lord ;
He shall stand at Armageddon with his brave old sword,
   When Heaven is marching on.
  Glory, glory, hallelujah, &c.
   For Heaven is marching on.

He shall file in front where the lines of battle form,
He shall face to front when the squares of battle form,
Time with the column, and charge in the storm,
   Where men are marching on.
  Glory, glory, hallelujah, &c.
   True men are marching on.

Ah ! foul tyrants ! do ye hear him where he comes ?
Ah ! black traitors ! do ye know him as he comes ?
In thunder of the cannon and roll of the drums,
   As we go marching on.
  Glory, glory, hallelujah, &c.
   We all are marching on.

Men may die, and moulder in the dust,
Men may die, and arise again from dust,
Shoulder to shoulder, in the ranks of the just,
        When Heaven is marching on.
      Glory, glory, hallelujah, &c.
        The Lord is marching on.

   April 17, 1862.

LULLABY.

BY E. JEFFERSON CUTLER.

Now the twilight shadows flit ;
Now the evening lamp is lit ;
   Sleep, baby, sleep !
Little head on mother's arm,
She will keep him safe from harm, —
Keep him safe and fold him warm :
   Sleep, baby, sleep !

Baby's father, far away,
Thinks of him at shut of day ;
   Sleep, baby, sleep !
He must guard the sleeping camp,
Hearkening, in the cold and damp,
For the foeman's stealthy tramp :
   Sleep, baby, sleep !

He can hear the lullaby,
He can see the laughing eye ;
   Sleep, baby, sleep !
And he knows, though we are dumb,
How we long to have him come
Back to baby, mother, home :
   Sleep, baby, sleep !
    7

Now the eyes are closing up;
Let their little curtains drop;
    Sleep, baby, sleep!
Softly on his father's bed
Mother lays her baby's head;
There, until the night be fled,
    Sleep, baby, sleep!

God, who driest the widow's tears,
God, who calms the orphan's fears,
    Guard baby's sleep!
Shield the father in the fray;
Help the mother wait and pray;
Keep us all by night and day:
    Sleep, baby, sleep!

Only Once.

THE RIVER FIGHT.

BY H. H. BROWNELL, U. S. N.

Do you know of the dreary land,
   If land such region may seem,
Where 't is neither sea nor strand,
Ocean nor good dry land,
   But the nightmare marsh of a dream?
Where the Mighty River his death-road takes,
Mid pools and windings that coil like snakes,
A hundred leagues of bayous and lakes,
   To die in the great Gulf Stream?

No coast-line clear and true,
Granite and deep-sea blue,
   On that dismal shore you pass,
Surf-worn boulder or sandy beach, —

But ooze-flats as far as the eye can reach,
  With shallows of water-grass;
Reedy savannahs, vast and dun,
Lying dead in the dim March sun;
Huge rotting trunks and roots that lie
Like the blackened bones of shapes gone by,
  And miles of sunken morass.

No lovely, delicate thing
  Of life o'er the waste is seen;
But the cayman, couched by his weedy spring,
  And the pelican, bird unclean,
Or the buzzard, flapping with heavy wing,
  Like an evil ghost o'er the desolate scene.

Ah! many a weary day
With our Leader there we lay,
  In the sultry haze and smoke,
Tugging our ships o'er the bar,
Till the Spring was wasted far,
  Till his brave heart almost broke.
For the sullen river seemed
As if our intent he dreamed, —
  All his sallow mouths did spew and choke.

But ere April fully passed,
All ground over at last,
And we knew the die was cast, —
  Knew the day drew nigh
To dare to the end one stormy deed,
Might save the land at her sorest need,
  Or on the old deck to die!

Anchored we lay, — and a morn the more,
  To his captains and all his men
Thus wrote our old Commodore —
  (He was n't Admiral then):

"GENERAL ORDERS.

" Send your to'gallant-masts down,
    Rig in each flying jib-boom !
    Clear all ahead for the loom
Of traitor fortress and town,
Or traitor fleet bearing down.

    " In with your canvas high ;
    We shall want no sail to fly !
Topsail, foresail, spanker, and jib,
(With the heart of oak in the oaken rib,)
    Shall serve us to win or die !

    " Trim every sail by the head,
    (So shall you spare the lead,)
Lest, if she ground, your ship swing round,
    Bows in shore, for a wreck.
See your grapnels all clear with pains,
And a solid kedge in your port main-chains,
    With a whip to the main yard :
    Drop it heavy and hard
        When you grapple a traitor deck !

" On forecastle and on poop
    Mount guns, as best you may deem.
If possible, rouse them up,
    (For still you must bow the stream.)
Also hoist and secure with stops
Howitzers firmly in your tops, .
    To fire on the foe a-beam.

" Look well to your pumps and hose ;
    Have water-tubs fore and aft,
    For quenching flame in your craft,
        And the gun-crews' fiery thirst.
See planks with felt fitted close,

To plug every shot-hole tight.
    Stand ready to meet the worst!
  For, if I have reckoned aright,
They will serve us shot, both cold and hot,
    Freely enough to-night.

" Mark well each signal I make, —
(Our life-long service at stake,
    And honor that must not lag !)
Whate'er the peril and awe,
In the battle's fieriest flaw,
Let never one ship withdraw
    Till the orders come from the flag ! "

———

Would you hear of the River Fight ?
It was two of a soft spring night;
    God's stars looked down on all;
And all was clear and bright
But the low fog's clinging breath :
Up the River of Death
    Sailed the Great Admiral.

On our high poop-deck he stood,
    And round him ranged the men
Who have made their birthright good
    Of manhood once and again, —
Lords of helm and of sail,
Tried in tempest and gale,
    Bronzed in battle and wreck.
Bell and Bailey grandly led
Each his line of the Blue and Red;
Wainwright stood by our starboard rail;
    Thornton fought the deck.

And I mind me of more than they,
    Of the youthful, steadfast ones,

That have shown them worthy sons
Of the seamen passed away.
Tyson conned our helm that day ;
  Watson stood by his guns.

What thought our Admiral then,
Looking down on his men ?
  Since the terrible day, —
    (Day of renown and tears !)
  When at anchor the Essex lay,
  Holding her foes at bay, —
When a boy by Porter's side he stood,
Till deck and plank-shear were dyed with blood :
    'T is half a hundred years, —
  Half a hundred years to a day !

Who could fail with him ?
Who reckon of life or limb ?
  Not a pulse but beat the higher !
There had you seen, by the starlight dim,
Five hundred faces strong and grim :
  The Flag is going under fire !
Right up by the fort, with her helm hard a-port,
  The Hartford is going under fire !

The way to our work was plain.
Caldwell had broken the chain,
(Two hulks swung down amain
  Soon as 't was sundered.)
Under the night's dark blue,
Steering steady and true,
Ship after ship went through,
Till, as we hove in view,
  "Jackson" out-thundered.

Back echoed "Philip !" Ah ! then
Could you have seen our men,

How they sprung, in the dim night haze,
To their work of toil and of clamor!
How the boarders, with sponge and rammer,
And their captains, with cord and hammer,
    Kept every muzzle a-blaze.
How the guns, as with cheer and shout
Our tackle-men hurled them out,
    Brought up on the water-ways!

First, as we fired at their flash,
    'T was lightning and black eclipse,
With a bellowing roll and crash.
But soon, upon either bow,
    What with forts, and fire-rafts, and ships,
(The whole fleet was hard at it, now,)
All pounding away! — and Porter
Still thundering with shell and mortar, —
    'T was the mighty sound and form!

(Such you see in the far South,
After long heat and drought,
    As day draws nigh to even,
Arching from north to south,
    Blinding the tropic sun,
    The great black bow comes on,
Till the thunder-veil is riven, —
When all is crash and levin,
And the cannonade of heaven
    Rolls down the Amazon!)

But, as we worked along higher,
    Just where the river enlarges,
Down came a pyramid of fire, —
    It was one of your long coal barges.
    (We had often had the like before.)
'T was coming down on us to larboard,
    Well in with the eastern shore;
    And our pilot, to let it pass round,

(You may guess we never stopped to sound,)
Giving us a rank sheer to starboard,
 Ran the Flag hard and fast aground!

'T was nigh abreast of the Upper Fort,
 And straightway a rascal Ram
 (She was shaped like the Devil's dam)
Puffed away for us, with a snort,
 And shoved it, with spiteful strength,
Right alongside of us to port.
 It was all of our ship's length, —
A huge crackling Cradle of the Pit!
 Pitch-pine knots to the brim,
 Belching flame red and grim, —
What a roar came up from it!

Well, for a little it looked bad:
 But these things are, somehow, shorter
In the acting than in the telling;
There was no singing out or yelling,
Or any fussing and fretting,
 No stampede, in short;
But there we were, my lad,
 All a-fire on our port quarter
Hammocks a-blaze in the netting,
 Flame spouting in at every port,
Our Fourth Cutter burning at the davit,
(No chance to lower away and save it.)

In a twinkling, the flames had risen
Half way to main-top and mizen,
 Darting up the shrouds like snakes!
 Ah, how we clanked at the brakes,
 And the deep steaming-pumps throbbed under,
 Sending a ceaseless flow.
Our top-men, a dauntless crowd,
Swarmed in rigging and shroud:
 There, ('t was a wonder!)

The burning ratlins and strands
They quenched with their bare hard hands ;
    But the great guns below
    Never silenced their thunder !

At last, by backing and sounding,
When we were clear of grounding,
    And under headway once more,
The whole rebel fleet came rounding
    The point. If we had it hot before,
    'T was now, from shore to shore,
    One long, loud thundering roar, —
Such crashing, splintering, and pounding,
    And smashing as you never heard before !

But that we fought foul wrong to wreck,
    And to save the land we loved so well,
You might have deemed our long gun-deck
    Two hundred feet of hell !

For above all was battle,
Broadside, and blaze, and rattle,
    Smoke and thunder alone ;
(But, down in the sick-bay,
Where our wounded and dying lay,
    There was scarce a sob or a moan.)
And at last, when the dim day broke,
And the sullen sun awoke,
    Drearily blinking
O'er the haze and the cannon smoke,
That ever such morning dulls, —
There were thirteen traitor hulls
    On fire and sinking !

Now, up the river ! — through mad Chalmette
Sputters a vain resistance yet.
Small helm we gave her, our course to steer, —
    'T was nicer work than you well would dream,

With cant and sheer to keep her clear
　　Of the burning wrecks that cumbered the stream.

The Louisiana, hurled on high,
Mounts in thunder to meet the sky!
Then down to the depths of the turbid flood, —
Fifty fathom of rebel mud!
The Mississippi comes floating down,
A mighty bonfire, from off the town;
And along the river, on stocks and ways,
A half-hatched devil's brood is a-blaze, —
The great Anglo-Norman is all in flames,
(Hark to the roar of her tumbling frames!)
And the smaller fry that Treason would spawn
Are lighting Algiers like an angry dawn!

From stem to stern, how the pirates burn,
　　Fired by the furious hands that built!
So to ashes forever turn
　　The suicide wrecks of wrong and guilt!

But as we neared the city,
　　By field and vast plantation,
　　(Ah, millstone of our Nation!)
With wonder and with pity,
　　What crowds we there espied
Of dark and wistful faces,
Mute in their toiling places,
　　Strangely and sadly eyed.
　　Haply, 'mid doubt and fear,
　　Deeming deliverance near.
　　(One gave the ghost of a cheer!)

And on that dolorous strand,
　　To greet the victor brave
　　One flag did welcome wave, —
Raised, ah me! by a wretched hand,

All outworn on our cruel Land, —
  The withered hand of a slave !

But all along the Levee,
  In a dark and drenching rain,
(By this, 't was pouring heavy,)
  Stood a fierce and sullen train.
A strange and frenzied time !
  There were scowling rage and pain,
    Curses, howls and hisses,
    Out of hate's black abysses, —
Their courage and their crime
  All in vain — all in vain !

For from the hour that the Rebel Stream,
With the Crescent City lying abeam,
  Shuddered under our keel,
Smit to the heart with self-struck sting,
Slavery died in her scorpion-ring,
  And Murder fell on his steel.

'T is well to do and dare ;
But ever may grateful prayer
Follow, as aye it ought,
When the good fight is fought,
  When the true deed is done.
Aloft in heaven's pure light,
(Deep azure crossed on white,)
Our fair Church pennant waves
O'er a thousand thankful braves,
  Bareheaded in God's bright sun.

Lord of mercy and frown,
  Ruling o'er sea and shore,
  Send us such scene once more !
    All in line of battle
When the black ships bear down

On tyrant fort and town,
　　Mid cannon cloud and rattle;
And the great guns once more
Thunder back the roar
Of the traitor walls ashore,
And the traitor flags come down!

New Orleans Era.

———◆———

THE BALLAD OF THE CRESCENT CITY.

I.

In the City of the Crescent, by red Mississippi's waves,
Dwells the haughty Creole matron with her daughters
　　and her slaves;
Round her throng the rebel knighthood, fierce of word
　　and proud of crest,
Slightly redolent of julep, cocktail, cobbler, and the rest
Of those miscellaneous tipples that the Southern heart
　　impel
To the mighty threats of prowess, whose dread fruits we
　　know so well.*
Round the matron and her daughters ring chivalric voices
　　high:
Not the meanest soul among them but is sworn to do or
　　die!
"Never to the Yankee Vandal, foul and hornéd thing of
　　mud,
Will they leave their maids and matrons while a single
　　vein holds blood!

---

* It is singular that the juleps, cocktails, and "miscellaneous
tipples" which European writers continually ridicule as a trait of
Yankee life, are all, as we know, of Southern invention.

Perish every Southron sooner! Death? They crave it
 as a boon!"
Then each desperate knight retires — to his favorite
 Quadroon!

II.

In the City of the Crescent, by red Mississippi's waves,
Sits the haughty Creole matron with her daughters and
 her slaves;
But her eye no longer flashes with the fire it held of late,
For, alas! the Yankee Vandals thunder at the city gate.
Proud on Mississippi's waters, looming o'er the dark levée,
Ride the gallant Northern war-ships, floats the Banner of
 the Free!
While a calm-eyed Captain paces through a sea of scowl-
 ing men,
To demand the full surrender of the city, there and then.
Yet the haughty Creole lady's sorest sorrow lies not there:
'T is not that the Yankee mudsills will pollute her sacred
 air; —
Though her delicate fibres shudder doubtless at the dread-
 ful thought
That her soft and fragrant breathings may by Yankee lips
 be caught; —
No! the cut of all unkindest — that which makes her
 heart dilate —
Is, her knights have all "skedaddled," and have left her
 to her fate!
Yes; no strength of smash or julep, nor the cocktail's
 bitterest heat,
Kept those recreant warriors steady when they saw the
 Yankee fleet;
All their desperate prowess vanished like a mist before
 the moon, —
Left the Creole maid and matron, even left the dear
 Quadroon!

III.

In the City of the Crescent, by red Mississippi's waves,
Walks the haughty Creole matron with her daughters and
her slaves;
Freedom's flag is floating o'er her, Freedom's sons she
passes by,
And the olden scornful fire burns rekindled in her
eye.
How dare Freedom thus insult her?   How dare mudsills
walk the pave
Whose each stone to her is hallowed by the toil-sweat of
the slave?
" What? you call that rag your banner?   You, sir, hire-
ling, hound, I mean!
Thus I spit upon your emblem!   Let your churl's blood
wash it clean!
Well you wear your liveried jacket, hireling bravo that
you are!
Lackey, paid to rob and murder in a thin disguise of
war!"
Thus, with many a taunting gesture, speaks she to the
Northern braves,
As she flaunts along the sidewalk with her daughters and
her slaves!
Naught reply the Northern soldiers, smiling, though they
feel the stings
Of the foul and meretricious taunts the Southern lady
flings;
So she passes, while the venom from her fragrant mouth
still slips
Like the loathsome toads and lizards from the enchanted
maiden's lips;
And her spotless soul joys, doubtless, soft her modest
bosom beats,
That she so has aped the harlot in her city's public
streets!

IV.

In the City of the Crescent, by red Mississippi's waves,
Walks the haughty Creole lady with her daughters and
 her slaves;
But her eye no longer flashes with its wonted fire of hate;
Her tongue is strangely silent now, and modest is her
 gait;
With quiet mien and humble she passes soldiers by,
Nor ever on our country's flag turns a defiant eye.
What wondrous glamour so hath changed the haughty
 lady's mien?
The crime of her rebellious heart hath she in sorrow
 seen?
Or has her spotless bosom owned that Yankees there
 may be
Worthy of even a Creole's love? Is hers no longer free?
No; it is none of these have tamed the lady's rebel soul;
On each mudsill she, *certes*, still breathes inward curse
 and dole!
And as for love, save for her knight, no love her heart
 can stir,
Since o'er a julep's sugared brink he swore to die for her;
For though he died not, but preferred another field to
 seek,
'T was only, as she knows, because the julep was too
 weak!
'T was none of these! A sterner cause for change of
 mien had she!
For spitting once too often at the Banner of the Free,
And once too oft through her pure lips the venom letting
 loose,
The haughty Creole dame was shown into — the Cala-
 boose!

Harpers' Weekly.

NEW ORLEANS WON BACK.

A LAY FOR OUR SAILORS.

BY ROBERT LOWELL.

[The opening words of the burden are a scrap of an old song caught up.]

CATCH — Oh! up in the morning, up in the morning,
   Up in the morning early!
  There lay the town that our guns looked down,
   With its streets all dark and surly.

God made three youths to walk unscathed
 In the furnace seven times hot;
And when smoky flames our squadron bathed,
 Amid horrors of shell and shot,
Then, too, it was God that brought them through
 That death-crowded thoroughfare:
So now, at six bells, the church pennons flew,
 And the crews went all to prayer.
Thank God! thank God! our men won the fight,
 Against forts, and fleets, and flame:
Thank God! they have given our flag its right,
 In a town that brought it shame.
   Oh! up in the morning, up in the morning,
    Up in the morning early!
   Our flag hung there, in the fresh, still air,
    With smoke floating soft and curly.

Ten days for the deep ships at the bar;
 Six days for the mortar-fleet,
That battered the great forts from afar;
 And then, to that deadly street!
A flash! Our strong ships snapped the boom
 To the fire-rafts and the forts,

To crush and crash, and flash and gloom,
  And iron beaks fumbling their ports.
From the dark came the raft, in flame and smoke ;
  In the dark came the iron beak ;
But our sailors' hearts were stouter than oak,
  And the false foe's iron weak.
        Oh ! up in the morning, up in the morning,
          Up in the morning early !
        Before they knew, they had burst safe through,
          And left the forts, grim and burly.

Though it be brute's work, not man's, to tear
  Live limbs like shivered wood ;
Yet, to dare, and to stand, and to take death for share,
  Are as much as the angels could.
Our men towed the blazing rafts ashore ;
  They battered the great rams down ;
Scarce a wreck floated where was a fleet before,
  When our ships came up to the town.
There were miles of batteries yet to be dared,
  But they quenched these all, as in play ;
Then with their yards squared, their guns' mouths bared,
  They held the great town at bay.
        Oh ! up in the morning, up in the morning,
          Up in the morning early !
        Our stout ships came through shell, shot, and
            flame,
          But the town will not always be surly ;

For this Crescent City takes to its breast
  The Father of Waters' tide ;
And here shall the wealth of our world, in the West,
  Meet wealth of the world beside :
Here the date-palm and the olive find
  A near and equal sun ;
And a hundred broad, deep rivers wind
  To the summer-sea in one :

8

Here the Fall steals all old Winter's ice,
    And the Spring steals all his snow;
While he but smiles at their artifice,
    And like his own nature go.
            Oh! up in the morning, up in the morning,
                Up in the morning early!
            May that flag float here till the earth's last
                year,
                With the lake mists, fair and pearly.

———◆———

THE VARUNA.

Sunk April 24th, 1862.*

BY GEORGE H. BOKER.

WHO has not heard of the dauntless Varuna?
    Who has not heard of the deeds she has done?
Who shall not hear, while the brown Mississippi
    Rushes along from the snow to the sun?

Crippled and leaking she entered the battle,
    Sinking and burning she fought through the fray;
Crushed were her sides, and the waves ran across her,
    Ere, like a death-wounded lion at bay,
Sternly she closed in the last fatal grapple,
    Then in her triumph moved grandly away.

Five of the rebels, like satellites round her,
    Burned in her orbit of splendor and fear;
One, like the pleiad of mystical story,
    Shot, terror-stricken, beyond her dread sphere.

We who are waiting with crowns for the victors,
    Though we should offer the wealth of our store,

* After sinking five of the enemy in the naval battle below New
Orleans.

Load the Varuna from deck down to kelson,
   Still would be niggard, such tribute to pour
On courage so boundless.   It beggars possession, —
   It knocks for just payment at heaven's bright door!

Cherish the heroes who fought the Varuna;
   Treat them as kings if they honor your way;
Succor and comfort the sick and the wounded;
   Oh! for the dead let us all kneel to pray.

———◆———

THE NEW BALLAD OF LORD LOVELL.*

LORD LOVELL he sat in St. Charles's Hotel, —
   In St. Charles's Hotel sat he;
As fine a case of a Southern swell
   As ever you 'd wish to see — see — see,
         As ever you 'd wish to see.

Lord Lovell the town had vowed to defend:
   A-waving his sword on high,
He swore thàt his last ounce of powder he 'd spend,
   And in the last ditch he 'd die.

He swore by black and he swore by blue,
   He swore by the stars and bars,
That never he 'd fly from a Yankee crew
   While he was a son of Mars.

He had fifty thousand gallant men, —
   Fifty thousand men had he,
Who had all sworn with him that they 'd never
   Surrender to any tarnation Yankee.

* Mansfield Lovell, of New York, commanded the Rebel troops
at New Orleans, and, on the approach of the national fleet and
army to that place, "led his forces out of the town."

He had forts that no Yankee alive could take;
    He had iron-clad boats a score;
And batteries all around the Lake,
    And all along the river-shore.

Sir Farragut came with a mighty fleet, —
    With a mighty fleet came he;
And Lord Lovell instanter began to retreat,
    Before the first boat he could see.

His fifty thousand gallant men
    Dwindled down to thousands six;
They heard a distant cannon, and then
    Commenced a-cutting their sticks.

" Oh, tarry, Lord Lovell! " Sir Farragut cried;
    " Oh, tarry, Lord Lovell! " said he;
" I rather think not," Lord Lovell replied,
    " For I 'm in a great hurry."

" I like the drinks at St. Charles's Hotel,
    But I never could bear strong Porter,
Especially when it 's served on the shell,
    Or mixed in an iron mortar."

" I reckon you 're right," Sir Farragut said;
    " I reckon you 're right," said he;
" For if my Porter should fly to your head,
    A terrible smash there 'd be."

Oh, a wonder it was to see them run!
    A wonderful thing to see;
And the Yankees sailed up without shooting a gun,
    And captured their great citie.

Lord Lovell kept running all day and night, —
    Lord Lovell a-running kept he;

For he swore he could n't abide the sight
Of the gun of a live Yankee.

When Lord Lovell's life was brought to a close
By a sharp-shooting Yankee gunner,
From his head there sprouted a red, red nose,
From his feet — a Scarlet Runner.

———◆———

GINERAL BUTLER.

[LINES RIT TU RICHARD YEADON, A RANK, PIZEN REBBEL, WHU
HES OFFERED TEN THAOUSAND DOLLARS FUR THE HED OV
GINERAL BUTLER. I ONLY WISH THE AMERIKAN EGLE MAY
LIVE TILL HE GITS IT!]

BY CHARITY GRIMES.

Yu offer us ten thaousand fur the hed ov Butler, du ye ?
Wa'al, I vaow I wunder at it ! But yu may jest spare
yure pains.
I tell yu (ef yu know enuff tu git the idee thru yu),
Yu 'd better wish, a tarnal site, fur Gineral Butler's
brains !

Here 's a fust-rate chance tu make a pile ! — a bribe fur
human natur !
Naow is the time fur Judases tu clap thare hands and
larf;
Ten thaousand dollars offered fur the sarvice ov a traitor ?
Why thare 's menny a poor scoundrel thet wood du the
work fur half !

Want the hed ov Gineral Butler ! Wa'al, I never ! 't is
surprisin !
Yu fellers daown in Dixie must be fallin off from grace.

Not hevin enny decent hed (that fact thare's no dis-
    guisin),
    Yu want tu take yure nabor's, es ef that wood help
        yure case !
Ten thaousand dollars offered !   Specie payment is 't, I
    wunder ?
    Bein a Yankee born, yu know, p'r'aps I *am* kind o' cute.
Yure promises air fair enuff; but fokes du sumtimes
    blunder,
    And them Confederate notes ov yourn, — 't ain't every
        wun they 'd suit !

Ten thaousand dollars offered fur the hed ov Butler !
    Reely !
    Haow long is 't sense yu larfed et him, and called him
        " Pickayune ? "
Did yu find he was tu big a coin fur yu tu hold genteely ?
    Or has he put yure notes ov war a leetle aout ov tune ?

Yu offer us ten thaousand fur the hed ov Butler, du yu ?
    Wa'al, I *don't* mutch wunder at it, — but yu may jest
        spare yure pains ;
But I 'll tell yu (ef yu know enuff to git the idee thru yu),
    Yu 'd better (fur yu need 'em) wish fur Gineral Butler's
        brains !

                        Harpers' Weekly.

RHODE ISLAND TO THE SOUTH.

BY GEN. F. W. LANDER.

ONCE on New England's bloody heights,
    And o'er a Southern plain,
Our fathers fought for sovereign rights,
    That working men might reign.

And by that only Lord we serve,
    The great Jehovah's name ;

By those sweet lips that ever nerve
   High hearts to deeds of fame;

By all that makes the man a king,
   The household hearth a throne, —
Take back the idle scoff ye fling,
   Where freedom claims its own.

For though our battle hope was vague
   Upon Manassas' plain,
Where Slocum stood with gallant Sprague,
   And gave his life in vain, —

Before we yield the holy trust
   Our old forefathers gave,
Or wrong New England's hallowed dust,
   Or grant the wrongs ye crave, —

We'll print in kindred gore so deep
   The shore we love to tread,
That woman's eyes shall fail to weep
   O'er man's unnumbered dead.

——◆——

THE PICKET-GUARD.

"ALL quiet along the Potomac," they say,
   "Except now and then a stray picket
Is shot, as he walks on his beat, to and fro,
   By a rifleman hid in the thicket.
'T is nothing: a private or two, now and then,
   Will not count in the news of the battle;
Not an officer lost, — only one of the men,
   Moaning out, all alone, the death-rattle."

All quiet along the Potomac to-night,
   Where the soldiers lie peacefully dreaming;

Their tents, in the rays of the clear autumn moon,
 Or the light of the watch-fires, are gleaming.
A tremulous sigh, as the gentle night-wind
 Through the forest leaves softly is creeping ;
While stars up above, with their glittering eyes,
 Keep guard, — for the army is sleeping.

There 's only the sound of the lone sentry's tread
 As he tramps from the rock to the fountain,
And thinks of the two in the low trundle-bed,
 Far away in the cot on the mountain.
His musket falls slack ; his face, dark and grim,
 Grows gentle with memories tender,
As he mutters a prayer for the children asleep, —
 For their mother, — may Heaven defend her !

The moon seems to shine just as brightly as then,
 That night, when the love yet unspoken
Leaped up to his lips, — when low, murmured vows
 Were pledged to be ever unbroken.
Then drawing his sleeve roughly over his eyes,
 He dashes off tears that are welling,
And gathers his gun closer up to its place,
 As if to keep down the heart-swelling.

He passes the fountain, the blasted pine-tree, —
 The footstep is lagging and weary ;
Yet onward he goes, through the broad belt of light,
 Toward the shades of the forest so dreary.
Hark ! was it the night-wind that rustled the leaves ?
 Was it moonlight so wondrously flashing ?
It looked like a rifle : " Ha ! Mary, good-bye ! "
 And the life-blood is ebbing and plashing.

All quiet along the Potomac to-night, —
 No sound save the rush of the river ;
While soft falls the dew on the face of the dead, —
 The picket 's off duty forever.

THE MARCH OF THE REGIMENT.

BY H. H. BROWNELL, U. S. N.

HERE they come ! — 't is the Twelfth, you know, —
　The colonel is just at hand ;
The ranks close up, to the measured flow
　Of music cheery and grand.
Glitter on glitter, row by row,
The steady bayonets, on they go
　For God and the right to stand :
Another thousand to front the foe !
And to die — if it must be even so —
　For the dear old fatherland !

O trusty and true ! O gay, warm heart !
　O manly and earnest brow !
Here, in the hurrying street, we part —
　To meet — ah ! where and how ?
O ready and stanch ! who, at war's alarm,
On lonely hill-side and mountain-farm
　Have left the axe and the plough !
That every tear were a holy charm,
To guard, with honor, some head from harm,
　And to quit some generous vow !
For, of valiant heart and of sturdy arm
　Was never more need than now.

Never a nobler morn to the bold,
　For God and for country's sake !
Lo ! a flag, so haughtily unrolled
On a hundred foughten fields of old,
　Now flaunts in a pirate's wake !
The lion coys in each blazoned fold,
　And leers on the blood-barred snake !

O base and vain ! that, for grudge and gain,
　Could a century's feud renew, —

Could hoard your hate for the coward chance
When a nation reeled in a wilder dance
   Of death, than the Switzer drew!
We have borne and borne — and may bear again
   With wrong, but if wrong from *you*.

Welcome, the sulphury cloud in the sky!
   Welcome, the crimson rain!
Act but the dream ye dared to form,
Strike a single spark! — and the storm
Of serried bayonets sweeping by,
   Shall swell to a hurricane!

O blind and bitter! that could not know,
Even in fight, a caitiff-blow,
(Foully dealt on a hard-set foe,)
   Ever is underwise;
Ever is ghosted with after fear, —
Ye might lesson it, — year by year,
   Looking, with fevered eyes,
For sail or smoke from the Breton shore,
Lest a land, so rudely wronged of yore,
   In flamy revenge should rise!

Office at outcry! — ah! wretched Flam!
   Vile Farce of hammer and prate!
Trade! bids Darby — and blood! smirks Pam —
Little ween they, each courtly Sham,
   Of the Terror lying in wait!
Little wot of the web he spins,
Their Tempter in purple, that darkly grins
   'Neath his stony visor of state,
O'er Seas, how narrow! — for, whoso wins,
At yon base Auction of Outs and Ins,
   The rule of his Dearest Hate;
Her point once flashing athwart her Kin's,
And the reckoning, ledgered for long, begins, —

The galling Glories and envied Sins
   Shall buzz in a mesh-like fate!

Ay, mate your meanest! — ye can but do
That permitted ; when Heaven would view
How Wrong, self-branded, her rage must rue
In wreck and ashes! — (such scene as you,
   If wise, shall witness afar) ;
How Guilt, o'erblown, her crest heaves high,
And dares the injured, with taunt, to try
   Ordeal of Fire in war ;
Blindfold and brazen, on God doth call —
Then grasps in horror, the glaring ball,
   Or treads on the candent bar!

Yet a little! — and men shall mark
This our Moloch, who sate so stark,
(These hundred winters through godless dark
   Grinning o'er death and shame) ;
Marking for murder each unbowed head,
Throned on his Ghizeh of bones, and fed
Still with hearts of the holy dead, —
Naught but a Spectre foul and dread,
   Naught but a hideous Name!
At last! — (ungloom, stern coffined frown !
Rest thee, Gray-Steel! — aye, dead Renown !
In flame and thunder, by field and town,
The Giant-Horror is going down, —
   Down to the Home whence it came !)

Deaf to the Doom that waits the Beast,
Still would she share the Harlot's Feast,
   And drink of her blood-grimed Cup!
Pause ! — the Accursed, on yon frenzied shore,
Buyeth your merchandise never more !
Mark, 'mid the Fiery Dew that drips,
Redder, faster, through black Eclipse,

How Sodom, to-night, shall sup!
(Thus the Kings, in Apocalypse,
The traders of souls, and crews of ships,
Standing afar, with pallid lips,
    While Babylon's smoke goes up!)

Yet, dree your weird! — though an hour may blight,
    In treason, a century's fame —
Trust Greed and Spite! — sith Reason and Right
    Lie cold, with Honor and Shame;
And learn anon — as on that dread night
    When, the dead around and the deck aflame,
From John Paul's lip the fierce word came, —
    " We have only *begun* to fight! "

Ay, 't is at hand! — foul lips, be dumb!
Our Armageddon is yet to come!
But cheery bugle and angry drum,
    With volleyed rattle and roar,
And cannon thunder-throb, shall be drowned,
That day, in a grander, stormier sound;
    The Land, from mountain to shore,
Hurling shackle and scourge and stake
Back to their Lender of pit and lake;
    ('T was Tophet leased them of yore), —
Hell, in her murkiest hold, shall quake,
    As they ring on the damned floor!
O mighty Heart! thou wast long to wake, —
'T is thine, to-morrow, to win or break
    In a deadlier close once more, —
If but for the dear and glorious sake
    Of those who have gone before.

O Fair and Faithful! that, sun by sun,
Slept on the field, or lost or won, —
Children dear of the Holy One!
    Rest in your wintry sod.

Rest, your noble devoir is done, —
Done — and forever !   Ours, to-day,
The dreary drift and the frozen clay
  By trampling armies trod ;
The smoky shroud of the War-Simoom,
The maddened Crime at bay with her Doom,
  And fighting it, clod by clod.
O Calm and Glory ! — beyond the gloom,
Above the bayonets bend and bloom
  The lilies and palms of God.

                     Hartford Evening Press.

THE LOYAL DEMOCRAT.

BY A. J. H. DUGANNE.

MOUTH not to me your Union rant,
Nor gloze mine ears with loyal cant !
Who stands this day in freedom's van,
He only is my Union man !
Who tramples Slavery's Gesler hat,
He is my loyal Democrat !

With whips, engirt by chains, too long
We strove to make our fasces strong ;
When rebel hands those fasces rend,
Must we with whips and chains still mend ?
If " Democrats " can stoop to *that*,
God help me ! *I'm* no Democrat !

Thank Heaven ! the lines are drawn this **hour**
'Twixt manly Right and despot Power ;
Who scowls in Freedom's pathway now
Bears " tyrant " stamped upon his brow ;
Who skulks aloof or shirks his part,
Hath " slave " imprinted in his heart.

In vain of " Equal Rights " ye prate,
Who fawn like dogs at Slavery's gate ;
Beyond the slave each slave-whip smites,
And codes for blacks are laws for whites ;
The chains that negro limbs encoil
Reach and enslave each child of toil !

O Northern men ! when will ye learn
'T is labor that these tyrants spurn ?
'T is not the blood or skin they brand,
But every poor man's toil-worn hand ;
And ye who serve them — knowing this —
Deserve the slave-lash that ye kiss !

While Northern blood remembrance craves
From twice ten thousand Southern graves,
Shall freeborn hearts — beneath the turf —
Lie always crushed by tramp of serf,
And pilgrims, at those graves, some day,
By Slavery's hounds be driven away ?

The green grass in the church-yard waves ;
The good corn grows o'er battle-graves ;
But, oh ! from crimson seeds now sown,
What crops — what harvest — shall be grown ?
On Shiloh's plain — on Roanoke's sod —
What fruits shall spring from blood, O God ?

Spring-time is here !   The past now sleeps —
The present sows — the future reaps !
Who plants good seed in Freedom's span
He only is my Union man !
Who treads the weeds of Slavery flat,
He is my loyal Democrat !

May 23, 1862.

THREE HUNDRED THOUSAND MORE.*

WE are coming, Father Abra'am, three hundred thousand
more,
From Mississippi's winding stream and from New Eng-
land's shore ;
We leave our ploughs and workshops, our wives and chil-
dren dear,
With hearts too full for utterance, with but a silent tear ;
We dare not look behind us, but steadfastly before :
We are coming, Father Abra'am, three hundred thousand
more.

If you look across the hill-tops that meet the northern sky,
Long moving lines of rising dust your vision may descry ;
And now the wind, an instant, tears the cloudy veil aside,
And floats aloft our spangled flag in glory and in pride ;
And bayonets in the sunlight gleam, and bands brave
music pour :
We are coming, Father Abra'am, three hundred thousand
more.

If you look all up our valleys, where the growing harvests
shine,
You may see our sturdy farmer boys fast forming into line ;
And children from their mothers' knees are pulling at the
weeds,
And learning how to reap and sow against their country's
needs ;
And a farewell group stands weeping at every cottage
door :
We are coming, Father Abra'am, three hundred thousand
more.

---

* President Lincoln issued a proclamation, July, 1862, calling for
three hundred thousand more volunteers.

You have called us, and we 're coming, by Richmond's
    bloody tide
To lay us down, for Freedom's sake, our brothers' bones
    beside ;
Or from foul treason's savage grasp to wrench the mur-
    derous blade,
And in the face of foreign foes its fragments to parade.
Six hundred thousand loyal men and true have gone
    before :
We are coming, Father Abra'am, three hundred thousand
    more.

                                 Evening Post.

THE DAY OF GOD.

BY GEORGE S. BURLEIGH.

ALL blessings walk with onward feet ;
    No day dawns twice, no night comes back ;
The car of doom, or slow or fleet,
    Rolls down an unreturned track.

What we have been, we cannot be ;
    Forward, inexorable Fate
Points mutely to her own decree,
    Beyond her hour is all too late.

God reaps his judgment field to-day,
    And sifts the darnel from the wheat ;
A whirlwind sweeps the chaff away,
    And fire the refuge of deceit.

Once in a century only blooms
    The flower of fortune so sublime
As now hangs budded o'er the tombs
    Of the great fathers of old time.

Eternal Justice sits on high
   And gathers in her awful scales
Our shame and glory — Slavery's lie
   And Freedom's starry countervails.

When falls her sword, as fall it must
   In red Bellona's fiery van,
Let the old anarch bite the dust,
   And rise the rescued rights of Man.

In vain a nation's bloody sweat,
   The sob of myriad hearts in vain,
If the scotched snake may live to set
   Its venom in our flesh again.

Priests of an altar fired once more
   For Freedom in His awful name,
Who trod the wine-press, dripping gore,
   And gave the Law in lurid flame, —

Oh, not in human wrath, that wreaks
   Revenge for wrong, and blood for blood
Not in the fiery will that seeks
   Brute power in battle's stormy flood, —

Go forth, redeemers of a land,
   Sad, stern, and fearless for the Lord,
Solemn and calm, with firm right hand
   Laid to the sacrificial sword.

The lords of treason and the whip
   Have called you to the dread appeal,
From the loud cannon's fevered lip,
   And the wide flash of bristling steel.

If now the echo of that voice
   Shake down their prison-house of wrong,
9

They have their own perfidious choice;
　For God is good, and Truth is strong.

Their steel draws lightning, and the bolt
　But fires their own volcanic mine;
God in their vineyard of Revolt
　Treads out his sacramental wine!

Be this our conquest, — as they gave
　Their all to Treason and the Chain,
We snap the fetter from the slave,
　And make our sole revenge their gain!

Independent, August, 1862.

—◆—

THE BATTLE AUTUMN OF 1862.

BY JOHN G. WHITTIER.

THE flags of war like storm-birds fly,
　The charging trumpets blow;
Yet rolls no thunder in the sky,
　No earthquake strives below.

And calm and patient nature keeps
　Her ancient promise well,
Though o'er her bloom and greenness sweeps
　The battle's breath of hell.

And still she walks in golden hours
　Through harvest-happy farms,
And still she wears her fruits and flowers
　Like jewels on her arms.

What means the gladness of the plain,
　This joy of eve and morn,
The mirth that shakes the beard of grain,
　And yellow locks of corn?

Ah! eyes may well be full of tears,
  And hearts with hate are hot;
But even paced come round the years,
  And Nature changes not.

She meets with smiles our bitter grief,
  With songs our groans of pain;
She mocks with tint of flower and leaf
  The war-field's crimson stain.

Still in the cannon's pause we hear
  Her sweet thanksgiving psalm;
Too near to God for doubt or fear,
  She shares the eternal calm.

She knows the seed lies safe below
  The fires that blast and burn;
For all the tears of blood we sow,
  She waits the rich return.

She sees, with clearer eye than ours,
  The good of suffering born, —
The hearts that blossom like her flowers,
  And ripen like her corn.

Oh! give to us, in times like these,
  The vision of her eyes;
And make her eyes and fruited trees
  Our golden prophecies!

Oh! give to us her finer ear!
  Above this stormy din;
We too would hear the bells of cheer
  Ring peace and freedom in.

Atlantic Monthly.

THE CRIPPLE AT THE GATE.*

Look! how the hoofs and wheels to-day
Scatter the dust on the broad highway,
Where Beauty and Fashion, and Wealth and Pride
On saddle and cushion serenely ride!
The very steeds have a conscious prance
Of pride in their elegant freight!
Love and laughter like jewels slip
From the sparkling eye and the merry lip;
You never would think that the Nation's life
Hung on the thread of a desperate strife,
Unless from these you should turn, by chance,
To the Cripple at the Gate.

Weary and footsore, and ragged and soiled,
Through the summer glare he has slowly toiled
Along the edge of the broad highway,
Since the early dawn of the westering day;
His rags are flecked with the dusty foam
That flew from the gilded bits
Of the champing steeds that passed him by;
And a haggard shadow is in his eye,
But it is not the gloom of an envious pain!
He has left a limb on the battle-plain,
And to win his way to his distant home
At my gate, a Beggar, he sits!

* We all remember one of the sad evidences of the unavoidable
insufficiency of our War Department to the demands made upon it
by a gigantic and protracted struggle which spread over such vast
distances and employed so many men, — the sight of discharged
soldiers, sometimes wounded or enfeebled by disease, without the
means of reaching their homes, which often were hundreds of miles
away. From this seeming reproach we were at last relieved by the
efforts of that noble organization, the Sanitary Commission.

He tells me his tale in a simple way:
" I had nothing," he says, " except my pay,
And a wife and four little girls, and so
I sent all my money to them, you know!
When I lost my limb, Sir — but that I 'm lame,
I do not complain, for, you see,
'T is the fortune of war, and it might be worse;
And I 'd lose the other to stop the curse
Of this terrible strife! — But I meant to say,
When I left the hospital t' other day,
I *did* think I had a kind of a claim
To be sent to my village free.

" Don't you think it hard yourself, Sir?   True,
There 's a hundred dollars of bounty due
In three years, or when the war 's ended; but how
Long may that be — can you tell me now?
I did not enlist for bounty, I trust, —
My conscience I never have sold;
But how does it look for a soldier to ' tramp,'
Begging his way like a vagabond scamp,
From the fields where he often risked his life,
To the home where he left his babes and wife,
In a uniform made of tatters and dust
Instead of the ' blue and gold ? '

" Whose fault this is, Sir, I do not know,"
Said the wayworn man as he rose to go;
" But of this, alas! I am sure — the sight
Of a soldier returning in such a plight
To the home whence, a few short months ago,
He marched in a gallant band,
With music, and banners, and shining steel,
Will dull more ears to the battle-peal,
And cause more bosoms with doubt to swell,
Than the secret traitor's deadliest spell.
Do'nt you see yourself, Sir, it must be so ? "
And he sighed as I held out my hand.

Lofty carriage and low *coupé*
Still whirl the dust on the broad highway;
Beauty and Fashion, and Wealth and Pride
Still through the roseate twilight ride,
With love, and laughter, and prancing steed,
As if Pleasure were all life's fate.
But I gaze no more on the joyous train,
For my eye is fixed with a steadfast strain
On the tattered soldier's halting stride,
Till his tall form sinks down the dark hill-side;
Then I cry, " Thank God! he hath *now* no need
To beg at the stranger's gate ! "

Harpers' Weekly.

WANTED — A MAN.

BY EDMUND C. STEDMAN.

BACK from the trebly crimson'd field
   Terrible words are thunder-tost;
Full of the wrath that will not yield,
   Full of revenge for battles lost!
   Hark to their echo as it crost
The Capital, making faces wan:
   " End this murderous holocaust;
Abraham Lincoln, give us a MAN !

" Give us a man of God's own mould,
   Born to marshal his fellow-men;
One whose fame is not bought and sold
   At the stroke of a politician's pen;
   Give us the man of thousands ten,
Fit to do as well as to plan;
   Give us a rallying-cry, and then, —
Abraham Lincoln, give us a MAN !

" No leader to shirk the boasting foe,
   And to march and countermarch our brave,
Till they fade like ghosts in the marshes low,
   And swamp-grass covers each nameless grave ;
   Nor another, whose fatal banners wave
Aye in Disaster's shameful van ;
   Nor another, to bluster, and lie, and rave ; —
Abraham Lincoln, give us a MAN !

" Hearts are mourning in the North,
   While the sister rivers seek the main,
Red with our life-blood flowing forth, —
   Who shall gather it up again ?
   Though we march to the battle-plain
Firmly as when the strife began,
   Shall all our offering be in vain ? —
Abraham Lincoln, give us a MAN !

" Is there never one in all the land,
   One on whose might the Cause may lean ?
Are all the common men so grand,
   And all the titled ones so mean ?
   What if your failure may have been
In trying to make good bread from bran —
   From worthless metal a weapon keen ? —
Abraham Lincoln, find us a MAN !

" Oh, we will follow him to the death,
   Where the foeman's fiercest columns are !
Oh, we will use our latest breath,
   Cheering for every sacred star !
   His to marshal us nigh and far,
Ours to battle, as patriots can
   When a Hero leads the Holy War ! —
Abraham Lincoln, give us a MAN ! "

   SEPTEMBER 8, 1862.
                              New York Tribune.

FREDERICKSBURGH.

BY W. F. W.

Eighteen hundred and sixty-two, —
  That is the number of wounded men
Who, if the telegraph's tale be true,
  Reached Washington City but yester e'en.

And it is but a handful, the telegrams add,
  To those who are coming by boats and by cars;
Weary and wounded, dying and sad;
  Covered — but only in front — with scars.

Some are wounded by Minié shot,
  Others are torn by the hissing shell,
As it burst upon them as fierce and as hot
  As a demon spawned in a traitor's hell.

Some are pierced by the sharp bayonet,
  Others are crushed by the horses' hoof;
Or fell 'neath the shower of iron which met
  Them as hail beats down on an open roof.

Shall I tell what they did to meet this fate?
  Why was this living death their doom?
Why did they fall to this piteous state
  'Neath the rifle's crack and the cannon's boom?

Orders arrived, and the river they crossed;
  Built the bridge in the enemy's face;
No matter how many were shot and lost,
  And floated — sad corpses — away from the place.

Orders they heard, and they scaled the height,
  Climbing right " into the jaws of death; "

Each man grasping his rifle-piece tight,
 Scarcely pausing to draw his breath.

Sudden flashed on them a sheet of flame
 From hidden fence and from ambuscade;
A moment more — (they say this is fame) —
 A thousand dead men on the grass were laid.

Fifteen thousand in wounded and killed,
 At least, is " our loss," the newspapers say.
This loss to our army must surely be filled
 Against another great battle-day.

" Our loss ! "   Whose loss ?   Let demagogues say
 That the Cabinet, President, all are in wrong :
What do the orphans and widows pray ?
 What is the burden of their sad song ?

'T is *their* loss !   But the tears in their weeping eyes
 Hide Cabinet, President, Generals, — all ;
And they only can see a cold form that lies
 On the hillside slope, by that fatal wall.

They cannot discriminate men or means, —
 They only demand that this blundering cease.
In their frenzied grief they would end such scenes,
 Though that end be — even with traitors — peace.

Is thy face from thy people turned, O God ?
 Is thy arm for the Nation no longer strong ?
We cry from our homes — the dead cry from the sod —
 How long, O our righteous God ! how long ?

   Nᴇᴡ Yᴏʀᴋ, December 17, 1862.

"MY MARYLAND." *

Ah me! I 've had enough of thee,
    Maryland, my Maryland!
Dear land, thou art too dear for me,
    Maryland, my Maryland!
I 'll take the nearest ford and go,
I 'll leave thee, darling, to the foe;
But do not let him kick me so,
    Maryland, my Maryland!

You 've dashed my hopes, ungrateful State,
    Maryland, my Maryland!
Go! bless your stars I came too late,
    Maryland, you understand!
I meant to dress you well in black,
And scar you with the battle's track,
And I had scourges for your back,
    Maryland, my contraband!

Oh, where are Longstreet, Hill, and Lee?
    Maryland, my Maryland!
And "Stonewall" Jackson, where is he?
    Maryland, my Maryland!
Four coat-tails streaming in the breeze,
And that is all a body sees;
Better than dangling from the trees,
    Maryland, my Maryland!

Gray geese are flying southward, ho!
    Maryland, O Maryland!

* This parody of the most spirited and most popular of the
Rebel Songs celebrates the failure of the insurgent forces to take
and hold Maryland, which was General Lee's object in his north-
ward march, and which was defeated by the battles of South Moun-
tain and Antie'am.

It 's getting cold up there, you know,
    Maryland, O Maryland !
I should have thought it rather warm, —
South Mountain yonder took by storm,
Antietam yielded in alarm, —
    Maryland, O Maryland !

Blood-red my hand, and dead my heart,
    Native land, my native land !
Columbia from her grave will start,
    Murder'd land, my murder'd land !
Thy flag is like a sword of fire,
I 'll fly, I 'll fly its vengeful ire ;
Beneath its stroke its foes expire,
    Native land, my native land !

Harpers' Weekly.

BOSTON HYMN.*

BY RALPH WALDO EMERSON.

THE word of the Lord by night
To the watching Pilgrims came,
As they sat by the sea-side,
And filled their hearts with flame.

God said, — I am tired of Kings,
I suffer them no more ;
Up to my ear the morning brings
The outrage of the poor.

Think ye I made this ball
A field of havoc and war,

* Read at the Emancipation Meeting at Boston, January 1,
1863.

Where tyrants great and tyrants small
Might harry the weak and poor?

My angel, — his name is Freedom, —
Choose him to be your king;
He shall cut pathways east and west,
And fend you with his wing.

Lo! I uncover the land
Which I hid of old time in the West,
As the sculptor uncovers his statue,
When he has wrought his best.

I show Columbia, of the rocks
Which dip their foot in the seas,
And soar to the air-borne flocks
Of clouds, and the boreal fleece.

I will divide my goods;
Call in the wretch and slave:
None shall rule but the humble,
And none but toil shall have.

I will have never a noble,
No lineage counted great:
Fishers and choppers and ploughmen
Shall constitute a State.

Go, cut down trees in the forest,
And trim the straightest boughs;
Cut down trees in the forest,
And build me a wooden house.

Call the people together,
The young men and the sires,
The digger in the harvest-field,
Hireling and him that hires.

And here in a pine State-House
They shall choose men to rule
In every needful faculty, —
In church and state and school.

Lo, now! if these poor men
Can govern the land and sea,
And make just laws below the sun, —
As planets faithful be.

And ye shall succor men;
'T is nobleness to serve;
Help them who cannot help again;
Beware from right to swerve.

I break your bonds and masterships,
And I unchain the slave:
Free be his heart and hand henceforth,
As wind and wandering wave.

I cause from every creature
His proper good to flow:
So much as he is and doeth,
So much he shall bestow.

But, laying his hands on another
To coin his labor and sweat,
He goes in pawn to his victim
For eternal years in debt.

Pay ransom to the owner,
And fill the bag to the brim!
Who is the owner? The slave is owner,
And ever was. Pay *him!*

O North! give him beauty for rags,
And honor, O South! for his shame;

Nevada! coin thy golden crags
With Freedom's image and name.

Up! and the dusky race
That sat in darkness long, —
Be swift their feet as antelopes,
And as behemoth strong.

Come East and West and North,
By races, as snow-flakes,
And carry My purpose forth,
Which neither halts nor shakes.

My will fulfilled shall be;
For, in daylight or in dark,
My thunderbolt has eyes to see
His way home to the mark.

Atlantic Monthly.

TREASON'S LAST DEVICE.

BY EDMUND C. STEDMAN.

"Who deserves greatness,
Deserves your hate.   .   .   .
You common cry of curs, whose breath I loathe
As reek o' the rotten fens."

Coriolanus.

"Hark! hark! the dogs do bark."
Nursery Rhyme.

Sons of New England in the fray,
    Do you hear the clamor behind your back?
Do you hear the yelping of Blanche and Tray,
    Sweetheart and all the mongrel pack?
Girded well with her ocean crags,
    Little our mother heeds their noise;

Her eyes are fixed on crimson flags:
　But you, — do you hear it, Yankee boys?

Do you hear them say that the patriot fire
　Burns on her altars too pure and bright,
To the darkened heavens leaping higher,
　Though drenched with the blood of every fight?
That in the light of its searching flame
　Treason and tyrants stand revealed,
And the yielding craven is put to shame
　On capitol floor or foughten field?

Do you hear the hissing voice which saith
　That she — who bore through all the land
The lyre of Freedom, the torch of Faith,
　And young Invention's mystic wand —
Should gather her skirts and dwell apart,
　With not one of her sisters to share her fate, —
A Hagar, wandering sick at heart?
　A Pariah, bearing the nation's hate?

Sons, who have peopled the gorgeous West,
　And planted the Pilgrim vine anew,
Where, by a richer soil carest,
　It grows as ever its parent grew, —
Say, do you hear — while the very bells
　Of your churches ring with her ancient voice,
And the song of your children sweetly tells
　How true was the land of your fathers' choice —

Do you hear the traitors who bid you speak
　The word that shall sever the sacred tie?
And ye who dwell by the golden Peak,
　Has the subtle whisper glided by?
Has it crossed the immemorial plains
　To coasts where the gray Pacific roars,
And the Pilgrim blood in the people's veins
　Is pure as the wealth of their mountain ores?

Spirits of sons who side by side
 In a hundred battles fought and fell,
Whom now no East and West divide,
 In the isles where the shades of heroes dwell, —
Say, has it reached your glorious rest,
 And ruffled the calm which crowns you there?
The shame that recreants have confest,
 The plot that floats in the troubled air?

Sons of New England, here and there,
 Wherever men are still holding by
The honor our fathers left so fair, —
 Say, do you hear the cowards' cry?
Crouching amongst her grand old crags,
 Lightly our mother heeds their noise,
With her fond eyes fixed on distant flags;
 But you, — do you hear it, Yankee boys?

WASHINGTON, Jan. 19, 1863.

New York Tribune.

LARRY'S RETURN FROM THE WAR.*

BY WILL S. HAYS.

THE black clouds were angrily chasing each other;
 The cold winter winds howling carelessly by
The cottage where sat Kitty Gray and her mother, —
 Poor Kitty looked sad, with a tear in her eye.
She thought of her lover, with whom she had parted, —
 Who had gone to the wars, — it was Larry O'More.
Oh, hark! she heard footsteps, and suddenly started;
 Then smiled, as she leaped like a fawn to the door.

 * Larry was one of those who withdrew from the contest be-
cause of the Proclamation of Freedom to the slaves in the States
under rebel rule, which was issued January 1, 1863.

And lo ! there stood Larry, as fresh and as cosy
  As when he left Kitty's bewitching young charms;
Whose eyes were so bright, and whose cheeks were so
    rosy, —
  " Arrah ! Kitty," said Larry, " love, come to me arms."
" O Larry ! you 're safe ! "   " Yes, thrue for ye, darlin';
  I 've been in the battles, whin the balance wor kilt,
An' the ribils, like haythens, come fightin' an' snarlin' —
  Arrah ! Kitty, no knowin' the blood that was spilt."

" Come, Larry, sit down."   " Faith, I will, an' close near
    you,
  For lonesome I 've been for many months past;
I often have wished — d' ye mind ? "   " Yes, I hear you."
  " That ivery big fight that we had was the last."
" And have you been wounded ? "   " Ah, no ! I wor
    lucky.
  The boys fought like divils, an' died in a hape;
An' since our last march, as we wint through Kintucky,
  How many brave fellows have laid down to slape !

" No longer a sojer, dear Kitty, I 'll tarry, —
  Faith, while I wor one, to the cause I wor thrue, —
An' now I 've come home, love, a swate girl to marry."
  " Pray, Larry, who is she ? "   " Arrah ! Kitty, 't is
    you !
I 've got me discharge, an' through life's wintry weather
  We 'll make the path aisy as aisy can be.
Me heart 's in me hand."   " I 'll take them together."
  " Presint arms, then, darlint ! "   " I will, love," says
    she.

" Ah, Larry ! I 'm glad — are you tired of fightin' ? "
  And sweet Kitty smiled — looked him full in the eyes.
" Oh ! no, Kitty, dear ; for I took a delight in
  Performin' me dooty, wherever it lies;
May me hand lave me body whin I pull the thrigger
    10

In battle again."   " Why, Larry ? "   " Because
The Goddess of Liberty 's turned to a nigger,
  An' ould Father Abram 's forgotten the laws ! "

HERMITAGE, January 8, 1863.

Louisville Sunday Democrat

AT PORT ROYAL.

BY JOHN GREENLEAF WHITTIER.

THE tent-lights glimmer on the land,
  The ship-lights on the sea;
The night-wind smooths with drifting sand
  Our track on lone Tybee.

At last our grating keels outslide,
  Our good boats forward swing;
And while we ride the land-locked tide,
  Our negroes row and sing.

For dear the bondman holds his gifts
  Of music and of song;
The gold that kindly Nature sifts
  Among his sands of wrong;

The power to make his toiling days
  And poor home-comforts please;
The quaint relief of mirth that plays
  With sorrow's minor keys.

Another glow than sunset's fire
  Has filled the West with light,
Where field and garner, barn and byre
  Are blazing through the night.

The land is wild with fear and hate,
  The rout runs mad and fast;
From hand to hand, from gate to gate,
  The flaming brand is passed.

The lurid glow falls strong across
  Dark faces broad with smiles:
Not theirs the terror, hate and loss
  That fire yon blazing piles.

With oar-strokes timing to their song,
  They weave in simple lays
The pathos of remembered wrong,
  The hope of better days; —

The triumph-note that Miriam sung,
  The joy of uncaged birds:
Softening with Afric's mellow tongue
  Their broken Saxon words.

SONG OF THE NEGRO BOATMEN.

O, PRAISE an' tanks! De Lord he come
  To set de people free;
An' massa tink de day ob doom,
  An' we ob jubilee.
De Lord dat heap de Red Sea waves
  He jus' as 'trong as den;
He say de word: we las' night slaves,
  To-day de Lord's freemen.
      De yam will grow, de cotton blow,
        We 'll hab de rice an' corn;
      O nebber you fear, if nebber you hear
        De driver blow his horn!

Ole massa on he trabbles gone;
  He leaf de land behind:

De Lord's breff blow him furder on,
  Like corn shuck in de wind.
We own de hoe, we own de plough,
  We own de hands dat hold ;
We sell de pig, we sell de cow,
  But nebber chile be sold.
      De yam will grow, de cotton blow,
        We 'll hab de rice an' corn ;
        O nebber you fear, if nebber you hear
        De driver blow his horn !

We pray de Lord ; he gib us signs
  Dat some day we be free ;
De Norf-wind tell it to de pines,
  De wild-duck to de sea ;
We tink it when de church-bell ring,
  We dream it in de dream ;
De rice-bird mean it when he sing,
  De eagle when he scream.
      De yam will grow, de cotton blow,
        We 'll hab de rice an' corn ;
        O nebber you fear, if nebber you hear
        De driver blow his horn !

We know de promise nebber fail,
  An' nebber lie de word ;
So, like de 'postles in de jail,
  We waited for de Lord ;
An' now he open ebery door,
  An' trow away de key ;
He tink we lub him so before,
  We lub him better free.
      De yam will grow, de cotton blow,
        He 'll gib de rice an' corn ;
        O nebber you fear, if nebber you hear
        De driver blow his horn !

So sing our dusky gondoliers;
  And with a secret pain,
And smiles that seem akin to tears,
  We hear the wild refrain.

We dare not share the negro's trust,
  Nor yet his hope deny;
We only know that God is just,
  And every wrong shall die.

Rude seems the song; each swarthy face,
  Flame-lighted, ruder still,
We start to think that hapless race
  Must shape our good or ill:

That laws of changeless justice bind
  Oppressor with oppressed;
And close as sin and suffering joined,
  We march to Fate abreast.

Sing on, poor hearts! your chant shall be
  Our sign of blight or bloom, —
The Vala-song of Liberty,
  Or death-rune of our doom!

LEFT ON THE BATTLE-FIELD.

BY SARAH T. BOLTON.

WHAT, was it a dream? am I all alone
  In the dreary night and the drizzling rain?
Hist! — ah, it was only the river's moan;
  They have left me behind, with the mangled slain.

Yes, now I remember it all too well!
   We met, from the battling ranks apart;
Together our weapons flashed and fell,
   And mine was sheathed in his quivering heart.

In the cypress gloom, where the deed was done,
   It was all too dark to see his face;
But I heard his death-groans, one by one,
   And he holds me still in a cold embrace.

He spoke but once, and I could not hear
   The words he said, for the cannon's roar;
But my heart grew cold with a deadly fear, —
   O God! I had heard that voice before!

Had heard it before at our mother's knee,
   When we lisped the words of our evening prayer!
My brother! would I had died for thee, —
   This burden is more than my soul can bear!

I pressed my lips to his death-cold cheek,
   And begged him to show me, by word or sign,
That he knew and forgave me: he could not speak,
   But he nestled his poor cold face to mine.

The blood flowed fast from my wounded side,
   And then for awhile I forgot my pain,
And over the lakelet we seemed to glide
   In our little boat, two boys again.

And then, in my dream, we stood alone
   On a forest path where the shadows fell;
And I heard again the tremulous tone,
   And the tender words of his last farewell.

But that parting was years, long years ago,
   He wandered away to a foreign land;

And our dear old mother will never know
  That he died to-night by his brother's hand.

    *   *   *   *   *   *

The soldiers who buried the dead away,
  Disturbed not the clasp of that last embrace,
But laid them to sleep till the Judgment-day,
  Heart folded to heart, and face to face.

    INDIANAOPLIS, Indiana, March, 1863.
                        Once a Week.

IN LOUISIANA.

BY J. W. DE FOREST, U. S. A.

WITHOUT a hillock stretched the plain ;
  For months we had not seen a hill ;
  The endless, flat savannas still
Wearied our eyes with waving cane.

One tangled cane-field lay before
  The ambush of the cautious foe ;
  Behind, a black bayou with low,
Reed-hidden, miry, treacherous shore ;

A sullen swamp along the right,
  Where alligators slept and crawled,
  And moss-robed cypress giants sprawled
Athwart the noontide's blistering light.

Quick, angry spits of musketry
  Proclaimed our skirmishers at work ;
  We saw their crouching figures lurk
Through thickets, firing from the knee.

Our Parrotts felt the distant wood
   With humming, shrieking, growling shell ;
   When suddenly the mouth of hell
Gaped fiercely for its human food.

A long and low blue roll of smoke
   Curled up a hundred yards ahead,
   And deadly storms of driving lead
From rifle-pits and cane-fields broke.

Then while the bullets whistled thick,
   And hidden batteries boomed and shelled,
   " Charge bayonets ! " the colonel yelled ;
" Battalion forward, — double quick ! "

With even slopes of bayonets
   Advanced — a dazzling, threatening crest —
   Right toward the rebels' hidden nest,
The dark-blue, living billow sets.

The color-guard was at my side ;
   I heard the color-sergeant groan ;
   I heard the bullet crush the bone ;
I might have touched him as he died.

The life-blood spouted from his mouth
   And sanctified the wicked land :
   Of martyred saviours what a band
Has suffered to redeem the South !

I had no malice in my mind ;
   I only cried, " Close up.   Guide right ! "
   My single purpose in the fight
Was steady march with ranks aligned.

I glanced along the martial rows,
   And marked the soldiers' eyeballs burn ;

Their eager faces, hot and stern, —
The wrathful triumph on their brows.

The traitors saw ; they reeled, they fled :
    Fear-stricken, gray-clad multitudes
    Streamed wildly toward the covering woods,
And left us victory and their dead.

Once more the march, the tiresome plain,
    The Father River fringed with dykes,
    Gray cypresses, palmetto spikes,
Bayous and swamps and yellowing cane ;

With here and there plantations rolled
    In flowers, bananas, orange-groves,
    Where laugh the sauntering negro droves,
Reposing from the task of old ;

And, rarer, half-deserted towns,
    Devoid of men, where women scowl,
    Avoiding us as lepers foul
With sidling gait and flouting gowns.

     THIBODEAUX, La., March, 1863.

                Harpers' Monthly.

—◆—

SONG OF NEW-ENGLAND SPRING BIRDS.

WHEN Robin, Swallow, Thrush, and Wren,
From " way down South " had come again,
I roamed through field and wood to see
If birds, like men, could Rebels be ;
I wondered if their tiny throats
Would circulate secession notes ;
I think, may be, my thoughts they knew,
So what they sang, I 'll sing to you.

First rising from a sedgy brook,
The stump, bold Bob-o' Lincoln took ;
" Well, now, I guess I 'm glad," said he,
" For my free speech a stump to see ;
They could n't hold me in the mesh
Of that strange net they call ' Secesh ';
To keep me down they need n't think on, —
Hurrah ! for Bob (and Abram) Lincoln ! "

The Robin Red-breast sang his song ;
" Ah, me ! I 've seen such fearful wrong !
I thought at first the storm would clear up,
But soon I had no heart to chirrup !
The ' Sunny South ' is fine, I know,
When Northern hills are white with snow ;
But oh, 't is full of grief and pain !
Cheer up ! chirrup I 'm home again."

The Wren piped forth her tiny cry ;
" A little thing, I know, am I ; —
But small, weak things, like you and me,
My sister Sparrow, love the free ! "
The Sparrow heard the lowly call,
And said, " Who heeds the sparrows' fall,
And keeps them always in His sight,
Shall hear ME sing ' God speed the Right ! ' "

Then Jay, the bluebird, joined the throng,
And bade the white Dove fly along ;
And Oriole with throat of red, —
And then exultantly, he said :
" Come, loyal birds, and as we stand,
Behold the colors of our Land !
Let every bird that 's brave and true,
Sing, cheer, the Red and White and Blue ! "

The sky o'erhead was clear and bright,
The North wind sang o'er plain and height ;

The rill went singing on its way,
And leaves and flowers were bright and gay;
The rock and wood and meadow rang,
As loud and clear and sweet they sang,
And every bird, it seemed to me,
Sang " Praise the Lord! We 're free! we 're free!"

Commonwealth.

THE WOOD OF CHANCELLORSVILLE.

THE ripe red berries of the wintergreen
    Lure me to pause awhile
In this deep, tangled wood.   I stop and lean
    Down where these wild flowers smile,
        And rest me in this shade; for many a mile,
Through lane and dusty street,
I 've walked with weary, weary feet,
And now I tarry 'mid this woodland scene,
'Mong ferns and mosses sweet.

Here all around me blows
The pale primrose.
I wonder if the gentle blossom knows
The feeling at my heart — the solemn grief,
    So whelming and so deep
That it disdains relief,
    And will not let me weep.
I wonder that the woodbine thrives and grows,
And is indifferent to the nation's woes.
For while these mornings shine, these blossoms bloom,
Impious rebellion wraps the land in gloom.

Nature, thou art unkind,
Unsympathizing, blind!
Yon lichen, clinging to th' o'erhanging rock,

Is happy, and each blade of grass
O'er which unconsciously I pass
Smiles in my face, and seems to mock
    Me with its joy.   Alas ! I cannot find
    One charm in bounteous Nature, while the wind
That blows upon my cheek bears on each gust
The groans of my poor country, bleeding in the dust.

The air is musical with notes
That gush from wingèd warblers' throats,
And in the leafy trees
I hear the drowsy hum of bees.
    Prone from the blinding sky
Dance rainbow-tinted sunbeams, thick with motes ;
    Daisies are shining, and the butterfly
Wavers from flower to flower ; — yet in this wood
The ruthless foeman stood,
And every turf is drenched with human blood !

O heartless flowers !
    O trees, clad in your robes of glistering sheen,
    Put off this canopy of gorgeous green !
These are the hours
For mourning, not for gladness.   While this smart
Of treason dire gashes the nation's heart,
Let birds refuse to sing,
And flowers to bloom upon the lap of spring.
Let Nature's face itself with tears o'erflow,
In deepest anguish for a people's woe.

While rank Rebellion stands
With blood of martyrs on his impious hands ;
While slavery and chains
    And cruelty and direst hate
    Uplift their heads within th' afflicted State,
And freeze the blood in every patriot's veins —
Let these old woodlands fair

Grow black with gloom, and from its thunder-lair
Let lightning leap, and scorch th' accursed air ;
Until the suffering earth,
Of treason sick, shall spew the monster forth, —
And each regenerate sod
Be consecrate anew, to Freedom and to God !

Delia R. German.

SONG OF THE COPPERHEAD.

THERE was glorious news, for our arms were victorious —
  'T was sometime ago — and 't was somewhere out
    West ;
The big guns were booming, — the boys getting glorious ;
  But one man was gloomy, and glad all the rest !
Intending emotions delightful to damp,
  He hummed and he hawed, and he sneered and he
    sighed, —
A snake in the grass, and a spy in the camp,
  While the honest were laughing, the Copperhead cried !

There was news of a battle, and sad souls were aching
  The fate of their brave and beloved ones to learn ;
Pale wives stood all tearless, their tender hearts breaking
  For the gallant good-man who would never return !
We had lost all but honor, — so ran the sad story, —
  Oh ! bitter the cup that the Patriot quaffed !
He had tears for our flag, — he had sighs for our glory, —
  He had groans for our dead, — but the Copperhead
    laughed !

The traitor ! the sneak ! say, what fate shall await him,
  Who forgets his fair land, and who spits on her fame ?
Let no woman love him ! Let honest men hate him !
  Let his children refuse to be known by his name !

In the hour of our sorrow all recreant we found him, —
   In the hour of his woe may he sigh for a friend!
Let his conscience upbraid, let his memory hound him,
   And no man take note of the Copperhead's end!

                        Vanity Fair.

—◆—

AT GETTYSBURG.*

LIKE a furnace of fire blazed the midsummer sun
   When to saddle we leaped at the order,
Spurred on by the boom of the deep-throated gun,
   That told of the foe on our border.
A mist in our rear lay Antietam's dark plain,
   And thoughts of its carnage came o'er us;
But smiling before us surged fields of ripe grain,
   And we swore none should reap it before us.

That night, with the ensign who rode by my side,
   On the camp's dreary edge I stood picket;
Our ears intent, lest every wind-rustle should hide
   A spy's stealthy tread in the thicket;
And, there, while we watched the first arrows of dawn
   Through the veil of the rising mist's quiver,
He told how the foeman had closed in upon
   His home by the Tennessee River.

He spoke of a sire in his weakness cut down,
   With last breath the traitor flag scorning, —
(And his brow at the mem'ry grew dark with a frown
   That paled the red light of the morning.)
For days he had followed the cowardly band;
   And when one lagged to forage or trifle,
Had seared in his forehead the deep Minié brand,
   And scored a fresh notch on his rifle.

  * The Battle of Gettysburg was fought July 1st, 2d, and 3d, 1863.

" But *one* of the rangers had cheated his fate, —
  For him he would search the world over."
Such cool-plotting passion, such keenness of hate,
  Ne'er saw I in woman-scorned lover.
O, who would have thought that beneath those dark curls
  Lurked vengeance as sure as death-rattle!
Or fancied those dreamy eyes — soft as a girl's —
  Could light with the fury of battle?

To horse! pealed the bugle, while grape-shot and shell
  Overhead through the forest were crashing.
A cheer for the flag! and the summer light fell
  On the blades from a thousand sheaths flashing.
As mad ocean waves to the storm-revel flock,
  So on we dashed, heedless of dangers;
A moment our long line surged back at the shock
  Then swept through the ranks of the Rangers.

I looked for our ensign: ahead of his troop,
  Pressing on through the conflict infernal,
His torn flag furled round him in festoon and loop,
  He spurred to the side of his Colonel.
And his clear voice rang out, as I saw his bright sword
  Through shako and gaudy plume shiver,
With " this for the last of the murderous horde!"
  And " this for the home by the river!"

At evening, returned from pursuit of the foe,
  By a shell-shattered caisson we found him;
And we buried him there in the sunset glow,
  With the dear old flag knotted around him.
Yet how could we mourn, when every proud strain
  Told of foemen hurled back in disorder;
When we knew that the North reaped her rich harvest
      grain
  Unharmed by a foe on her border!
                                    Harpers' Weekly.

HOW ARE YOU, GENERAL LEE?

Of General Lee, the Rebel chief, you all perhaps do
    know
How he came North, a short time since, to spend a month
    or so ?
But soon he found the climate warm, although a Southern
    man,
And quickly hurried up his cakes,* and toddled home
    again.
Chorus — How are you, General Lee ? it is ; why don't
            you longer stay ?
        How are your friends in Maryland and Penn-
            sylvani–a ?

Jeff. Davis met him coming back : " Why, General Lee,"
    he said,
" What makes you look and stagger so ? there 's whiskey
    in your head."
" Not much, I think," says General Lee ; " No whiskey 's
    there, indeed ;
What makes me feel so giddy is, I 've taken too much
    Meade ! "
Chorus — How are you, General ? &c.

" But you seem ill yourself, dear Jeff. You look quite
    sad enough ;
I think, while I 've been gone, Old Abe has used you
    rather rough."
" Well, yes, he has, and that 's a fact ; it makes me feel
    downcast,

---

* As long as the importance of hurrying buckwheat pancakes
from the griddle to the table is impressed upon the American mind,
this vile slang will need no explanation. But the fame of the
rebel march into Pennsylvania and of the victory of Gettysburg
will probably outlive even the taste for those alluring compounds.

For they 've bothered us at Vicksburg, so 't is Granted
   them at last."
Chorus — Then, how are you, Jeff. Davis ? What is it
     makes you sigh ?
     How are your friends at Vicksburg and in
     Mississippi–i ?

" Yes, Vicksburg they have got quite sure, and Richmond
   soon they 'll take ;
At Port Hudson, too, they have some Banks I fear we
   cannot break :
While Rosecrans, in Tennessee, swears he 'll our army
   flog,
And prove if Bragg 's a terrier good, Holdfast 's a better
   dog."
Chorus — How are you, Jeff. Davis ? Would you not
     like to be
     A long way out of Richmond and the Con-
     fede—ra—cy ?
     For, with " Porter " on the river, and " Meade "
     upon the land,
     I guess you 'll find that these mixed drinks are
     more than you can stand.

HYMN

FOR THE FOURTH OF JULY, 1863.

BY GEORGE H. BOKER.

Lord, the people of the land
In Thy presence humbly stand ;
On this day, when Thou didst free
Men of old from tyranny,
We, their children, bow to Thee.
   Help us, Lord, our only trust !
   We are helpless, we are dust !

11

All our homes are red with blood;
Long our grief we have withstood;
Every lintel, each door-post
Drips, at tidings from the host,
With the blood of some one lost.
    Help us, Lord, our only trust!
    We are helpless, we are dust!

Comfort, Lord, the grieving one
Who bewails a stricken son!
Comfort, Lord, the weeping wife,
In her long, long widowed life,
Brooding o'er the fatal strife!
    Help us, Lord, our only trust!
    We are helpless, we are dust!

On our Nation's day of birth,
Bless Thy own long-favored earth!
Urge the soldier with Thy will!
Aid their leaders with Thy skill!
Let them hear Thy trumpet thrill!
    Help us, Lord, our only trust!
    We are helpless, we are dust!

Lord, we only fight for peace, —
Fight that freedom may increase.
Give us back the peace of old,
When the land with plenty rolled,
And our banner awed the bold!
    Help us, Lord, our only trust!
    We are helpless, we are dust!

Lest we pray in thoughtless guilt
Shape the future as Thou wilt!
Purge our realm from hoary crime
With Thy battles, dread, sublime,
In Thy well-appointed time!

Help us, Lord, our only trust!
We are helpless, we are dust!

With one heart the Nation's cries
From our choral lips arise;
Thou didst point a noble way
For our Fathers through the fray:
Lead their children thus to-day!
　Help us, Lord, our only trust!
　We are helpless, we are dust!

In His name who bravely bore
Cross and crown begemmed with gore,
By His last immortal groan
Ere He mounted to His throne, —
Make our sacred cause Thine own!
　Help us, Lord, our only trust!
　We are helpless, we are dust!

———◆———

LEFT ON THE BATTLE-FIELD.

BY HOWARD GLYNDON.

Oh, my darling! my darling! never to feel
　Your hand going over my hair!
Never to lie in your arms again, —
　Never to know where you are!
Oh, the weary miles that stretch between
　My feet and the battle-ground,
Where all that is left of my dearest love
　Lies under some yellow mound!

It is but little I might have done
　To lighten your parting pain;
But 't is bitter to think that you died alone,
　Out in the dark and the rain!

Oh, my hero love! — to have kissed the pain
   And the mist from your fading eyes!
To have saved one only passionate look
   To sweeten these memories!

And thinking of all, I am strangely stunned,
   And cannot believe you dead.
You loved me, dear! And I loved you, dear!
   And your letter lies there unread!
You are not dead! You are not dead!
   God never could will it so —
To craze my brain and break my heart —
   And shatter my life — I know!

Dead! dead! and never a word,
   Never a look for me!
Dead! dead! and our marriage-day
   Never on earth to be!
I am left alone, and the world is changed,
   So dress me in bridal white,
And lay me away in some quiet place
   Out of the hateful light.

                Harpers' Weekly, Aug 29, 1863.

———◆———

LAY OF THE MODERN "KONSERVATIVS."

BY CHARITY GRIMES.

I AM a gay "Konservativ,"
   I stand by the old Konstitushun, I du;
I go for the Union ez it was,
   With the old Dimmycrat ticket, rite thru.
These Black Republikans don't suit me,
Fur I'm a Konservativ man, yu see!

I am a Dimmycrat, dyed in the wool;
  I go fur free trade, and that sort ov thing;
I think it 's rite tu let slavery rule —
  Sooner 'n hev Lincoln, I 'd vote fur a king,
And hev the Saouth fur an aristockracy,
To rule the hull North, (except the Dimmockracy.)

Shuttin' up folks fur speekin' their mind,
  In my opinion 's a piece ov knavery, —
I go fur free speech ov every kind,
  Except when it interferes with slavery !
(Sich kind ov free speech all Dimmykrats fight, —
Ef Brooks hed *killed* Sumner, he 'd done jest right.)

I go fur aour konstitush'nal rights,
  With the rite ov *habeas corpus* invi'late ;
I 'll show 'em haow a Dimmykrat fights,
  Ef Abram Lincoln attempts tu spile it !
I 've a right to *tawk* treason, ez I understand, —
Tawk 's tawk ; it 's *money* that buys the land!

I go fur the vigorous conduct ov war ; —
  Of course with a decent regard tu figgers,
So ez not tu inkreese aour national debt,
  And abuv all *not* to free the niggers.
I 'd ruther the North hed not pulled a trigger,
Than see a traitor shot down by a nigger.

Yes, I am a real Konservativ ;
  I stand by the Konstitushun, I du !
Ef enny wun sez I 'm frends with the Saouth,
  I 'll sware by hokey it is n't true !
I *an't* a rebel ; but he—m ! — *speak low* —
I *kinder* beleeve in Vallandigham, though !

SAYS PRIVATE MAGUIRE.

BY T. B. ALDRICH.

[I must beg the pardon of Private Maguire, of the ——— New York Regiment, for thus publicly putting his sentiments into verse. The following lyric will assure him that I have not forgotten how generously he shared his scanty blanket with me, one terrible night in the Virginia woods, when a blanket was worth fifty dollars an inch.]

" Och ! 't is nate to be captain or colonel,
    Divil a bit would I want to be higher ;
But to rust as a private, I think 's an infernal
    Predicament surely," says Private Maguire.

" *They* can go sparkin' and playin' at billiards,
    With greenbacks to spend for their slightest desire,
Loafin' and atin', and dthrinkin' at Willard's.
    While *we 're* on the pickets," says Private Maguire.

" Livin' in clover, they think it 's a thrifle
    To stand out all night in the rain and the mire,
And a Rebel hard by with a villainous rifle
    Jist ready to pop ye," says Private Maguire.

" Faith, now, it 's not that I 'm afther complainin' ;
    I 'm spilin' to meet ye, Jeff. Davis, Esquire !
Ye blag-gard ! — it 's only I 'm weary of thrainin',
    And thrainin', and thrainin'," says Private Maguire.

" O Lord, for a row ! but, Maguire, be aisy,
    Keep yourself sweet for the inemy's fire,
McClellan 's the saplin' that shortly will plaze ye,
    Be the holy St. Pathrick ! " says Private Maguire.

" And, lad, if ye 're hit, (O, bedad, that eternal
    Jimmy O'Dowd would make up to Maria !)
Whether ye 're sargeant, or captain, or colonel,
    Ye 'll die with the best, then ! " says Private Maguire.

SPRING AT THE CAPITAL.

THE poplar drops beside the way
    Its tasselled plumes of silver gray ;
The chestnut points its green brown buds, impatient for
    the laggard May.

    The honeysuckles lace the wall ;
    The hyacinths grow fair and tall ;
And mellow sun and pleasant wind and odorous bees are
    over all.

    Down-looking in this snow-white bud,
    How distant seems the war's red flood !
How far remote the streaming wounds, the sickening
    scent of human blood !

    Nor Nature does not recognize
    This strife that rends the earth and skies ;
No war-dreams vex the winter sleep of clover-heads and
    daisy-eyes.

    She holds her even way the same,
    Though navies sink or cities flame ;
A snow-drow is a snow-drop still, despite the nation's joy
    or shame.

    When blood her grassy altar wets,
    She sends the pitying violets
To heal the outrage with their bloom, and cover it with
    soft regrets.

    O, crocuses with rain-wet eyes,
    O, tender-lipped anemones,
What do you know of agony, and death and blood-won
    victories ?

No shudder breaks your sunshine trance,
  Though near you rolls, with slow advance,
Clouding your shining leaves with dust, the anguish-laden
        ambulance.

Yonder a white encampment hums;
  The clash of martial music comes;
And now your startled stems are all a-tremble with the
        jar of drums.

Whether it lessen or increase,
  Or whether trumpets shout or cease,
Still deep within your tranquil hearts the happy bees are
        humming "Peace!"

O flowers! the soul that faints or grieves,
  New comfort from your lips receives;
Sweet confidence and patient faith are hidden in your
        healing leaves.

Help us to trust, still on and on,
  That this dark night will soon be gone,
And that these battle-stains are but the blood-red trouble
        of the dawn —

Dawn of a broader, whiter day
  Than ever blessed us with its ray, —
A dawn beneath whose purer light all guilt and wrong
        shall fade away.

Then shall our nation break its bands,
  And, silencing the envious lands,
Stand in the searching light unshamed, with spotless robe,
        and clean, white hands.

A WOMAN'S WAITING.

Under the apple-tree blossoms, in May,
   We sat and watched as the sun went down;
Behind us the road stretched back to the east,
   On, through the meadows, to Danbury town.

Silent we sat, for our hearts were full,
   Silently watched the reddening sky,
And saw the clouds across the west
   Like the phantoms of ships sail silently.

Robert had come with a story to tell,
   I knew it before he had said a word, —
It looked from his eye, and it shadowed his face, —
   He was going to march with the Twenty-third.

We had been neighbors from childhood up, —
   Gone to school by the self-same way,
Climbed the same steep woodland paths,
   Knelt in the same old church to pray.

We had wandered together, boy and girl,
   Where wild flowers grew and wild grapes hung;
Tasted the sweetness of summer days
   When hearts are true, and life is young.

But never a love-word had crossed his lips,
   Never a hint of pledge or vow,
Until, as the sun went down that night,
   His tremulous kisses touched my brow.

" Jenny," he said, " I 've a work to do
   For God and my country and the right, —
True hearts, strong arms, are needed now,
   I dare not stay away from the fight.

" Will you give me a pledge to cheer me on, —
  A hope to look forward to by-and-by ?
Will you wait for me, Jenny, till I come back ? "
  " I will wait," I answered, " until I die."

The May moon rose as we walked that night
  Back through the meadows to Danbury town,
And one star rose and shone by her side, —
  Calmly and sweetly they both looked down.

The scent of blossoms was in the air,
  The sky was blue and the eve was bright,
And Robert said, as he walked by my side,
  " Old Danbury town is fair to-night.

" I shall think of it, Jenny, when far away,
  Placid and still 'neath the moon as now, —
I shall see it, darling, in many a dream,
  And you with the moonlight on your brow."

No matter what else were his parting words, —
  They are mine to treasure until I die,
With the clinging kisses and lingering looks,
  The tender pain of that fond good-bye.

I did not weep, — I tried to be brave, —
  I watched him until he was out of sight, —
Then suddenly all the world grew dark,
  And I was blind in the bright May night.

Blind and helpless I slid to the ground,
  And lay with the night-dews on my hair,
Till the moon was down and the dawn was up,
  And the fresh May morn rose clear and fair.

He was taken and I was left, —
  Left to wait and to watch and pray, —

Till there came a message over the wires,
  Chilling the air of the August day.

"Killed in a skirmish eight or ten;"
  "Wounded and helpless;" as many more, —
All of them our Connecticut men,
  From the little town of Danbury, four.

But I only saw a single name,
  Of one who was all the world to me;
I promised to wait for him till I died, —
  O God, O Heaven, when will it be!

                              Harpers' Magazine.

——◆——

BY JOHN GREENLEAF WHITTIER.

UP from the meadows rich with corn,
Clear in the cool September morn,

The clustered spires of Frederick stand
Green-walled by the hills of Maryland.

Round about them orchards sweep,
Apple and peach-tree fruited deep,

* The incident upon which this ballad is founded took place literally as it is told by the poet upon the occupation of Frederick in Maryland on the second march northward of the insurgent forces. The heroine, as I am informed by Mr. Whittier, was ninety-six years old at the time of the occurrence. The title of the ballad on this page is a fac-simile of her autograph signature to a receipt which is in my possession.

Fair as the garden of the Lord
To the eyes of the famished rebel horde,

On that pleasant morn of the early fall
When Lee marched over the mountain-wall, —

Over the mountains winding down,
Horse and foot, into Frederick town.

Forty flags with their silver stars,
Forty flags with their crimson bars,

Flapped in the morning wind : the sun
Of noon looked down and saw not one.

Up rose Barbara Fritchie then,
Bowed with her fourscore years and ten ;

Bravest of all in Frederick town,
She took up the flag the men hauled down ;

In her attic-window the staff she set,
To show that one heart was loyal yet.

Up the street came the rebel tread,
Stonewall Jackson riding ahead.

Under his slouched hat left and right
He glanced : the old flag met his sight.

" Halt ! " — the dust-brown ranks stood fast.
" Fire ! " — out blazed the rifle-blast.

It shivered the window, pane and sash ;
It rent the banner with seam and gash.

Quick, as it fell, from the broken staff,
Dame Barbara snatched the silken scarf ;

She leaned far out on the window-sill,
And shook it forth with a royal will.

"Shoot, if you must, this old gray head,
But spare your country's flag," she said.

A shade of sadness, a blush of shame,
Over the face of the leader came;

The nobler nature within him stirred
To life at that woman's deed and word:

"Who touches a hair of yon gray head
Dies like a dog! March on!" he said.

All day long through Frederick street
Sounded the tread of marching feet:

All day long that free flag tost
Over the heads of the rebel host.

Ever its torn folds rose and fell
On the loyal winds that loved it well;

And through the hill-gaps sunset light
Shone over it with a warm good-night.

Barbara Fritchie's work is o'er,
And the Rebel rides on his raids no more.

Honor to her! and let a tear
Fall for her sake on Stonewall's bier.

Over Barbara Fritchie's grave
Flag of Freedom and Union wave!

Peace and order and beauty draw
Round thy symbol of light and law;

And ever the stars above look down
On thy stars below in Frederick town !

Atlantic Monthly.

A THANKSGIVING RAILROAD BALLAD FOR
1863.

BY E. PLURIBUS UNUM, ESQ.

IT was a sturdy engineer,
   The Union train had he,
But slippery tracks and heavy grades,
   In eighteen sixty-three.

He wiped the sweat from off his brow :
   " These drivin' wheels will do,
A better ingine never ran,
   She's bound to put us through.

" Ho ! Fireman, Fireman Chase, I mean,
   Down in the tender there !
We've used a powerful sight of wood,
   How much have we to spare ? "

" Oh ! " out then spoke that fireman bold,
   " We've wood and water still ;
Old Legal Tender holds enough
   To make what steam you will."

" Ho ! Seward, ho ! — conductor yet,
   In spite of all the row —
That Frenchman and that Englishman,
   How fare these worthies now ? "

" Quiet enough, these blustering coves,
   That carried it so high ;

A great big Russian up and blazed
   The Frenchman in the eye.

" His friend, John Bull, did not ' pitch in,'
   He drew it very mild,
And sat him in the corner down,
   Submissive as a child."

" Two stations back, conductor say,
   What made that heavy strain ?
It felt to me as though you had
   Hitched on an extra train."

" Confound that rascal Copperhead,
   And all his brood of snakes !
Just at the heaviest of the grade
   They put on all the brakes ! "

The old wheel-tapper goes his round,
   While waits the engineer,
Tink, tink, tink, tink ! the tested wheel,
   Sound music in his ear.

" I thought as how some wheels were cracked,
   But nary one I find,
All right, save that old Jersey one,
   And that we need n't mind.

" Ha ! here 's a telegram from Grant,
   The news, he says, is prime,
All clear along the track once more,
   We 'll yet be in on time."
    .   .   .   .

The bell now rings, the whistle blows,
   The signal given, " All right ; "
On thunders now the Union train,
   On streams its flag of light,

Which, like the beacon on the main,
　Flings hope athwart the night.
　　　　Halloo!
　The grand old iron train
　　Has swept clean out of sight.

THE DEAD DRUMMER-BOY.

'MIDST tangled roots that lined the wild ravine,
　Where the fierce fight raged hottest through the day,
And where the dead in scattered heaps were seen,
Amid the darkling forests' shade and sheen,
　　Speechless in death he lay.

The setting sun, which glanced athwart the place
　In slanting lines, like amber-tinted rain,
Fell sidewise on the drummer's upturned face,
Where Death had left his gory finger's trace
　　In one bright crimson stain.

The silken fringes of his once bright eye
　Lay like a shadow on his cheek so fair;
His lips were parted by a long-drawn sigh,
That with his soul had mounted to the sky
　　On some wild martial air.

No more his hand the fierce tattoo shall beat,
　The shrill reveillé, or the long-roll's call,
Or sound the charge, when in the smoke and heat
Of fiery onset foe with foe shall meet,
　　And gallant men shall fall.

Yet maybe in some happy home, that one —
　A mother — reading from the list of dead,
Shall chance to view the name of her dear son,

And move her lips to say, " God's will be done ! "
    And bow in grief her head.

But more than this what tongue shall tell his story ?
    Perhaps his boyish longings were for fame ?
He lived, he died ; and so, *memento mori* —
Enough if on the page of War and Glory
    Some hand has writ his name.

                    Harpers' Weekly.

THE SENTINEL ON MORRIS ISLAND.

WITH measured tread along his lonely beat,
    At twilight, dawn, or in the darksome night,
Or when at noon the sun, with growing heat,
    Lets fall his dazzling light, —

The watchful sentinel, up and down the shore,
    Paces with weary feet the yielding sand,
While the salt waves, with deep and sullen roar,
    Shout hoarsely to the land.

At dawn he sees the glitt'ring morning star
    Set like a jewel in the roseate sky ;
And glimmering to the sight, within the bar,
    The fleet at anchor lie.

He sees the city, distant, dull, and gray,
    Its quaint old roofs, and slender, tapering spires,
When darkly painted at the close of day
    Against the sunset's fires.

At night he sees the heavens all spangled o'er
    With shining gems that like bright watch-fires burn ;
And though far off, and on a hostile shore,
    His thoughts to home will turn.

Or maybe, in the pitiless, cold storm,
   While moans the wind like some poor soul in pain,
With drooping head and weary, bended form,
      He braves the pelting rain,

And in his mind there dwells a picture fair :
   A cottage-room with walls like purest snow,
And round the hearthstone friendly faces there
      Shine in the fire's warm glow.

An aged man, with locks all silver white ;
   An aged dame, his helpmate she through life;
And still a third, with mild eyes beaming bright, —
      Perhaps the soldier's wife ;

And rosy children climb upon her knee —
   With smiling face looks on the aged dame —
They, laughing, clap their little hands in glee,
      And sweetly lisp his name.

Now from the frowning batteries' bristling side
   Peals forth the murderous cannon's awful roar,
Waking the answering echoes, far and wide,
      From shore to farthest shore.

So fades the picture : each loved form is fled, —
   That waking vision, beautiful, yet brief; —
And up the beach with solid, steady tread
      Comes on the brave " Relief."

Then on his bed, while falls the chilly rain
   And other sentinels their vigils keep,
Sweet thoughts of home go flitting through his brain,
      And fill his dreamful sleep.

                               Harpers' Weekly.

" SHODDY."

OLD Shoddy sits in his easy-chair,
　And cracks his jokes and drinks his ale,
Dumb to the shivering soldier's prayer,
　Deaf to the widows' and orphans' wail.
His coat is as warm as the fleece unshorn ;
　Of the " golden fleece " he is dreaming still ;
And the music that lulls him night and morn
　Is the hum-hum-hum of the shoddy-mill.

Clashing cylinders, whizzing wheels,
　Rend and ravel and tear and pick ;
What can resist these hooks of steel,
　Sharp as the claws of the ancient Nick ?
Cast-off mantle of millionaire,
　Pestilent vagrant's vesture chill,
Rags of miser or beggar bare,
　All are "grist" for the shoddy-mill.

Worthless waste and worn-out wool,
　Flung together, a spacious *sham !*
With just enough of the "fleece" to pull
　Over the eyes of poor Uncle Sam.
Cunningly twisted through web and woof,
　Not " shirt of Nessus " such power to kill ;
Look, how the prints of his hideous hoof
　Track the fiend of the shoddy-mill !

A soldier lies on the frozen ground,
　While crack his joints with aches and ails ;
A 'shoddy' blanket wraps him round,
　His 'shoddy' garments the wind assails.
His coat is 'shoddy,' well 'stuffed' with 'flocks ; '
　He dreams of the flocks on his native hill ;
His feverish sense the demon mocks, —
　The demon that drives the shoddy-mill.

Ay! pierce his tissues with shooting pains,
   Tear the muscles, and rend the bone,
Fire with frenzy the heart and brain, —
   Old Rough Shoddy, your work is done:
Never again shall the bugle blast
   Waken the sleeper that lies so still;
His dream of home and glory past,
   Fatal's the 'work' of the shoddy-mill.

Struck by 'shoddy' and not by 'shells,'
   And not by shot our brave ones fall;
Greed of gold the story tells,
   Drop the mantle and spread the pall.
Out on the vampires! out on those
   Who of our life-blood take their fill!
No *meaner* 'traitor' the nation knows,
   Than the greedy ghoul of the shoddy-mill!

LINT.

FIBRE by fibre, shred by shred,
   It falls from her delicate hand
In feathery films, as soft and slow
As fall the flakes of a vanishing snow
   In the lap of a summer land.

There are jewels of price in her roseate ears,
   And gold round her white wrist coils;
There are costly trifles on every hand,
And gems of art from many a land
   In the chamber where she toils.

A rare bird sings in a gilded cage
   At the open casement near;
A sun-ray glints through a swaying bough,
And lights with a diamond radiance now
   The dew of a falling tear!

A sob floats out to the summer air
  With the song-bird's latest trill ;
The gossamer folds of the drapery
Are waved by the swell of a long, low sigh,
  And the delicate hands are still.

" Ah ! beauty of earth is naught, is naught !
  And a gilded youth is vain !
I have seen a sister's scarred face shine
With a youth and beauty all divine
  By the soldier's couch of pain ! "

" I have read of another whose passing shade
  On their pillows the mangled kissed
In the far Crimea ! "   There are no more tears,
But she plucks the gems from her delicate ears,
  And the gold from her slender wrist.

The bird still sings in his gilded cage ;
  But the Angel in her heart
Hath stung her soul with a noble pain ;
And beauty is naught, and youth is vain,
  While the Patriot's wounds still smart !
  .   .   .   .   .
Fibre by fibre, shred by shred,
  Still fall from her delicate hand
The feathery films, as soft and slow
As fall the flakes of a vanishing snow
  In the lap of a summer land.

There are crimson stains on breasts and brows,
  And fillets in ghastly coils ;
The walls are lofty, and white, and bare,
And moaning echoes roll ever there
  Through the chamber where she toils.

No glitter of gold on her slender wrist,
  Nor gem in her roseate ears ;

But a youth and a beauty all divine
In the face of the Christian maiden shine,
And her gems are the soldier's tears!

Harpers' Weekly.

THE "PEACE DEMOCRACY."

BY "CHARITY GRIMES."

RESOLUSHUNS OV THE CONCORD, N. H., "DIMMOCKRASSY," (SO-
KALLED *NOT* IN HONOR OV GINERAL JACKSON.) DEDI-
KATED TU HON. FRANKLIN PIERCE, THE HERO OV MEX-
ICCO, AND CHAIRMAN OV THE KONVENSHUN.

Resolved, — This nation's goin' tu reuin, —
   Old Abram Lincoln's baound tu strand it.
Thare's sum awlfired mischief brewin',
   We Dimmykrats can't no way stand it!
We make a vaow, from this time forth,
Tu stop awl warfare in the North.

Resolved, — Thet Lincoln's a userper —
   An awful skeery wun et that, —
He shall not lead us wun step further
   Then we've a mind tu go, — thet's flat!
We luv the Guverment ov the nation,
But go agin its administrashun.

Resolved, — This war shood be conduckted
   Most viggorous, by the laws ov peece.
Thet nigger folks may be abduckted
   Whereso aour Suthern brethren please ;
And whereso'er a tremblin' slave is,
He shood be given tu Jeff Davis.

Resolved, — The stones we've thrown in Dixie
   Hev brought us tu an orful pass.

We let aour dander rise too quickly;
    We shood hev gone on throwin' grass.
We b'lieve Vallandigham a saint:
Woe tu the man whu sez he ain't!

Resolved, — We will rekord the story,
    Thet in this war *we 've* acted wust:
It 's true, the Saouth fired on " Old Glory; " *
    But did n't we go and histe it fust?
We might hev missed the war's mischances
Ef we hed histed olive-branches!

Tharefore we form a resolushun
    Tu make all Lincoln's auders void;
Tu put his ginerals tu konfushun,
    So thet aour own sha'n't be annoyed;
And fortify aour strong position
By firing guns on abbolition!

We 'll grasp the fiery suthern cross,
    And bid sich fokes ez Butler bear it!
We 'll kover aour defeat and loss
    With treason's garb (naow Davis wears it).
We skorn deceit, detest hypockracy —
Make way thare fur the Peace Dimmockrassy!

                              Harpers' Weekly.

——————◆——————

THE LATEST WAR–NEWS.

Oh pale, pale face!   Oh helpless hands!
    Sweet eyes by fruitless watching wronged,
Yet turning ever towards the lands
    Where war's red hosts are thronged.

* This name, fondly given by our volunteer soldiers to the flag,
is one of the phrases born of the war for the Republic.

She shudders when they tell the tale
  Of some great battle lost and won!
Her sweet child-face grows old and pale,
  Her heart falls like a stone!

She sees no conquering flag unfurled,
  She hears no victory's brazen roar,
But a dear face, — which was her world, —
  Perchance she 'll kiss no more!

Ever there comes between her sight
  And the glory that they rave about
A boyish brow, and eyes whose light
  Of splendor hath gone out.

The midnight glory of his hair,
  Where late her fingers, like a flood
Of moonlight, wandered, lingering there,
  Is stiff and dank — with blood!

She must not shriek, she must not moan,
  She must not wring her quivering hands;
But sitting dumb and white alone,
  Be bound with viewless bands.

Because her suffering life enfolds
  Another dearer, feebler life,
In death-strong grasp her heart she holds,
  And stills its torturing strife.

Yester eve, they say, a field was won.
  Her eyes asks tidings of the fight;
But tell her of the dead alone
  Who lay out in the night!

In mercy tell her that *his* name
  Was not upon that fatal list;

That not among the heaps of slain
　Dumb are the lips she 's kissed.

Oh, poor, pale child!　Oh, woman heart!
　Its weakness triumphed o'er by strength!
Love teaching pain discipline's art,
　And conquering at length!

———◆———

THE CAVALRY CHARGE.

BY EDMUND C. STEDMAN.

OUR good steeds snuff the evening air,
　Our pulses with their purpose tingle;
The foeman's fires are twinkling there;
　He leaps to hear our sabres jingle!
　　　　Halt!
　Each carbine sent its whizzing ball:
　Now, cling! clang! forward all,
　　　　Into the fight!

Dash on beneath the smoking dome:
　Through level lightnings gallop nearer!
One look to Heaven!　No thoughts of home,
　The guidons that we bear are dearer.
　　　　Charge!
　Cling! clang! forward all!
　Heaven help those whose horses fall, —
　　　　Cut left and right!

They flee before our fierce attack!
　They fall! they spread in broken surges.
Now, comrades, bear our wounded back,
　And leave the foeman to his dirges.
　　　　Wheel!

The bugles sound the swift recall :
Cling ! clang ! backward all !
    Home, and good-night !

———◆———

THE FISHERMAN OF BEAUFORT.

BY MRS. FRANCES D. GAGE.

THE tide comes up, and the tide goes down,
    And still the fisherman's boat,
At early dawn and at evening shade,
    Is ever and ever afloat :
His net goes down, and his net comes up,
    And we hear his song of glee ;
" De fishes dey hates de ole slave nets,
    But comes to de nets ob de free."

The tide comes up, and the tide goes down,
    And the oysterman below
Is picking away, in the slimy sands,
    In the sands " ob de long ago."
But now if an empty hand he bears,
    He shudders no more with fear ;
There 's no stretching-board for the aching bones,
    And no lash of the overseer.

The tide comes up, and the tide goes down,
    And ever I hear a song,
As the moaning winds through the moss-hung oaks,
    Sweep surging ever along.
" O massa white man ! help de slave,
    And de wife and chillen too ;
Eber dey 'll work, wid de hard worn hand,
    Ef ell gib 'em de work to do."

The tide comes up, and the tide goes down,
   But it bides no tyrant's word,
As it chants unceasing the anthem grand
   Of its Freedom to the Lord.
The fisherman floating on its breast
   Has caught up the key-note true :
" De sea works, massa, for 't sef and God,
   And so must de brack man too.

" Den gib him de work, and gib him de pay,
   For de chillen an' wife him love,
And de yam shall grow, and de cotton shall blow,
   And him nebber, nebber rove ;
For him love de ole Carlina State,
   And de ole magnolia tree :
Oh ! nebber him trouble de icy Norf,
   Ef de brack folks — am go free."

SEWARD.

BY A. D. F. RANDOLPH.

WELL, be it so ! The not uncommon fate
   Of greatness overtakes thee in thy prime :
He who is mighty will have foes who hate, —
Thou hast false friends, who only consummate
   Their own destruction in attempting thine.
O, peerless Champion of the Cause so Just,
   When some, o'er zealous now, were cold or mute,
Thou, with sublimest courage, took the Trust
And priceless venture, conscious that thou must
   Bear scorn of those who would thy cause dispute.
   Keep heart ! the Great Hereafter will refute
Each slander born of envy or of hate,
   And thus thy final labors will compute :
" He Freedom saved, by saving first the State ! "

THE SONG OF THE CAMPS.

BY J. R. M.

FAR away in the piney woods,
  Where the dews fall heavy and damp,
A soldier sat by the smouldering fire
  And sang the song of the camp.

" It is not to be weary and worn,
  It is not to feel hunger and thirst,
It is not the forced march nor the terrible fight,
  That seems to the soldier the worst.

" But to sit through the comfortless hours, —
  The lonely, dull hours that will come, —
With his head in his hands and his eyes on the fire,
  And his thoughts on visions of home.

" To wonder how fares it with those
  Who mingled so late with his life, —
Is it well with my little children three ?
  Is it well with my sickly wife ?

" This night-air is chill to be sure,
  But logs lie in plenty around ;
How is it with *them* where wood is so dear,
  And the cash for it hard to be found ?

" Oh, that North air cuts bitterly keen,
  And the ground is hard as a stone ;
It would comfort me just to know that they sit
  By a fire as warm as my own.

" And have they enough to eat ?
  My lads are growing boys,

And my girl is a little tender thing,
　　With her mother's smile and voice.

" My wife she should have her tea,
　　Or maybe a sup of beer;
It went to my heart to look on her face,
　　So white, with a smile and a tear.

" Her form it is weak and thin, —
　　She would gladly work if she could, —
But how can a woman have daily strength
　　Who wants for daily food?

" My oldest boy *he* can cut wood,
　　And Johnny can carry it in;
But then, how frozen their feet must be
　　If their shoes are worn and thin!

" I hope they don't cry with the cold —
　　Are there tears in my little girl's eyes?
O God! say *peace!* to these choking fears,
　　These fears in my heart that rise.

" Many rich folks are round them, I know,
　　And their hearts are not hard nor cold;
They would give to my wife if they only knew,
　　And my little one three years old.

" They would go, like God's angels fair,
　　And enter the lowly door,
And make the sorrowful glad with gifts
　　From their abundant store.

" In this blessed Christmas-time,
　　When the great gift came to men,
They would show, by their gentle and generous deeds,
　　How He cometh in hearts again.

" And my sickly, patient wife,
　　And my little children three,
Would be kindly warmed and fed and clothed
　　As part of Christ's family.

" Well, I leave it all with God,
　　For my sight is short and dim;
He cares for the falling sparrow,
　　My dear ones are safe with Him."

So the soldier watched through the night,
　　Through the dew-fall, heavy and damp;
And as he sat by the smouldering fire,
　　He sang the song of the camp.
Sᴛ. Pᴀᴜʟ, Minn.　　　　　　　　　*Church Journal.*

---◆---

SOLDIER'S TALK.

ʙʏ ᴄʜᴀʀʟᴇs ɢ. ʜᴀʟᴘɪɴ.

Wᴇ have heard the rebel yell,
　　We have heard the Union shout,
We have weighed the matter very well,
　　And mean to fight it out;
In victory's happy glow,
　　In the gloom of utter rout,
We have pledged ourselves — Come weal or woe,
　　By Heaven! we fight it out.

'T is now too late to question
　　What brought the war about;
'T is a thing of pride and passion
　　And we mean to fight it out.
Let the " big wigs " use the pen,
　　Let them caucus, let them spout,

We are half a million weaponed men
  And mean to fight it out.

Our dead, our loved, are crying
  From many a stormed redoubt,
In the swamps and trenches lying, —
  " Oh, comrades, fight it out!
'T was our comfort as we fell
  To hear your gathering shout,
Rolling back the rebels' weaker yell, —
  God speed you, fight it out!"

The negro — free or slave —
  We care no pin about,
But for the flag our fathers gave
  We mean to fight it out;
And while that banner brave
  One rebel rag shall flout,
With volleying arm and flashing glaive
  By Heaven! we fight it out!

Oh, we 've heard the rebel yell,
  We have heard the Union shout,
We have weighed the matter very well,
  And mean to fight it out;
In the flush of perfect triumph,
  And the gloom of utter rout,
We have sworn on many a bloody field —
  We mean to fight it out!

Harpers' Weekly.

PER TENEBRAS LUMINA.

BY MRS. WHITNEY.

I KNOW how, through the golden hours,
　When summer sunlight floods the deep,
The fairest stars of all the heaven
　Climb up, unseen, the effulgent steep.

Orion girds him with a flame;
　And king-like, from the eastward seas,
Comes Aldebaran, with his train
　Of Hyades and Pleiades.

In far meridian pride, the Twins
　Build, side by side, their luminous thrones;
And Sirius and Procyon pour
　A splendor that the day disowns.

And stately Leo, undismayed,
　With fiery footstep tracks the Sun,
To plunge adown the western blaze,
　Sublimely lost in glories won.

I know, if I were called to keep
　Pale morning watch with grief and pain,
Mine eyes should see their gathering might
　Rise grandly through the gloom again.

And when the winter solstice holds
　In his diminished path the sun, —
When hope, and growth, and joy are o'er,
　And all our harvesting is done, —

When, stricken like our mortal life,
　Darkened and chill, the year lays down

The summer beauty that she wore,
    Her summer stars of harp and crown, —

Thick trooping with their golden tread
    They come, as nightfall fills the sky,
Those strong and solemn sentinels,
    To hold their mightier watch on high.

Ah ! who shall shrink from dark and cold,
    Or fear the sad and shortening days,
Since God doth only so unfold
    The wider glory to his gaze ?

Since loyal Truth, and holy Trust,
    And kingly Strength defying Pain,
Stern Courage, and sure Brotherhood
    Are born from out the depths again ?

Dear country of our love and pride !
    So is thy stormy winter given !
So, through the terrors that betide,
    Look up, and hail thy kindling heaven !

                                    Atlantic Monthly.

———◆———

THE CONFEDERATE PRIMER.*

            AT Nashville's fall
            We sinned all.

* Only those can appreciate this burlesque who know the Alphabet Rhymes in the old New-England Primer, beginning —

            In Adam's fall
            We sinned all.

And containing also these impressive rhymes,

            The cat doth play
            And after slay.

            The royal oak it was the tree
            That saved his royal majesty.
            13

At Number Ten
We sinn'd again.

Thy purse to mend
Old Floyd attend.

Abe Lincoln bold
Our ports doth hold.

Jeff Davis tells a lie,
And so must you and I.

Isham doth mourn
His case forlorn.

Brave Pillow's flight
Is out of sight.

Buell doth play
And after slay.

Yon oak will be the gallows-tree
Of Richmond's fallen majesty.

Nashville Union.

AN IDYL.*

Dedicated to the Georgia Regiments, and others of the C. S. R.,
that is, the Confederate States Resurrectionists.

BY H. BEDLOW.

You, forsooth, and valor brothers!
You the types of knighthood's braves!

* I should willingly have omitted these verses, which seem like
a rhymed combination of the Papal anathema with a treatise on
purulent diseases. But they are the expression, gross and fiendish
though it be, of a feeling excited in some people by the language

Offspring of degraded mothers, —
 Suckled at the dugs of slaves !
You at Freedom's holy altars,
 Chanting your blaspheming psalm ;
Candidates for loyal halters ;
 Confed'rates in a monstrous sham !

Catiline's own spawn and scions,
 Daring what no manhood dares ;
Gascons with the lungs of lions,
 But the speed and hearts of hares !
Apostates from the faith of sages ;
 Fools, confounding wrong and right ;
Rushing on the thick-bossed ægis
 Of fair Freedom's belted knight !

Swaggering braggarts, peculators !
 Swindlers of the swell-mob grade !
Fratricidal, perjured traitors !
 Heroes of an ambuscade !
Miscreants, scorn of all the nation ;
 Priesthood of the gyves and lash ;
Ruffians, worthier flagellation
 Than the nobler slaves you gash !

As 'gainst hell's insurgent banners,
 Ithuriel to the battle posts,
Freemen march with loud hosannas,
 Freedom lord of loyal hosts.
Some must fall in this endeavor,
 But where each sacred corse is found,
To the nation's heart forever,
 That dear spot is holy ground.

of most and the acts of many rebels during the war. There was not
a little of such writing on the rebel side, as the reader may see; but
in all the multitudinous mass of verses that I have examined I have
found only this example of its kind among loyal writers. The fact
that it is unique is another reason for its preservation.

Were you littered, whelps inhuman,
  To bay great freedom's climbing moon?
Abortions of the womb of woman!
  Dear saints in heaven! a boon, a boon!
Curse me now, each foul hyena,
  Charnel burglar, ghoul or worse;
Make his leprous body leaner,
  Than a three-months' buried corse.

In each joint's articulation,
  Plant an anguish fixed and sore;
Through the ducts of circulation,
  Madness and delirium pour.
In idiot frenzy let him tattle,
  How he rifled loyal graves;
Let his limbs with palsy rattle,
  Like a gibbet swinging knaves.

Pain and spasm lancinating,
  Fill his days and nights with moans;
Cramp and rack excruciating,
  Twitch his curséd coward bones.
In foretaste of meed hereafter,
  Mock his fevered thirst with streams;
Let him hear hell's goblin laughter,
  In convulsed and nightmare dreams.

By disease's vitiation,
  Corrupt his scoundrel carcass more;
Loathsome forms of suppuration —
  Abscess, ulcer, cancerous sore.
In his own putrescence stifled;
  By a gangrene agonized;
Horrors of the graves he's rifled,
  In his own flesh — vitalized.

Let him — seeming dead — but lying
  In trance's awful consciousness,

Yield the grave its rights — undying —
   Corruption claiming its redress.
With his death-glazed sight, beholding
   All the dark funereal show ;
Feeling living fibre mouldering,
   And the crawling worms also.

Let him see grim insurrection,
   (Rebellion by rebellion paid,)
Arson, pillage, fierce defection,
   Blazing homestead, murderous raid.
Or hear to merry music treading,
   Ransomed slaves, rejoicing well,
For *him*, an undersong pervading
   Mutterings of defrauded hell.

Failing this — then retribution
   Blight his hopes, disgrace his name,
Blast his roof-tree with pollution,
   Drag his household down to shame.
Let consuming hate and malice
   Gnaw his heart like vultures — then
Commend unto his lips a chalice,
   Poisoned with the scorn of men.

Skulking, (guilty fear confounding,)
   In his forests dank and grim,
Every loyal bugle sounding
   Like the judgment trump to him.
Let his last breath be, when dying,
   Miasma from his Southern bogs ;
Dead, then leave his carrion lying,
   " In that last ditch " — like a dog's.

THE OLD SERGEANT.*

THE Carrier cannot sing to-day the ballads
    With which he used to go,
Rhyming the grand-rounds of the happy New-Years
    That are now beneath the snow ;

For the same awful and portentous shadow
    That overcast the earth,
And smote the land last year with desolation,
    Still darkens every hearth.

And the Carrier hears Beethoven's mighty death-march
    Come up from every mart,
And he hears and feels it breathing in his bosom,
    And beating in his heart.

And to-day, like a scarred and weatherbeaten veteran,
    Again he comes along,
To tell the story of the Old Year's struggles,
    In another New-Year's song.

And the song is his, but not so with the story ;
    For the story, you must know,
Was told in prose to Assistant-Surgeon Austin,
    By a soldier of Shiloh :

By Robert Burton, who was brought up on the *Adams*,
    With his death-wound in his side ;
And who told the story to the Assistant-Surgeon
    On the same night that he died :

But the singer feels it will better suit the ballad,
    If all should deem it right,

* This poem was distributed on the first day of the year, 1863,
by the carriers of the *Louisville Journal.*

To sing the story as if what it speaks of
   Had happened but last night :

" Come a little nearer, Doctor — Thank you! let me take
   the cup !
Draw your chair up — draw it closer — just another little
   sup !
Maybe you may think I 'm better, but I 'm pretty well
   used up —
Doctor, you 've done all you could do, but I 'm just a
   going up.

" Feel my pulse, sir, if you want to, but it is no use to
   try."
" Never say that," said the surgeon, as he smothered down
   a sigh,
" It will never do, old comrade, for a soldier to say die ! "
" What you say will make no difference, Doctor, when
   you come to die.

" Doctor, what has been the matter ? "   " You were very
   faint, they say ;
You must try to get to sleep now."   " Doctor, have I
   been away ? "
" No, my venerable comrade."   " Doctor, will you please
   to stay ?
There is something I must tell you, and you won't have
   long to stay !

" I have got my marching orders, and am ready now to
   go ;
Doctor, did you say I fainted ? — but it could n't have
   been so —
For as sure as I 'm a sergeant and was wounded at
   Shiloh,
I 've this very night been back there — on the old field
   of Shiloh !

" You may think it all delusion — all the sickness of the
      brain —
If you do, you are mistaken, and mistaken to my pain ;
For upon my dying honor, as I hope to live again,
I have just been back to Shiloh, and all over it again !

" This is all that I remember : the last time the Lighter
      came,
And the lights had all been lowered, and the noises much
      the same ;
He had not been gone five minutes before something
      called my name —
' ORDERLY SERGEANT ROBERT BURTON !' — just that
      way it called my name.

" Then I thought, who could have called me so distinctly
      and so slow ?
It can't be the Lighter, surely ; he could not have
      spoken so ;
And I tried to answer, ' Here, sir !' but I could n't make
      it go,
For I could n't move a muscle, and I could n't make it
      go !

" Then I thought, it 's all a nightmare — all a humbug
      and a bore !
It is just another *grapevine*,* and it won't come any
      more ;
But it came, sir, notwithstanding, just the same words as
      before, —
' ORDERLY SERGEANT ROBERT BURTON !' — more dis-
      tinctly than before !

" That is all that I remenber, till a sudden burst of light,
And I stood beside the river, where we stood that Sun-
      day night,

_____

* I am unable to explain this slang, which appears to be Western,
and born of the war.

Waiting to be ferried over to the dark bluffs opposite,
When the river seemed perdition and all hell seemed
    opposite !

" And the same old palpitation came again with all its
    power,
And I heard a bugle sounding as from heaven or a tower;
And the same mysterious voice said : ' It is—the elev-
    enth hour !
Orderly Sergeant — Robert Burton — it is the
    eleventh hour !'

" Doctor Austin, what *day* is this ? " " It is Wednesday
    night, you know."
" Yes ! To-morrow will be New-Year's, and a right good
    time below !
What *time* is it, Doctor Austin ? " " Nearly twelve."
    " Then don't you go !
Can it be that all this happened — all this — not an hour
    ago !

" There was where the gunboats opened on the dark,
    rebellious host,
And where Webster semicircled his last guns upon the
    coast ;
There were still the two log-houses, just the same, or else
    their ghost ;
And the same old transport came and took me over — or
    its ghost !

" And the whole field lay before me, all deserted far and
    wide :
There was where they fell on Prentiss — there McCler-
    nand met the tide ;
There was where stern Sherman rallied, and where Hurl-
    but's heroes died ;
Lower down, where Wallace charged them, and kept
    charging till he died !

" There was where Lew Wallace showed them he **was of**
    the canny kin ;
There was where old Nelson thundered, and where Rous-
    seau waded in ;
There McCook ' sent them to breakfast,' and we all began
    to win ;
There was where the grape-shot took me just as we began
    to win.

" Now a shroud of snow and silence over everything was
    spread ;
And but for this old blue mantle, and the old hat on my
    head,
I should not have even doubted, to this moment, I was
    dead ;
For my footsteps were as silent as the snow upon the
    dead.

" Death and silence ! Death and silence ! starry silence
    overhead !
And behold a mighty tower, as if builded to the dead,
To the heaven of the heavens lifted up its mighty head !
Till the Stars and Stripes of heaven all seemed waving
    from its head !

" Round and mighty-based, it towered — up into the in-
    finite !
And I knew no mortal mason could have built a shaft so
    bright ;
For it shone like solid sunshine ; and a winding stair of
    light
Wound around it and around it, till it wound clear out of
    sight !

" And behold ! as I approached it with a rapt and daz-
    zled stare,
Thinking that I saw old comrades just ascending the
    great stair,

Suddenly the solemn challenge broke of, 'Halt!' and
    'Who goes there?'
'I'm a friend,' I said, 'if you are.' 'Then advance, sir,
    to the stair.'

"I advanced; that sentry, Doctor, was Elijah Ballan-
    tyne —
First of all to fall on Monday, after we had formed the
    line.
'Welcome! my old sergeant, welcome! Welcome by that
    countersign!'
And he pointed to the scar there under this old cloak of
    mine!

"As he grasped my hand I shuddered — thinking only of
    the grave;
But he smiled and pointed upward, with a bright and
    bloodless glaive:
'That's the way, sir, to headquarters.' 'What head-
    quarters?' 'Of the brave!'
'But the great tower?' 'That was builded of the great
    deeds of the brave!'

"Then a sudden shame came o'er me at his uniform of
    light;
At my own so old and tattered, and at his so new and
    bright:
'Ah!' said he, 'you have forgotten the new uniform
    to-night!
Hurry back, for you must be here at just twelve o'clock
    to-night!'

"And the next thing I remember, you were sitting there,
    and I —
Doctor, it is hard to leave you — Hark! God bless you
    all! Good-bye!

Doctor, please to give my musket and my knapsack, when
      I die,
To my son — my son that 's coming — he won't get here
      till I die !

" Tell him his old father blessed him as he never did
      before ;
And to carry that old musket — Hark ! a knock is at the
      door ! —
Till the Union — see ! it opens !"   " Father ! father !
      speak once more !"
" Bless you !" gasped the old gray Sergeant ; and he lay
      and said no more !

When the surgeon gave the heir-son the old Sergeant's
      last advice,
And his musket and his knapsack, how the fire flashed
      in his eyes !
He is on the march this morning, and will march on till
      he dies ;
He will save this bleeding country, or will fight until he
      dies !

———◆———

IN THE SEPULCHRE.

O KEEPER of the Sacred Key
And the Great Seal of Destiny !
Whose eye is the blue canopy,
Look down upon the world once more, and tell us what
      the end will be.

Three cold bright moons have filled and wheeled,
And the white cerement that concealed
The lifeless Figure on the shield
Is turned to verdure, and the land is now one mighty
      battle-field.

And the twin brothers that we said
Had clashed above the fallen head,
Heedless of all on which they tread,
Now crimson with each other's blood the vernal drapery
    of the dead.

And all their children, far and wide,
That are so greatly multiplied,
Rise up in frenzy and divide,
And all, according to their might, unsheathe the sword
    and choose their side.

I see the champion sword-strokes flash,
I see them fall and hear them clash,
I hear the murderous engines crash,
I see a brother stoop to loose his foeman-brother's bloody
    sash.

I hear the curses and the thanks,
I see the mad charge on the flanks, —
The rents — the gaps — the broken ranks, —
And seen the vanquished driven headlong down the
    river's bridgeless banks.

I see the death-gripe on the plain,
The grappling monsters on the main;
I see the thousands that are slain,
And all the speechless suffering and agony of heart and
    brain.

I see the torn and mangled corpse,
The dead and dying heaped in scores,
The heedless rider by his horse,
The wounded captives bayoneted through and through
    without remorse.

I see the dark and bloody spots,
The crowded rooms and crowded cots,

The bleaching bones, the battle-blots ;
And write on many a nameless grave a legend of forget-
        me-nots.

I see the assassin crouch and fire ;
I see his victim fall — expire —
I see the victor creeping nigher,
To strip the dead — he turns the head — the face ! — the
        son beholds his sire !

I hear the dying sufferer cry,
With his crushed face turned to the sky ;
I see him crawl in agony
To the foul pool, and bow his head into its bloody slime
        and die.

And in the low sun's bloodshot rays —
Portentous of the coming days —
I see the oceans blush and blaze,
And the emergent continent between them wrapt in
        crimson haze.

And I foreorder and ordain,
That ere the sixth red moon shall wane
Those brothers' swords shall cross again,
And the True shall smite down the False within the Vir-
        gin's waste domain.

And lo ! the bloody dew shall fall,
And my great darkness, like a pall
Of deep compassion, cover all,
Till the dead nation rise, transformed by truth, to tri-
        umph over all.

Thus saith the Keeper of the Key
And the Great Seal of Destiny,

Whose eye is the blue canopy,
And casts the pall of his great darkness over all the land
    and sea.

Louisville Journal.

UNCLE SAM.

AIR — "*Tom Brown.*"

THE king will take the queen,
    And the queen will take the jack ;
And down we march to Dixie's land,
    With knapsacks at our back.
Chorus — Here's to you, Uncle Sam,
        And your flag shall be our chart ;
        Here's to you, with hand and heart ;
        And for you we'll win a battle or two,
        And that before we part ;
        Here's to you, Uncle Sam ! [*Repeat.*

The jack will take the ten,
    And the ten will take the nine ;
And over Richmond's rebel walls
    The Stars and Stripes must shine.
Chorus — Here's to you, etc.

The nine will take the eight,
    And the eight will take the seven ;
And out of Old Virginia's soil
    Secession shall be driven.
Chorus — Here's to you, etc.

The seven will take the six,
    And the six will take the five ;
King Davis and his wretched crew
    From Dixie's land we'll drive.
Chorus — Here's to you, etc.

The five will take the four,
    And the four will take the tray ;
And all the ragged rebel rogues
    We 'll shortly sweep away.
Chorus — Here 's to you, etc.

The tray will take the deuce,
    But the deuce can't take the ace ;
And so the Devil and Davis both
    Must leave their power and place.
Chorus — Here 's to you, etc.

———◆———

WHEN JOHNNY COMES MARCHING HOME.*

WHEN Johnny comes marching home again,
    Hurrah ! hurrah !
We 'll give him a hearty welcome then,
    Hurrah ! hurrah !
The men will cheer, the boys will shout,
The ladies, they will all turn out,
    And we 'll all feel gay,
When Johnny comes marching home.

CHORUS TO EACH VERSE.

The men will cheer, the boys will shout,
    The ladies, they will all turn out,
        And we 'll all feel gay,
    When Johnny comes marching home.

The old church-bell will peal with joy,
    Hurrah ! hurrah !
To welcome home our darling boy,
    Hurrah ! hurrah !

* A very popular street-song during the last two years of the
war. It was sung to a kind of jig, in the minor key.

The village lads and lasses say,
With roses they will strew the way;
 And we 'll all feel gay,
When Johnny comes marching home.

Get ready for the jubilee,
 Hurrah! hurrah!
We 'll give the hero three times three,
 Hurrah! hurrah!
The laurel-wreath is ready now
To place upon his loyal brow;
 And we 'll all feel gay,
When Johnny comes marching home.

Let love and friendship on that day,
 Hurrah! hurrah!
Their choicest treasures then display,
 Hurrah! hurrah!
And let each one perform some part,
To fill with joy the warrior's heart;
 And we 'll all feel gay,
When Johnny comes marching home.
Chorus — The men will cheer, the boys will shout,
 The ladies, they will all turn out,
  And we 'll all feel gay,
When Johnny comes marching home.

SONNET.

BY GEORGE H. BOKER.

BLOOD, blood! the lines of every printed sheet
Through their dark arteries reek with running gore;
At hearth, at board, before the household door,
'T is the sole subject with which neighbors meet.
Girls at the feast, and children in the street
14

Prattle of horrors — flash their little store
Of simple jests against the cannon's roar,
As if mere slaughter kept existence sweet.
Oh, Heaven! I quail at the familiar way
   This fool — the world — disports his jingling cap;
   Murdering or dying, with one grin agap!
Our very Love comes draggled from the fray, —
   Smiling at victory, scowling at mishap,
   With gory Death companioned and at play.

———◆———

SONNET.

BY GEORGE H. BOKER.

Oh! craven, craven! while my brothers fall
   Like grass before the mower, in the fight,
   I, easy vassal to my own delight,
Am bound with flowers, — a far too willing thrall.
Day after day along the streets I crawl,
   Shamed in my manhood, reddening at the sight
   Of every soldier who upholds the Right,
With no more motive than his country's call.
I love thee more than honor; ay, above
   That simple duty, conscience plain and clear
   To dullest minds, whose summons all men hear.
Yet, as I blush and loiter, who should move
   In the grand marches, I cannot but fear
   That thou wilt scorn me for my very love.

———◆———

THE BRAVE AT HOME.

BY THOMAS BUCHANAN READ.

The maid who binds her warrior's sash
   With smile that well her pain dissembles,

The while beneath her drooping lash
 One starry tear-drop hangs and trembles,
Though Heaven alone records the tear,
 And Fame shall never know her story,
Her heart shall shed a drop as dear
 As ever dewed the field of glory.

The wife who girds her husband's sword
 'Mid little ones who weep or wonder,
And gravely speaks the cheering word,
 What though her heart be rent asunder;
Doomed nightly in her dreams to hear
 The bolts of war around him rattle,
Hath shed as sacred blood as e'er
 Was poured upon a field of battle.

The mother who conceals her grief
 When to her breast her son she presses,
Then breathes a few brave words and brief,
 Kissing the patriot brow she blesses,
With no one but her secret God
 To know the pain that weighs upon her,
Sheds holy blood as e'er the sod
 Received on Freedom's field of honor.

———◆———

WHEN THIS CRUEL WAR IS OVER.*

DEAREST love, do you remember
 When we last did meet,

---

* Of all the songs which the war produced, this was the most
sung, except, perhaps, the John Brown Song. At one time the air
was heard out of doors and in public places constantly, — sung,
whistled, hummed, or played on barrel-organs. Sitting with open
windows one evening in the summer of 1863, I heard this air at
intervals of not more than five minutes (it seemed without inter-
mission) from eight o'clock until long after midnight.

How you told me that you loved me,
    Kneeling at your feet?
O, how proud you stood before me
    In your suit of blue,
When you vowed to me and country
    Ever to be true.
Chorus — Weeping, sad and lonely,
        Hopes and fears, how vain;
      Yet praying
          When this cruel war is over,
        Praying that we meet again.

When the summer breeze is sighing
    Mournfully along,
Or when autumn leaves are falling,
    Sadly breathes the song.
Oft in dreams I see thee lying
    On the battle-plain,
Lonely, wounded, even dying,
    Calling, but in vain.
Chorus — Weeping, sad, &c.

If, amid the din of battle,
    Nobly you should fall,
Far away from those who love you,
    None to hear you call,
Who would whisper words of comfort?
    Who would soothe your pain?
Ah, the many cruel fancies
    Ever in my brain!
Chorus — Weeping, sad, &c.

But our country called you, darling,
    Angels cheer your way!
While our nation's sons are fighting,
    We can only pray.
Nobly strike for God and liberty,

Let all nations see
How we love the starry banner,
Emblem of the free!
Chorus — Weeping, sad and lonely,
        Hopes and fears, how vain;
    Yet praying
        When this cruel war is over,
        Praying that we meet again.

——◆——

APRIL 20, 1864.

BY CHARLES G. HALPIN.

THREE years ago to-day
  We raised our hands to heaven,
And on the rolls of muster
  Our names were thirty-seven;
There were just a thousand bayonets,
  And the swords were thirty-seven,
As we took the oath of service
  With our right hands raised to heaven.

Oh, 't was a gallant day,
  In memory still adored,
That day of our sun-bright nuptials
  With the musket and the sword!
Shrill rang the fifes, the bugles blared,
  And beneath a cloudless heaven
Twinkled a thousand bayonets,
  And the swords were thirty-seven.

Of the thousand stalwart bayonets
  Two hundred march to-day;
Hundreds lie in Virginia swamps,
  And hundreds in Maryland clay;
And other hundreds, less happy, drag
  Their shattered limbs around,

And envy the deep, long, blessèd sleep
  Of the battle-field's holy ground.

For the swords — one night, a week ago,
  The remnant, just eleven,
Gathered around a banqueting board
  With seats for thirty-seven;
There were two limped in on crutches,
  And two had each but a hand
To pour the wine and raise the cup
  As we toasted " Our flag and land ! "

And the room seemed filled with whispers
  As we looked at the vacant seats,
And, with choking throats, we pushed aside
  The rich but untasted meats;
Then in silence we brimmed our glasses,
  As we rose up — just eleven —
And bowed as we drank to the loved and the dead
  Who had made us thirty-seven !

Harpers' Weekly.

GRANT.

BY GEORGE H. BOKER.

As Moses stood upon the flaming hill,
  With all the people gathered at his feet,
  Waiting in Sinai's valley, there to meet
The awful bearer of Jehovah's will, —
So, Grant, thou stand'st, amidst the trumpets shrill,
  And the wild fiery storms that flash and beat
  In iron thunder and in leaden sleet,
Topmost of all, and most exposed to ill.
O, stand thou firm, great leader of our race,
  Hope of our future, till the times grow bland,
  And into ashes drops war's dying brand;

Then let us see thee, with benignant grace,
Descend thy height, God's glory on thy face,
   And the law's tables safe within thy hand!

THE BOUNTY–JUMPER.*

BY J. CROSS CASTEN.

MY song is of a fast young man whose name was Billy
      Wires;
He used to run with the machine and go to all the fires:
But as he loved a Soldier's life, and wished strange things
      to see,
So the thought struck him that he would go and jump
      the Bounti–e.

At once he went to see a friend, whose maiden name
      was Cal,
When they started to the office of the Provost Marshi–al.
The Surgeon found that they would pass, as either had no
      scars,
And they received the Bounty of Five Hundred Dol–li–ars.

They were then marched into a room that was extremely
      near,
Where they were dressed in the latest style as Union
      Cavaliers;
Into this room they were locked up, no longer to be free:
Says Billy, "the first chance that I get I'll jump the
      Bounti–e!"

Three days elapsed, when they were marched to the depot
      through the street:
Says Cal to Billy, "Let's get away, for nimble are our
      feet."

---

* The author calls this song "A pathetic ditty, written for Pony
Smith, the favorite Ethiopian Comedian," which perhaps means
negro minstrel.

As they got near the depot the guard told all to stop;
When Billy and Cal as quick as you please popped into
     a Policy shop.

When the guard found out that they were gone they
     did n't know what to do :
They went in every Gin-mill, and searched the place all
     through ;
But their search was fruit–i–less, as you may plainly see,
For, says Billy to Cal, " We 're hunkey boys that have
     jumped the Bounti–e."

As soon as they found that the guard had gone they
     resolved upon a spree ;
They travelled all around the town the Elephant to see ;
They treated everybody, and to please all they tried
     hard ;
But there was one whom they could not please, for he
     happened to be the guard.

Poor Cal was seized and hurried to jail, his time there to
     serve out ;
But Billy escaped through the back door, for he knew
     that route.
That night, as Billy lay on his couch, his sin he plainly
     did see,
In cheating the Government out of funds in jumping the
     Bounti–e.

He rolled all over that night in bed — to sleep he vainly
     tried ;
He pitied Cal who in pris–u–on was, and resolved on
     suicide ;
He bought six dozen wrought-iron spikes, and swallowed
     them three by three,
And that was the last of Billy Wires, who jumped the
     Bounti–e.

THE SONG OF KILPATRICK'S TROOPERS.

Up from the ground at break of day,
   When the bugle's note is heard, —
From the cold, hard ground, where all night we lay,
   To rise with the waking bird.
Right merrily our sabres ring
   As we scour along on our steeds;
Oh, true and tried are the hearts of those
   Whom the brave Kilpatrick leads!

Away, away, o'er the plain we go,
   Away on our steeds so fleet!
Ah, well the foeman's path we know
   By the print of the foeman's feet!
So on we ride while our sabres ring
   A merrily sounding tune,
By field and river and wooded steep,
   To the halt which comes with noon.

And then in the forest's welcome shade,
   'Neath the pine-trees dark and high,
We rest till the burning heat is past
   From the Southern noonday sky.
Then up and away o'er the rolling plain,
   Away on our gallant steeds!
What foe is there whom we would not dare
   When the brave Kilpatrick leads?

Of Northern steel our good blades are,
   Our carbines are true of aim;
The Southern traitor hears with dread
   The sound of our leader's name.
Oh, wild is the life we troopers live,
   But a merrier none may know,
To scour the plain on our gallant steeds
   In search of the traitorous foe!

And when on the battle-field we meet,
    And loud on the echoing air
The bugles sound, and quick in the sun
    Our blades gleam bright and bare,
Away we go at the one word *charge*,
    With a cheer, at the flying foe ;
While the bullets sing, and our scabbards ring,
    And the bugles loudly blow !

Oh, long shall the tale of our deeds be told
    When this cruel war shall cease,
On winter eves, by the glowing hearth,
    When the land shall be blessed with peace.
And long shall live in the hearts of all
    Our valiant leader's fame,
And our children lisp with their infant lips
    The brave Kilpatrick's name.

Harpers' Weekly.

THE SONG OF GRANT'S SOLDIERS.

PILE on the rails !   Come, comrades, all,
    We 'll sing a song to-night ;
To-morrow, when the bugles call,
    Be ready for the fight.
Be ready then with loud hurrah
    To battle or to die ;
When Grant shall yield, the Northern star
    Will fade from out the sky.
        Hurrah ! hurrah ! hurrah !

Before us lies the rebel host,
    Their watch-fires we can see ;

We laugh to hear the traitor boast
   Of Southern victory.
Three cheers for Grant, and one more cheer,
   Until the woods ring back !
Ah, well the rebel chief may fear
   The blood-hound on his track.
        Hurrah ! hurrah ! hurrah !

In Freedom's cause our blades were drawn :
   The traitor yet shall feel
Before the day of Peace shall dawn
   How strong is Northern steel.
Three cheers for Grant, my gallant men !
   Give three loud, roaring cheers !
Until the foe within his den
   Shall tremble while he hears.
        Hurrah ! hurrah ! hurrah !

Thus far we 've come through fire and flood ;
   Still further on we 'll press,
Although the way be red with blood
   As through the wilderness.
Then cheer, brave comrades ; let the night
   Ring with your loud hurrahs
For Grant, who knows so well to fight,
   And for the Stripes and Stars.
        Hurrah ! hurrah ! hurrah !

Our longing eyes shall yet behold
   Proud Richmond's slender spires ;
Our children's children will be told
   How fought their valiant sires.
Look well to cap and cartridge, too ;
   And as we onward press
We 'll cheer for Grant, who brought us through
   The bloody wilderness.
        Hurrah ! hurrah ! hurrah !

Brave soldiers of the Lord are we,
  In solid ranks we come!
The Southern traitors yet shall see
  How fight the Northern "scum."
Be ready, then, with loud hurrah,
  To battle or to die;
When Grant shall yield, the Northern star
  Will drop from out the sky.
            Hurrah! hurrah! hurrah!

Harpers' Weekly.

————◆————

DRIVING HOME THE COWS.

OUT of the clover and blue-eyed grass,
  He turned them into the river-lane;
One after another he let them pass,
  Then fastened the meadow bars again.

Under the willows and over the hill,
  He patiently followed their sober pace;
The merry whistle for once was still,
  And something shadowed the sunny face.

Only a boy! and his father had said
  He never could let his youngest go!
Two already were lying dead,
  Under the feet of the trampling foe.

But after the evening work was done,
  And the frogs were loud in the meadow-swamp,
Over his shoulder he slung his gun
  And stealthily followed the foot-path damp.

Across the clover and through the wheat,
  With resolute heart and purpose grim,

Though cold was the dew on his hurrying feet,
  And the blind bats flitting startled him.

Thrice since then had the lanes been white,
  And the orchards sweet with apple-bloom;
And now, when the cows came back at night,
  The feeble father drove them home.

For news had come to the lonely farm
  That three were lying where two had lain;
And the old man's tremulous, palsied arm
  Could never lean on a son's again.

The summer day grew cool and late;
  He went for the cows when the work was done;
But down the lane, as he opened the gate,
  He saw them coming, one by one.

Brindle, Ebony, Speckle, and Bess,
  Shaking their horns in the evening wind;
Cropping the buttercups out of the grass —
  But who was it following close behind?

Loosely swang in the idle air
  The empty sleeve of army blue;
And worn and pale, from the crisping hair,
  Looked out a face that the father knew;

For Southern prisons will sometimes yawn,
  And yield their dead unto life again; *

---

* Yet there are twelve thousand nine hundred and nineteen graves of Union soldiers at the one rebel prison-pen of Andersonville; while from the comfortable quarters in which the rebel prisoners were kept, there went back into the rebel armies some of "the finest fighting material" the rebel Commissioner of Exchange ever saw.

And the day that comes with a cloudy dawn
  In golden glory at last may wane.

The great tears sprang to their meeting eyes;
  For the heart must speak when the lips are dumb,
And under the silent evening skies
  Together they followed the cattle home.

                      Harpers' Magazine.

ON PICKET DUTY.

WITHIN a green and shadowy wood,
Circled with spring, alone I stood:
The nook was peaceful, fair, and good.

The wild-plum blossoms lured the bees,
The birds sang madly in the trees,
Magnolia-scents were on the breeze.

All else was silent; but the ear
Caught sounds of distant bugle clear,
And heard the bullets whistle near, —

When from the winding river's shore
The Rebel guns began to roar,
And ours to answer, thundering o'er;

And echoed from the wooded hill,
Repeated and repeated still,
Through all my soul they seemed to thrill.

For, as their rattling storm awoke,
And loud and fast the discord broke,
In rude and trenchant *words* they spoke.

"*We hate!*" boomed fiercely o'er the tide;
"*We fear not!*" from the other side;
"*We strike!*" the Rebel guns replied.

Quick roared our answer, "We defend!"
"*Our rights!*" the battle-sounds contend;
"The rights of all!" we answer send.

"*We conquer!*" rolled across the wave;
"We persevere!" our answer gave;
"*Our Chivalry!*" they wildly rave.

"*Ours are the brave!*" "Be ours the free!"
"*Be ours the slave, the masters we!*"
"On us their blood no more shall be!"

As when some magic word is spoken,
By which a wizard spell is broken,
There was a silence at that token.

The wild birds dared once more to sing,
I heard the pine bough's whispering,
And trickling of a silver spring.

Then, crashing forth with smoke and din,
Once more the rattling sounds begin,
Our iron lips roll forth, "We win!"

And dull and wavering in the gale
That rushed in gusts across the vale
Came back the faint reply, "*We fail!*"

And then a word, both stern and sad,
From throat of huge Columbiad, —
"Blind fools and traitors! ye are mad!"

Again the Rebel answer came,
Muffled and slow, as if in shame, —
" *All, all is lost !* " in smoke and flame.

Now bold and strong and stern as Fate
The Union guns sound forth, " We wait ! "
Faint comes the distant cry, " *Too late !* "

" Return ! return ! " our cannon said ;
And, as the smoke rolled overhead,
" *We dare not !* " was the answer dread.

Then came a sound, both loud and clear,
A godlike word of hope and cheer, —
" Forgiveness ! " echoed far and near ;

As when beside some death-bed still
We watch, and wait God's solemn will,
A bluebird warbles his soft trill.

I clenched my teeth at that blest word,
And, angry, muttered, " Not so, Lord !
The only answer is the sword ! "

I thought of Shiloh's tainted air,
Of Richmond's prisons, foul and bare,
And murdered heroes, young and fair, —

Of block and lash and overseer,
And dark, mild faces pale with fear,
Of baying hell-hounds panting near.

But then the gentle story told
My childhood, in the days of old,
Rang out its lessons manifold.

O prodigal, and lost! arise
And read the welcome blest that lies
In a kind Father's patient eyes!

Thy elder brother grudges not
The lost and found should share his lot,
And wrong in concord be forgot.

Thus mused I, as the hours went by,
Till the relieving guard drew nigh,
And then was challenge and reply.

And as I hastened back to line,
It seemed an omen half divine
That " Concord " was the countersign.

Atlantic Monthly.

THE HEART OF THE WAR.

PEACE in the clover-scented air,
   And stars within the dome ;
And underneath, in dim repose,
   A plain New-England home.
Within, a murmur of low tones
   And sighs from hearts oppressed,
Merging in prayer at last, that brings
   The balm of silent rest.

I 've closed a hard day's work, Marty, —
   The evening chores are done ;
And you are weary with the house,
   And with the little one.

15

But he is sleeping sweetly now,
  With all our pretty brood;
So come and sit upon my knee,
  And it will do me good.

Oh, Marty! I must tell you all
  The trouble in my heart,
And you must do the best you can
  To take and bear your part.
You 've seen the shadow on my face,
  You 've felt it day and night;
For it has filled our little home,
  And banished all its light.

I did not mean it should be so,
  And yet I might have known
That hearts that live as close as ours
  Can never keep their own.
But we are fallen on evil times,
  And, do whate'er I may,
My heart grows sad about the war,
  And sadder every day.

I think about it when I work,
  And when I try to rest,
And never more than when your head
  Is pillowed on my breast;
For then I see the camp-fires blaze,
  And sleeping men around,
Who turn their faces toward their homes,
  And dream upon the ground.

I think about the dear, brave boys,
  My mates in other years,
Who pine for home and those they love,
  Till I am choked with tears.
With shouts and cheers they marched away
  On glory's shining track,

But, ah! how long, how long they stay!
  How few of them come back!

One sleeps beside the Tennessee,
  And one beside the James,
And one fought on a gallant ship
  And perished in its flames.
And some, struck down by fell disease,
  Are breathing out their life;
And others, maimed by cruel wounds,
  Have left the deadly strife.

Ah, Marty! Marty! only think
  Of all the boys have done
And suffered in this weary war!
  Brave heroes, every one!
Oh! often, often in the night,
  I hear their voices call:
"Come on and help us!   Is it right
  That we should bear it all?"

And when I kneel and try to pray,
  My thoughts are never free,
But cling to those who toil and fight
  And die for you and me.
And when I pray for victory,
  It seems almost a sin
To fold my hands and ask for what
  I will not help to win.

Oh! do not cling to me and cry,
  For it will break my heart;
I'm sure you'd rather have me die
  Than not to bear my part.
You think that some should stay at home
  To care for those away;
But still I'm helpless to decide
  If I should go or stay.

For, Marty, all the soldiers love,
   And all are loved again ;
And I am loved, and love, perhaps,
   No more than other men.
I cannot tell — I do not know —
   Which way my duty lies,
Or where the Lord would have me build
   My fire of sacrifice.

I feel — I know — I am not mean ;
   And though I seem to boast,
I'm sure that I would give my life
   To those who need it most.
Perhaps the Spirit will reveal
   That which is fair and right ;
So, Marty, let us humbly kneel
   And pray to Heaven for light.

———

Peace in the clover-scented air,
   And stars within the dome ;
And, underneath, in dim repose,
   A plain, New-England home.
Within, a widow in her weeds,
   From whom all joy is flown,
Who kneels among her sleeping babes,
   And weeps and prays alone !

                 Atlantic Monthly.

———◆———

THE DRUMMER–BOY'S BURIAL.

ALL day long the storm of battle through the startled
    valley swept ;
All night long the stars in heaven o'er the slain sad vigils
    kept.

Oh the ghastly, upturned faces gleaming whitely through
the night!
Oh the heaps of mangled corses in that dim sepulchral
light!

One by one the pale stars faded, and at length the morn-
ing broke;
But not one of all the sleepers on that field of death
awoke.

Slowly passed the golden hours of that long bright sum-
mer day,
And upon that field of carnage still the dead unburied
lay:

Lay there stark and cold, but pleading with a dumb, un-
ceasing prayer,
For a little dust to hide them from the staring sun and
air.

But the foemen held possession of that hard-won battle
plain,
In unholy wrath denying even burial to our slain.

Once again the night dropped round them — night so
holy and so calm
That the moonbeams hushed the spirit, like the sound of
prayer or psalm.

On a couch of trampled grasses, just apart from all the
rest,
Lay a fair young boy, with small hands meekly folded on
his breast.

Death had touched him very gently, and he lay as if in
sleep;
Even his mother scarce had shuddered at that slumber
calm and deep.

For a smile of wondrous sweetness lent a radiance to the
      face,
And the hand of cunning sculptor could have added
      nought of grace

To the marble limbs so perfect in their passionless repose,
Robbed of all save matchless purity by hard, unpitying
      foes.

And the broken drum beside him all his life's short story
      told :
How he did his duty bravely till the death-tide o'er him
      rolled.

Midnight came with ebon garments and a diadem of stars,
While right upward in the zenith hung the fiery planet
      Mars.

Hark ! a sound of stealthy footsteps and of voices whisper-
      ing low, —
Was it nothing but the young leaves, or the brooklet's
      murmuring flow ?

Clinging closely to each other, striving never to look
      round
As they passed with silent shudder the pale corses on the
      ground,

Came two little maidens, — sisters, — with a light and
      hasty tread,
And a look upon their faces, half of sorrow, half of dread.

And they did not pause nor falter till, with throbbing
      hearts, they stood
Where the Drummer-Boy was lying in that partial soli-
      tude.

They had brought some simple garments from their ward-
    robe's scanty store,
And two heavy iron shovels in their slender hands they
    bore.

Then they quickly knelt beside him, crushing back the
    pitying tears,
For they had no time for weeping, nor for any girlish
    fears.

And they robed the icy body, while no glow of maiden
    shame
Changed the pallor of their foreheads to a flush of lam-
    bent flame.

For their saintly hearts yearned o'er it in that hour of
    sorest need,
And they felt that Death was holy, and it sanctified the
    deed.

But they smiled and kissed each other when their new,
    strange task was o'er,
And the form that lay before them its unwonted garments
    wore.

Then with slow and weary labor a small grave they hol-
    lowed out,
And they lined it with the withered grass and leaves that
    lay about.

But the day was slowly breaking ere their holy work was
    done,
And in crimson pomp the morning again heralded the sun.

And then those little maidens — they were children of
    our foes —
Laid the body of our Drummer-Boy to undisturbed repose.
                    Harpers' Magazine.

THE BAY FIGHT.

(*Mobile Bay, August* 5, 1864.)

BY H. H. BROWNELL, U. S. N.

" On the forecastle, Ulf the Red
    Watched the lashing of the ships.
 ' If the Serpent lie so far ahead,
  We shall have hard work of it here,'
    Said he."

THREE days through sapphire seas we sailed,
    The steady Trade blew strong and free,
The Northern Light his banners paled,
The Ocean Stream our channels wet,
    We rounded low Canaveral's lee,
And passed the isles of emerald set
    In blue Bahamas turquoise sea.

By reef and shoal obscurely mapped,
    And hauntings of the gray sea-wolf,
The palmy Western Key lay lapped
    In the warm washing of the Gulf.

But weary to the hearts of all
    The burning glare, the barren reach
    Of Santa Rosa's withered beach,
And Pensacola's ruined wall.

And weary was the long patrol,
    The thousand miles of shapeless strand,
From Brazos to San Blas that roll
    Their drifting dunes of desert sand.

Yet, coastwise as we cruised or lay,
    The land-breeze still at nightfall bore,
By beach and fortress-guarded bay,
    Sweet odors from the enemy's shore,

Fresh from the forest solitudes,
  Unchallenged of his sentry lines, —
The bursting of his cypress buds,
  And the warm fragrance of his pines.

Ah, never braver bark and crew,
  Nor bolder Flag a foe to dare,
Had left a wake on ocean blue
  Since Lion-Heart sailed *Trenc-le-mer*! *

But little gain by that dark ground
  Was ours, save, sometime, freer breath
For friend or brother strangely found,
  'Scaped from the drear domain of death.

And little venture for the bold,
  Or laurel for our valiant Chief,
  Save some blockaded British thief,
Full fraught with murder in his hold,

Caught unawares at ebb or flood;
  Or dull bombardment, day by day,
  With fort and earth-work, far away,
Low couched in sullen leagues of mud.

A weary time — but to the strong
  The day at last, as ever, came;
And the volcano, laid so long,
  Leaped forth in thunder and in flame!

" Man your starboard battery ! "
  Kimberly shouted;
The ship, with her hearts of oak,
Was going, mid roar and smoke,
    On to victory!
  None of us doubted, —

* The flag-ship of Richard I.

No, not our dying, —
Farragut's Flag was flying!

Gaines growled low on our left,
    Morgan roared on our right —
Before us, gloomy and fell,
With breath like the fume of hell,
Lay the Dragon of iron shell,
    Driven at last to the fight!

Ha, old ship! do they thrill,
    The brave two hundred scars
    You got in the River-Wars?
That were leeched with clamorous skill,
    (Surgery savage and hard,)
Splinted with bolt and beam,
Probed in scarfing and seam,
    Rudely linted and tarred
With oakum and boiling pitch,
And sutured with splice and hitch,
    At the Brooklyn Navy-Yard!

Our lofty spars were down,
To bide the battle's frown,
(Wont of old renown,) —
But every ship was drest
In her bravest and her best,
    As if for a July day;
Sixty flags and three,
    As we floated up the bay, —
Every peak and mast-head flew
The brave Red, White, and Blue, —
    We were eighteen ships that day.

With hawsers strong and taut,
The weaker lashed to port,
    On we sailed, two by two, —

That if either a bolt should feel
Crash through caldron or wheel,
Fin of bronze or sinew of steel,
    Her mate might bear her through.

Steadily nearing the head,
The great Flag-Ship led, —
    Grandest of sights!
On her lofty mizen flew
Our Leader's dauntless Blue,
    That had waved o'er twenty fights.
So we went, with the first of the tide,
    Slowly, mid the roar
    Of the rebel guns ashore,
And the thunder of each full broadside.

Ah, how poor the prate
Of statute and state,
    We once held with these fellows:
Here, on the flood's pale-green,
    Hark how he bellows, —
    Each bluff old Sea-Lawyer!
Talk to them Dahlgren,
    Parrott, and Sawyer!

On in the whirling shade
    Of the cannon's sulphury breath,
    We drew to the Line of Death
That our devilish Foe had laid;
Meshed in a horrible net,
    And baited villainous well,
Right in our path were set
    Three hundred traps of hell!

And there, O sight forlorn!
    There, while the cannon
        Hurtled and thundered, —

(Ah what ill raven
Flapped o'er the ship that morn!)
Caught by the under-death,
In the drawing of a breath,
  Down went dauntless Craven,
    He and his hundred!

A moment we saw her turret,
  A little heel she gave,
And a thin white spray went o'er her,
  Like the crest of a breaking wave;
In that great iron coffin,
  The channel for their grave,
  The fort their monument,
(Seen afar in the offing,)
Ten fathom deep lie Craven
  And the bravest of our brave.

Then, in that deadly track,
A little the ships held back,
  Closing up in their stations:
There are minutes that fix the fate
  Of battles and of nations,
    (Christening the generations,)
When valor were all too late,
  If a moment's doubt be harbored;
From the main-top, bold and brief,
Came the word of our grand old Chief, —
  " Go on!" — 't was all he said;
    Our helm was put to the starboard,
    And the Hartford passed ahead.

Ahead lay the Tennessee, —
  On our starboard bow he lay,
With his mail-clad consorts three,
  (The rest had run up the Bay), —
There he was, belching flame from his bow,

And the steam from his throat's abyss
Was a Dragon's maddened hiss, —
  In sooth a most cursèd craft! —
In a sullen ring, at bay,
By the Middle Ground they lay,
  Raking us, fore and aft.

  Trust me, our berth was hot,
   Ah, wickedly well they shot;
How their death-bolts howled and stung!
   And the water-batteries played
   With their deadly cannonade
Till the air around us rung;
So the battle raged and roared —
Ah, had you been aboard
  To have seen the fight we made!
How they leaped, the tongues of flame,
  From the cannon's fiery lip!
How the broadsides, deck and frame,
  Shook the great ship!

  And how the enemy's shell
   Came crashing, heavy and oft,
   Clouds of splinters flying aloft
And falling in oaken showers:
  But ah, the pluck of the crew!
Had you stood on that deck of ours,
  You had seen what men may do.

Still, as the fray grew louder,
  Boldly they worked and well, —
Steadily came the powder,
  Steadily came the shell.
And if tackle or truck found hurt,
  Quickly they cleared the wreck;
And the dead were laid to port,
  All a-row, on our deck.

Never a nerve that failed,
Never a cheek that paled,
Not a tinge of gloom or pallor:
  There was bold Kentucky's grit,
And the old Virginian valor,
  And the daring Yankee wit.

There were blue eyes from turfy Shannon,
  There were black orbs from palmy Niger, —
But there alongside the cannon,
  Each man fought like a tiger!

A little, once, it looked ill,
  Our consort began to burn;
They quenched the flames with a will,
But our men were falling still,
  And still the fleet was astern.

Right abreast of the Fort
  In an awful shroud they lay,
  Broadsides thundering away,
And lightning from every port —
  Scene of glory and dread!
A storm-cloud all aglow
  With flashes of fiery red;
The thunder raging below,
  And the forest of flags o'erhead!

So grand the hurly and roar,
  So fiercely their broadsides blazed,
The regiments fighting ashore
  Forgot to fire as they gazed.

There, to silence the Foe,
  Moving grimly and slow,
They loomed in that deadly wreath,
  Where the darkest batteries frowned, —

Death in the air all round,
And the black torpedoes beneath!

And now, as we looked ahead,
　　All for'ard, the long white deck
Was growing a strange dull red;
　　But soon, as once and agen
Fore and aft we sped,
　　(The firing to guide or check,)
You could hardly choose but tread
　　On the ghastly human wreck
(Dreadful gobbet and shred
　　　That a minute ago were men!)

Red, from main-mast to bitts!
　　Red, on bulwark and wale!
Red, by combing and hatch!
　　Red, o'er netting and rail!
And ever, with steady con,
　　The ship forged slowly by;
And ever the crew fought on,
　　And their cheers rang loud and high.

Grand was the sight to see
　　　How by their guns they stood,
Right in front of our dead
　　Fighting square abreast —
　　Each brawny arm and chest
All spotted with black and red, —
　　　Chrism of fire and blood!

Worth our watch, dull and sterile,
　　Worth all the weary time;
Worth the woe and the peril,
　　To stand in that strait sublime!

Fear?　A forgotten form!
　　Death?　A dream of the eyes!

We were atoms in God's great storm
    That roared through the angry skies.

One only doubt was ours,
    One only dread we knew:
Could the day that dawned so well
    Go down for the Darker Powers?
    Would the fleet get through?
And ever the shot and shell
Came with the howl of hell,
The splinter-clouds rose and fell,
    And the long line of corpses grew:
    Would the fleet win through?

They are men that never will fail,
    (How aforetime they've fought!)
But Murder may yet prevail, —
      They may sink as Craven sank.
    Therewith one hard fierce thought,
    Burning on heart and lip,
    Ran like fire through the ship:
      Fight her, to the last plank!

A dimmer Renown might strike
    If Death lay square alongside;
But the Old Flag has no like,
    She must fight, whatever betide:
When the War is a tale of old,
And this day's story is told,
    They shall hear how the Hartford died!

But as we ranged ahead,
    And the leading ships worked in,
    Losing their hope to win,
The enemy turned and fled:
And one seeks a shallow reach,
    And another, winged in her flight,

Our mate, brave Jouett, brings in ;
　And one, all torn in the fight,
Runs for a wreck on the beach,
　Where her flames soon fire the night.

And the Ram, — when well up the Bay,
　And we looked that our stems should meet,
(He had us fair for a prey,)
Shifting his helm midway,
　Sheered off, and ran for the fleet;
There, without skulking or sham,
　He fought them, gun for gun,
And ever he sought to ram,
　But could finish never a one.

From the first of the iron shower
　Till we sent our parting shell,
'T was just one savage hour
　Of the roar and the rage of hell.
With the lessening smoke and thunder,
　Our glasses around we aim, —
What is that burning yonder ?
　Our Philippi — aground and in flame !

Below, 't was still all a-roar,
As the ships went by the shore,
　But the fire of the Fort had slacked,
(So fierce their volleys had been) ;
And now, with a mighty din,
The whole fleet came grandly in,
　Though sorely battered and wracked.

So, up the Bay we ran,
　The Flag to port and ahead,
And a pitying rain began
　To wash the lips of our dead.
16

A league from the Fort we lay,
  And deemed that the end must lag;
When lo! looking down the Bay,
  There flaunted the Rebel Rag:
The Ram is again under way,
  And heading dead for the Flag!

Steering up with the stream,
  Boldly his course he lay,
Though the fleet all answered his fire,
And, as he still drew nigher,
  Ever on bow and beam
    Our Monitors pounded away, —
    How the Chickasaw hammered away!

Quickly breasting the wave,
  Eager the prize to win,
First of us all the brave
  Monongahela went in,
Under full head of steam;
Twice she struck him abeam,
Till her stem was a sorry work;
  (She might have run on a crag!)
The Lackawana hit fair;
He flung her aside like cork, —
  And still he held for the Flag.

High in the mizzen-shroud,
  (Lest the smoke his sight o'erwhelm,)
Our Admiral's voice rang loud:
  "Hard-a-starboard your helm!
Starboard! and run him down!"
  Starboad it was; and so,
Like a black squall's lifting frown,
Our mighty bow bore down
  On the iron beak of the Foe.

We stood on the deck together,
   Men that had looked on death
In battle and stormy weather;
   Yet a little we held our breath,
   When, with the hush of death,
The great ships drew together.

Our Captain strode to the bow,
   Drayton, courtly and wise,
   Kindly cynic, and wise,
(You hardly had known him now, —
   The flame of fight in his eyes!)
His brave heart eager to feel
How the oak would tell on the steel!

   But, as the space grew short,
     A little he seemed to shun us;
Out peered a form grim and lanky,
   And a voice yelled: "Hard-a-port!
Hard-a-port! — here's the damned Yankee
     Coming right down on us!"

He sheered, but the ships ran foul;
With a gnarring shudder and growl,
   He gave us a deadly gun;
But, as he passed in his pride,
(Rasping right alongside!)
   The Old Flag, in thunder-tones,
Poured in her port broadside,
Rattling his iron hide,
   And cracking his timber bones!

Just then, at speed on the Foe,
   With her bow all weathered and brown,
   The great Lackawana came down
Full tilt for another blow:
We were forging ahead,
   She reversed; but, for all our pains,

Rammed the old Hartford instead,
  Just for'ard the mizzen-chains!

Ah! how the masts did buckle and bend,
  And the stout hull ring and reel,
As she took us right on end!
  (Vain were engine and wheel, —
  She was under full steam), —
With the roar of a thunder-stroke
Her two thousand tons of oak
  Brought up on us, right abeam!

A wreck, as it looked, we lay;
(Rib and plankshear gave way
  To the stroke of that giant wedge!)
Here, after all, we go;
The old ship is gone! — ah, no,
  But cut to the water's edge.

Never mind then; at him again!
  His flurry now can't last long;
He 'll never again see land;
Try that on *him*, Marchand!
  On him again, brave Strong!

Heading square at the hulk,
  Full on his beam we bore;
But the spine of the huge Sea-Hog
Lay on the tide like a log, —
  He vomited flame no more.

By this, he had found it hot:
  Half the fleet, in an angry ring,
  Closed round the hideous thing,
Hammering with solid shot,
And bearing down, bow on bow —
  He has but a minute to choose;

Life or renown? — which now
   Will the Rebel Admiral lose?

Cruel, haughty, and cold,
He ever was strong and bold, —
   Shall he shrink from a wooden stem?
He will think of that brave band
He sank in the Cumberland:
   Ay, he will sink like them.

Nothing left but to fight
Boldly his last sea-fight!
   Can he strike? By Heaven, 't is true!
   Down comes the traitor Blue,
And up goes the captive White!

Up went the White! Ah, then,
The hurrahs that, once and agen,
Rang from three thousand men,
   All flushed and savage with fight!
Our dead lay cold and stark,
But our dying, down in the dark,
   Answered as best they might, —
Lifting their poor lost arms,
   And cheering for God and Right!

Ended the mighty noise,
   Thunder of forts and ships,
     Down we went to the hold!
Oh, our dear dying boys!
   How we pressed their poor brave lips,
     (Ah, so pallid and cold!)
And held their hands to the last
     (Those that had hands to hold).

Still thee, O woman heart!
   (So strong an hour ago), —

If the idle tears must start,
　'T is not in vain they flow.

They died, our children dear,
　On the drear berth-deck they died ;
Do not think of them here, —
Even now their footsteps near
The immortal, tender sphere, —
(Land of love and cheer !
　Home of the Crucified !)

And the glorious deed survives.
　Our threescore, quiet and cold,
Lie thus, for a myriad lives
　And treasure-millions untold, —
(Labor of poor men's lives,
Hunger of weans and wives,
　Such is war-wasted gold.)

Our ship and her fame to-day
　Shall float on the storied Stream,
When mast and shroud have crumbled away,
　And her long white deck is a dream.

One daring leap in the dark,
　Three mortal hours, at the most, —
And hell lies stiff and stark
　On a hundred leagues of coast.

For the mighty Gulf is ours, —
　The bay is lost and won,
　　An Empire is lost and won !
Land, if thou yet hast. flowers,
Twine them in one more wreath
　Of tenderest white and red,
(Twin buds of glory and death !)
　For the brows of our brave dead, —
　　For thy Navy's noblest Son.

Joy, O Land, for thy sons,
   Victors by flood and field!
The traitor walls and guns
   Have nothing left but to yield —
(Even now they surrender!)

And the ships shall sail once more,
   And the cloud of war sweep on
To break on the cruel shore, —
   But Craven is gone, —
   He and his hundred are gone.

The flags flutter up and down,
   At sunrise and twilight dim,
The cannons menace and frown, —
   But never again for him, —
   Him and the hundred.

The Dalgrens are dumb,
   Dumb are the mortars;
Never more shall the drum
   Beat to colors and quarters:
   The great guns are silent.

O brave heart and loyal!
   Let all your colors dip;
   Mourn him, proud Ship!
From main-deck to royal.
   God rest our Captain, —
   Rest our lost hundred.

Droop, flag and pennant!
   What is your pride for?
   Heaven, that he died for,
Rest our Lieutenant, —
   Rest our brave threescore.

O Mother Land! this weary life
　　We led, we lead, is 'long of thee;
Thine the strong agony of strife,
　　And thine the lonely sea.

Thine the long decks all slaughter-sprent,
　　The weary rows of cots that lie
With wrecks of strong men, marred and rent,
　　'Neath Pensacola's sky.

And thine the iron caves and dens
　　Wherein the flame our war-fleet drives;
The fiery vaults, whose breath is men's
　　Most dear and precious lives.

Ah, ever, when with storm sublime
　　Dread Nature clears our murky air,
Thus in the crash of falling crime
　　Some lesser guilt must share.

Full red the furnace fires must glow
　　That melt the ore of mortal kind:
The Mills of God are grinding slow,
　　But ah, how close they grind!

To-day the Dahlgren and the drum
　　Are dread Apostles of His Name;
His Kingdom here can only come
　　By chrism of blood and flame.

Be strong: already slants the gold
　　Athwart these wild and stormy skies;
From out this blackened waste, behold,
　　What happy homes shall rise!

But see thou well no traitor gloze,
　　No striking hands with Death and Shame,

Betray the sacred blood that flows
　So freely for thy name.

And never fear a victor foe, —
　Thy children's hearts are strong and high;
Nor mourn too fondly, — well they know
　On deck or field to die.

Nor shalt thou want one willing breath,
　Though, ever smiling round the brave,
The blue sea bear us on to death,
　The green were one wide grave.

U. S. Flag Ship Hartford,
　Mobile Bay, August, 1864.

Harpers' Magazine.

THE CHICAGO SURRENDER.*

BY BAYARD TAYLOR.

WHAT! hoist the white flag when our triumph is nigh?
What! crouch before Treason? make Freedom a lie?
What! spike all our guns when the foe is at bay,
And the rags of his black banner dropping away?
Tear down the strong name that our nation has won,
And strike her brave bird from his home in the sun?

* The Democratic Party Convention for the nomination of a candidate to oppose President Lincoln, of which Mr. August Belmont was temporary chairman, and Mr. Horatio Seymour permanent chairman, and which resolved, among other things, that "four years of failure to restore the Union by the experiment of war," and "public liberty and private right alike stricken down," "demand that immediate efforts be made for a cessation of hostilities;" — also that "the sympathy of the Democratic party is heartily and earnestly extended to the soldiers of our army," was held on the 20th of August, 1864.

He 's a coward who shrinks from the lift of the sword;
He 's a traitor who mocks at the sacrifice poured;
Nameless and homeless the doom that should blast
The knave who stands idly till peril is past;
But he who submits when the thunders have burst
And victory dawns, is of cowards the worst!

Is the old spirit dead?   Are we broken and weak,
That cravens so shamelessly lift the white cheek
To court the swift insult, nor blush at the blow,
The tools of the treason and friends of the foe?
See! Anarchy smiles at the Peace which they ask,
And the eyes of Disunion flash out through the mask!

Give thanks, ye brave boys, who by vale and by crag
Bear onward, unfaltering, our noble old flag, —
Strong arms of the Union, heroes living and dead,
For the blood of your valor is uselessly shed!
No soldier's green laurel is promised you here,
But the white rag of "*sympathy*" softly shall cheer!

And you, ye war-martyrs, who preach from your graves
How captives are nursed by the masters of slaves,
Or, living, still linger in shadows of Death, —
Puff out the starved muscle, recall the faint breath,
And shout, till those cowards rejoice at the cry,
" By the hands of the Union we fought for we die!"

By the God of our fathers! this shame we must share;
But it grows too debasing for freemen to bear;
And Washington, Jackson, will turn in their graves,
When the Union shall rest on two races of slaves;
Or, spurning the spirit which bound it of yore,
And sundered, exist as a nation no more!

New York Tribune.

SHERIDAN'S RIDE.

BY T. BUCHANAN READ.

Up from the South at break of day,
Bringing to Winchester fresh dismay,
The affrighted air with a shudder bore,
Like a herald in haste to the chieftain's door,
The terrible grumble and rumble and roar,
Telling the battle was on once more,
And Sheridan was twenty miles away.

And wider still those billows of war
Thundered along the horizon's bar,
And louder yet into Winchester rolled
The war of that red sea uncontrolled,
Making the blood of the listener cold,
As he thought of the stake in that fiery fray,
And Sheridan twenty miles away.

But there 's a road from Winchester town,
A good, broad highway leading down, —
And there, through the flush of the morning light,
A steed, as black as the steeds of night,
Was seen to pass as with eagle flight;
As if he knew the terrible need,
He stretched away with his utmost speed;
Hills rose and fell, but his heart was gay,
With Sheridan fifteen miles away.

Still sprung from those swift hoofs thundering South
The dust, like the smoke from the cannon's mouth,
Or the trail of a comet sweeping faster and faster,
Foreboding to traitors the doom of disaster;
The heart of the steed and the heart of the master
Were beating like prisoners assaulting their walls,
Impatient to be where the battle-field calls;

Every nerve of the charger was strained to full play,
With Sheridan only ten miles away.

Under his spurning feet, the road
Like an arrowy Alpine river flowed ;
And the landscape sped away behind,
Like an ocean flying before the wind ;
And the steed, like a bark fed with furnace ire,
Swept on, with his wild eyes full of fire.
But lo ! he is nearing his heart's desire ;
He is snuffing the smoke of the roaring fray,
With Sheridan only five miles away.   ·

The first that the General saw were the groups
Of stragglers, and then the retreating troops :
What was done — what to do — a glance told him both ;
Then striking his spurs, with a terrrible oath,
He dashed down the line mid a storm of huzzas,
And the wave of retreat checked its course there, because
The sight of the master compelled it to pause.
With foam and with dust the black charger was gray ;
By the flash of his eye, and his red nostrils' play,
He seemed to the whole great army to say :
" I have brought you Sheridan all the way
From Winchester down to save the day ! "

Hurrah, hurrah for Sheridan !
Hurrah, hurrah for horse and man !
And when their statues are placed on high
Under the dome of the Union sky,
The American Soldier's Temple of Fame,
There, with the glorious General's name,
Be it said in letters both bold and bright :
" Here is the steed that saved the day
By carrying Sheridan into the fight,
From Winchester — twenty miles away ! "

AFTER ALL.

BY WILLIAM WINTER.

THE apples are ripe in the orchard,
　The work of the reaper is done,
And the golden woodlands redden
　In the blood of the dying sun.

At the cottage-door the grandsire
　Sits pale in his easy-chair,
While the gentle wind of twilight
　Plays with his silver hair.

A woman is kneeling beside him;
　A fair young head is pressed,
In the first wild passion of sorrow,
　Against his aged breast.

And far from over the distance
　The faltering echoes come
Of the flying blast of trumpet,
　And the rattling roll of drum.

And the grandsire speaks in a whisper .
　" The end no man can see;
But we gave him to his country,
　And we give our prayers to Thee."

The violets star the meadows,
　The rose-buds fringe the door,
And over the grassy orchard
　The pink-white blossoms pour.

But the grandsire's chair is empty,
　The cottage is dark and still;
There 's a nameless grave in the battle-field,
　And a new one under the hill.

And a pallid, tearless woman
  By the cold hearth sits alone,
And the old clock in the corner
  Ticks on with a steady drone.

———◆———

THE YEAR OF JUBILEE.*

SAY, darkies, hab you seen de massa,
  Wid de muffstash on he face,
Go 'long de road some time dis mornin',
  Like he gwine to leabe de place?
He see de smoke way up de ribber
  Whar de Lincum gun-boats lay;
He took he hat and leff berry sudden,
  And I 'spose he 's runned away.
     De massa run, ha! ha!
      De darky stay, ho! ho!
      It mus' be now de kingdum comin',
      An' de yar ob Jubilo.

He six foot one way and two foot todder,
  An' he weigh six hundred poun';
His coat so big he could n't pay de tailor,
  An' it won't reach half way roun';
He drill so much dey calls him cap'n,
  An' he git so mighty tan'd,
I spec he 'll try to fool dem Yankees
  For to tink he contraband.
     De massa run, ha! ha!
      De darkey stay, ho! ho!
      It mus' be now de kingdum comin',
      An' de yar ob Jubilo.

---

* In 1864 the negro slaves began to see that the year of jubilee
was certainly coming, and this song, expressive of their views upon
the subject, appeared. In April, 1865, a detachment of negro troops
sang it as they marched into Richmond.

De darkies got so lonesome libb'n
    In de log hut on de lawn,
Dey move dere tings into massa's parlor
    For to keep it while he gone.
Dar's wine and cider in de kichin,
    And de darkies dey hab some,
I spec it will all be 'fiscated,
      When de Lincum sojers come.
        De massa run, ha! ha!
          De darkey stay, ho! ho!
        It mus' be now de kingdum comin',
          An' de yar ob Jubilo.

De oberseer, he makes us trubble,
    An' he dribe us roun' a spell,
We lock him up in de smoke-house cellar,
    Wid de key flung in de well.
De whip am lost, de han'-cuff broke,
    But de massa hab his pay;
He big an' ole enough for to know better
    Dan to went an' run away.
        De massa run, ha! ha!
          De darkey stay, ho! ho!
        It mus' be now de kingdum comin',
          An' de yar ob Jubilo.

ABOLITION OF SLAVERY BY CONSTITU-TIONAL AMENDMENT.*

Not unto us who did but seek,
The word that burned within to speak;
Not unto us this day belong
The triumph and exulting song.

* Passed the House of Representatives, January 31st, 1865, by a vote of 119 to 56.

Upon us fell in early youth
The burden of unwelcome truth,
And left us, weak and frail, and few,
The censor's painful work to do.

Thenceforth our life a fight became;
The air we breathed was hot with blame;
For not with gauged and softened tone
We made the bondman's cause our own.

We bore, as Freedom's hope forlorn,
The private hate, the public scorn;
Yet held through all the paths we trod
Our faith in man and trust in God.

We prayed and hoped; but still with awe
The coming of the sword we saw;
We heard the nearing steps of doom,
And saw the shade of things to come.

We hoped for peace: our eyes survey
The blood-red dawn of Freedom's day;
We prayed for love to loose the chain;
'T was shorn by battle-axe in twain.

Nor skill nor strength nor zeal of ours
Has mined and heaved the hostile towers;
Not by our hands is turned the key
That sets the sighing captive free.

A redder sea than Egypt's wave
Is piled and parted for the slave;
A darker cloud moves on in light;
A fiercer fire is guide by night!

The praise, O Lord! be Thine alone;
In Thy own way Thy work be done!
Our poor gifts at Thy feet we cast,
To whom be glory, first and last.

BROTHER JONATHAN AND TAXES.

I GUESS I mean to tax myself,
  In every jot and tittle,
Of all I eat and drink and wear,
  And all I chew and whittle ;
In flour and sperrits, ale and wine,
  In oils and in tobackers ;
In papers, gas, salt, soap, and skins,
  And meal and malt and crackers.
        Yankee Doodle, etc.

The leather that we walk upon, —
  The upper and the under, —
The electric fluid in the wires,
  (Guess I can't catch the thunder ;)
Each passenger that takes the cars,
  Each 'bus that runs on tramrods,
Advertisements and steamboats too,
  And guns, locks, stocks, and ramrods.
        Yankee Doodle, etc.

There 's not a billiard-ball shall spin,
  But into Guv'ment's pockets ;
No draughts or pill cure human ill,
  Without the Guv'ment dockets ;
All carriages taxed carts shall be ;
  Watches go tick for taxes ;
And messages shall pay, — both eends, —
  Who answers and who axes.
        Yankee Doodle, etc.

No banker shall shinplasters make,
  No pedler cheat the farmers,
No liquor-store shall sell its drams,
  No theatres its dramers ;
17

No rider spring round the circus-ring,
  No bowling-alley roll up,
But shall to Guv'ment needs help bring
  The totle of the whole up.
      Yankee Doodle, etc.

London Punch.

A LITTLE JEU D'ESPRIT:

SHOWING HOW AUGUST BECAME JULY AND MARCH, AND A LITTLE MAN GREW TO A GREAT HEIGHT.

THE august name Auguste,
  (From the Emperor Augustus,)
With its late associations
  Doth mightily disgust us, —
    Doth mightily disgust us.

For the snobbish individual,
  To whom it *don't* apply,
Since the falsehoods of Chicago
  Should be surely named July, —
    Should be surely named July.

The elections of November
  Will take out all his starch;
Then all our friends, and he himself,
  Will wish to make him March, —
    Will wish to make him March.

For his vile and nasty politics,
  Let him take his carcass hence;
He is, indeed, a little man,
  Yet the height of Impudence, —
    Yet the height of Impudence.

Evening Post.

A HAIR-DRESSER'S STORY.

The story runs, that to a certain town
   Of much renown
For teas æsthetic, and for streets that wind,
With his fair wife, a whilom General came,
   Well known to fame,
Whose tactics were of the defensive sort,
Whose masterly retreats and memory short
Had proved him fitted for a sphere confined.

At least the people thought him not designed,
   In spite of his refined
And gentlemanly manners, for the place
Of President. They voted that too large
   For little George :
Thus snubbed, disgusted he has left his home
To join his sympathizing friends at Rome,
In papal patriarchism finding his solace.

Nor shall we care again to see his face
   Who in disgrace-
ful forced inaction kept an army tried,
And trained to war. Whose mole-like strategy
   And sullen vanity,
Whose organizing skill and nice precision,
Whose imperturbable, slow indecision,
Deceived the trust that in him most relied.

But to my story. In this city, where
   The very air
Dampens your soul with intellectual dew,
The General's friends, with just appreciation,
   Did an " ovation "
Of costly banquet and " reception " offer,
For his delight ; and frowned down any scoffer
Who thought at his campaigns to glance askew.

For this *reunion*, — where professors drew
       Out ladies blue, —
A hair-dresser was sent for, to arrange
The lady's tresses in the newest fashion,
       (Braids *à discrétion*)
Regardless of expense, that should amaze
The souls of all men privileged to gaze
Upon that head of complications strange.

And while his well-trained fingers swiftly range
       And deftly change
From rats to mice, from curl to smoothest roll, —
Before a glass that in a corner stood,
       In thoughtful mood,
The General his razor did prepare,
And with a cautious, meditative care
His coat and waistcoat from his trunk unfold.

And then the lady, thoughtful of her spouse,
       Did him arouse
In gentle accents: " General, are you ready? "
(She had her back turned to him that the light
       Might fall aright.)
The General, waking from a reverie,
(In Spain he often won a victory,)
Answered her, " No," in tone composed and steady.

But soon again: " Now, General are you ready? "
       Said his good lady,
With slight impatience. " It is nearly time
That we were off. You know of all the guests
       We should be first;
And I am much afraid you will be late."
He plainly saw that she would be irate,
Yet answered " No," with constancy sublime.

This answer did not with her humor chime:
       The clock struck nine.

She scarcely her impatience could control.
At last, her head completed, round she turned,
  With eyes that burned,
Upon her lord: " Why, are you not yet ready ?
Oh, dear! You know, George, you are *never* ready ! "
Broke in sad truth from that long wearied soul.

        A. M. W.

SHERMAN'S MARCH.

BY A SOLDIER.

THEIR lips are still as the lips of the dead,
The gaze of their eyes is straight ahead ;
The tramp, tramp, tramp of ten thousand feet
Keep time to that muffled, monotonous beat, —
   Rub-a-dub-dub! rub-a-dub-dub!

Ten thousand more ! and still they come
To fight a battle for Christendom !
With cannon and caissons, and flags unfurled,
The foremost men in all the world !
   Rub-a-dub-dub! rub-a-dub-dub!

The foe is intrenched on the frowning hill, —
A natural fortress, strengthened by skill ;
But vain are the walls to those who face
The champions of the human race !
   Rub-a-dub-dub! rub-a-dub-dub!

" By regiment! Forward into line ! "
Then sabres and guns and bayonets shine.
Oh ye who feel your fate at last
Repeat the old prayer as your hearts beat fast
   Rub-a-dub-dub! rub-a-dub-dub!

Oh ye who 've waited and prayed so long
That Right might have a fair fight with Wrong,
No more in fruitless marches shall plod,
But smite the foe with the wrath of God!
      Rub-a-dub-dub! rub-a-dub-dub!

O Death! what a charge that carried the hill!
That carried, and kept, and holds it still!
The foe is broken and flying with fear,
While far on their route our drummers I hear,—
      Rub-a-dub-dub! rub-a-dub-dub!

Harper's Weekly.

THE CRAVEN.

FROM AN UNPUBLISHED POEM BY ALFRED ANDHISON.

ON that mighty day of battle, 'mid the booming and the
    rattle,
Shouts of victory and of anguish, wherewith Malvern's
    hill did roar,
Did a General now quite fameless, who in these lines
    shall be nameless,
Show himself as rather gameless,— gameless on the James's
    shore,—
Safely smoking on a gunboat, while the tempest raged on
    shore,
      Only this, and nothing more.

The Congressional Committee sat within the nation's city,
And each Congressman so witty did the General implore:
" Tell us if thou at that battle, 'mid the booming and the
    rattle,
Wert on a gunboat or in saddle, while the tempest raged
    ashore ? "

Answered he : " I don't remember, — might have been."
    What more ?
        Only this, and nothing more.

" By the truth which is eternal, by the lies that are
    diurnal,
By our Abraham paternal, General, we thee implore,
Tell the truth and shame the devil, — parent of old Jeff.
    and evil ;
Give us no more of such drivel.   Tell us, wert thou on
    the shore."
" Don't remember, — might have been ; " thus spoke ho
    o'er and o'er, —
        Only this, and nothing more.

" On that day, sir, had you seen a gunboat of the name
    Galena,
In an anchorage, to screen a man from danger on the
    shore ?
Was a man about your inches, smoking with those three
    French Princes,
With a caution which evinces care for such a *garde de-*
    corps ?
Were you that man on the gunboat ? " " Don't remem-
    ber, — might have been.   The bore."
        Only this, and nothing more.
                Evening Post.

THE HOUR OF NORTHERN VICTORY.

BY FANNY KEMBLE.

ROLL not a drum, sound not a clarion note
    Of haughty triumph to the silent sky ;
Hush'd be the shout of joy in ev'ry throat,
    And veil'd the flash of pride in ev'ry eye.

Not with *Te Deums* loud and high Hosannas
  Greet we the awful victory we have won ;
But with our arms revers'd and lower'd banners
  We stand, — our work is done!

Thy work is done, God, terrible and just,
  Who laidst upon our hearts and hands this task ;
And kneeling, with our foreheads in the dust,
  We venture Peace to ask.

Bleeding and writhing underneath our sword,
  Prostrate our brethren lie, Thy fallen foe,
Struck down by Thee through us, avenging Lord, —
  By Thy dread hand laid low.

For our own guilt have we been doomed to smite
  These our kindred, Thy great laws defying, —
These, our own flesh and blood, who now unite
  In one thing only with us, — bravely dying.

Dying how bravely, yet how bitterly!
  Not for the better side, but for the worse, —
Blindly and madly striving against Thee,
  For the bad cause where Thou hast set Thy curse.

At whose defeat we may not raise our voice,
  Save in the deep thanksgiving of our prayers :
" Lord! we have fought the fight!" But to rejoice
  Is ours no more than theirs.

Call back thy dreadful ministers of wrath
  Who have led on our hosts to this great day ;
Let our feet halt now in the avenger's path,
  And bid our weapons stay.

Upon our land, Freedom's inheritance,
  Turn Thou once more the splendor of Thy face,

Where nations serving Thee to light advance,
 Give us again our place.

Not our bewildering past prosperity,
 Not all thy former ill-requited grace,
But this one boon, — Oh! grant us still to be
 The home of Hope to the whole human race.
 April 25th, 1865.   *London Spectator.*

———◆———

COTTON AND CORN.

Cotton and Corn were mighty kings,*
Who differed at times on certain things,
 To the country's dire confusion :
Corn was peaceable, mild, and just,
But Cotton was fond of saying " you must " ;
So, after he 'd boasted, bullied, and cussed,
 He got up a revolution.
But in the course of time the bubble is bursted,
And Corn is the King, and Cotton is worsted.

———◆———

THE FREEDMAN'S SONG.

De Lord, He make us free indeed
 In His own time an' way ;

* The phrase " King Cotton " was brought into use by the fol-
lowing passage in a speech Senator Hammond, of South Carolina,
made in the Senate, March 4th, 1858 : — " No, you dare not make
war upon cotton; no power upon earth dares to make war upon
it. *Cotton is king :* until lately the Bank of England was king;
but she tried to put her screws, as usual, the fall before last, on the
cotton crop, and was utterly vanquished. The last power has been
conquered : who can doubt, that has looked at recent events, that
cotton is supreme! "

We plant de rice an' cotton seed,
    An' see de sprout some day;
We know it come, but not de why, —
    De Lord know more dan we;
We 'spected freedom by-an'-by,
    An' now we all are free.
        Praise de Lord! Praise de Lord!
          For now we all are free.

De Norf is on de side of right,
    An' full of men, dey say;
An' dere, when poor man work, at night
    He sure to get his pay;
De Lord, He glad dey are so good,
    An' make dem bery strong;
An' when dey called to give deir blood
    Dey all come right along.
        Praise de Lord! Praise de Lord!
          Dey all come right along.

Deir blue coats cover all de groun',
    An' make it like de sky;
An' ebery grayback loafing roun'
    He tink it time to fly:
We not afraid; we bring de child
    An' stan' beside de door,
An' oh! we hug it bery wild,
    An' keep it ebermore.
        Praise de Lord! Praise de Lord!
          We keep it ebermore.

De mas'er 's come back from his tramp,
    'Pears he is broken quite;
He takes de basket to de camp
    For rations ebery night;
Dey fought him when he loud and strong,
    Dey feed him when he low,

Dey say dey will forgive de wrong
　And bid him 'pent and go.
　　Praise de Lord! Praise de Lord!
　　Dey bid him 'pent and go.

De rice is higher far dis year,
　De cotton taller grow;
De lowest corn-silk on de ear
　Is higher dan de hoe;
De Lord He lift up ebery ting
　'Cept rebel in his grave;
De negro bress de Lord, an' sing
　He is no longer slave.
　　Praise de Lord! Praise de Lord!
　　De negro no more slave.

Harpers' Weekly.

ABRAHAM LINCOLN.

ASSASSINATED GOOD FRIDAY, 1865.

BY EDMUND C. STEDMAN.

" Forgive them, for they know not what they do!"
　He said, and so went shriven to his fate, —
Unknowing went, that generous heart and true.
　Even while he spoke the slayer lay in wait;
　And when the morning opened Heaven's gate
There passed the whitest soul a nation knew.
　Henceforth all thoughts of pardon are too late;
They, in whose cause that arm its weapon drew,
　Have murdered Mercy. Now alone shall stand
Blind Justice, with the sword unsheathed she wore.
　Hark! from the eastern to the western strand,
The swelling thunder of the people's roar, —
　What words they murmur: Fetter not her hand!
So let it smite: such deeds shall be no more!

　April 15, 1865.　　　　　*New York Tribune.*

ABRAHAM LINCOLN.

BY WILLIAM CULLEN BRYANT.

O, SLOW to smite and swift to spare,
   Gentle and merciful and just!
Who, in the fear of God, didst bear
   The sword of power — a nation's trust.

In sorrow by thy bier we stand,
   Amid the awe that hushes all,
And speak the anguish of a land
   That shook with horror at thy fall.

Thy task is done — the bond are free;
   We bear thee to an honored grave,
Whose noblest monument shall be
   The broken fetters of the slave.

Pure was thy life; its bloody close
   Hath placed thee with the sons of light,
Among the noble host of those
   Who perished in the cause of right.

              Evening Post.

REUNION.

BY JOHN NICHOL.

AN end at last! The echoes of the war —
   The weary war beyond the western waves —
Die in the distance. Freedom's rising star
   Beacons above a hundred thousand graves:

The graves of heroes who have won the fight,
   Who in the storming of the stubborn town

Have rung the marriage-peal of might and right,
    And scaled the cliffs and cast the dragon down.

Pæans of armies thrill across the sea,
    Till Europe answers: " Let the struggle cease, —
The bloody page is turned; the next may be
    For ways of pleasantness and paths of peace ! "

A golden morn — a dawn of better things —
    The olive-branch — clasping of hands again —
A noble lesson read to conquering kings —
    A sky that tempests had not scoured in vain.

This from America we hoped, and him
    Who ruled her " in the spirit of his creed."
Does the hope last when all our eyes are dim,
    As history records her darkest deed ?

The pilot of his people through the strife,
    With his strong purpose turning scorn to praise,
E'en at the close of battle reft of life,
    And fair inheritance of quiet days.

Defeat and triumph found him calm and just;
    He showed how clemency should temper power;
And, dying, left to future times in trust
    The memory of his brief victorious hour.

O'ermastered by the irony of fate,
    The last and greatest martyr of his cause;
Slain like Achilles at the Scæan gate,
    He saw the end, and fixed " the purer laws."

May these endure, and, as his work, attest
    The glory of his honest heart and hand:
The simplest, and the bravest, and the best, —
    The Moses and the Cromwell of his land.

Too late the pioneers of modern spite,
  Awe-stricken by the universal gloom,
See his name lustrous in Death's sable night,
  And offer tardy tribute at his tomb.

But we who have been with him all the while,
  Who knew his worth, and loved him long ago,
Rejoice that in the circuit of our isle
  There is no room at last for Lincoln's foe.

London Spectator.

ABRAHAM LINCOLN.

FOULLY ASSASSINATED, APRIL 14, 1865.

You lay a wreath on murdered LINCOLN's bier, —
  You, who with mocking pencil wont to trace,
Broad for the self-complacent British sneer,
  His length of shambling limb, his furrowed face,

His gaunt, gnarled hands, his unkempt, bristling hair,
  His garb uncouth, his bearing ill at ease,
His lack of all we prize as debonair,
  Of power or will to shine, of art to please:

You, whose smart pen backed up the pencil's laugh,
  Judging each step, as though the way were plain;
Reckless, so it could point its paragraph,
  Of chief's perplexity, or people's pain.

Beside this corpse, that bears for winding-sheet
  The Stars and Stripes he lived to rear anew,
Between the mourners at his head and feet, —
  Say, scurrile-jester, is there room for *you*?

Yes, he had lived to shame me from my sneer,
  To lame my pencil and confute my pen;
To make me own this hind of princes peer, —
  This rail-splitter, a true-born king of men.

My shallow judgment I had learnt to rue,
  Noting how to occasion's height he rose;
How his quaint wit made home-truth seem more true, —
  How, iron-like, his temper grew by blows.

How humble, yet how hopeful, he could be, —
  How in good fortune and in ill the same:
Nor bitter in success, nor boastful he,
  Thirsty for gold, nor feverish for fame.

He went about his work — such work as few
  Ever had laid on head and heart and hand —
As one who knows, where there's a task to do,
  Man's honest will must Heaven's good grace command;

Who trusts the strength will with the burden grow,
  That God makes instruments to work His will,
If but that will we can arrive to know,
  Nor tamper with the weights of good and ill.

So he went forth to battle on the side
  That he felt clear was Liberty's and Right's,
As in his peasant boyhood he had plied
  His warfare with rude Nature's thwarting mights, —

The uncleared forest, the unbroken soil;
  The iron-bark, that turns the lumberer's axe;
The rapid, that o'erbears the boatman's toil;
  The prairie, hiding the mazed wanderer's tracks;

The ambushed Indian, and the prowling bear, —
  Such were the needs that helped his youth to train:

Rough culture, but such trees large fruit may bear,
  If but their stocks be of right girth and grain.

So he grew up, a destined work to do,
  And lived to do it : four long suffering years'
Ill-fate, ill-feeling, ill-report, lived through,
  And then he heard the hisses change to cheers,

The taunts to tribute, the abuse to praise,
  And took both with the same unwavering mood ;
Till, as he came on light from darkling days,
  And seemed to touch the goal from where he stood,

A felon hand, between the goal and him,
  Reached from behind his back, a trigger prest, —
And those perplexed and patient eyes were dim,
  Those gaunt, long-laboring limbs were laid to rest !

The words of mercy were upon his lips,
  Forgiveness in his heart and on his pen,
When this vile murderer brought swift eclipse
  To thoughts of peace on earth, good-will to men.

The Old World and the New, from sea to sea,
  Utter one voice of sympathy and shame !
Sore heart, so stopped when it at last beat high :
  Sad life, cut short just as its triumph came.

A deed accurst ! Strokes have been struck before
  By the assassin's hand, whereof men doubt
If more of horror or disgrace they bore ;
  But thy foul crime, like CAIN'S, stands darkly out.

Vile hand, that brandest murder on a strife,
  Whate'er its grounds, stoutly and nobly striven ;
And with the martyr's crown crownest a life
  With much to praise, little to be forgiven !

                              London Punch.

ABRAHAM LINCOLN.

INSCRIBED TO THE LONDON PUNCH, BY ALICE CARY.

No glittering chaplet brought from other lands!
   As in his life, this man, in death, is ours;
His own loved prairies o'er his " gaunt gnarled hands "
   Have fitly drawn their sheet of summer flowers!

What need hath he now of a tardy crown,
   His name from mocking jest and sneer to save?
When every ploughman turns his furrow down
   As soft as though it fell upon his grave.

He was a man whose like the world again
   Shall never see, to vex with blame or praise;
The landmarks that attest his bright, brief reign,
   Are battles, not the pomps of gala-days!

The grandest leader of the grandest war
   That ever time in history gave a place, —
What were the tinsel flattery of a star
   To such a breast! or what a ribbon's grace!

'T is to th' man, and th' man's honest worth,
   The nation's loyalty in tears upsprings;
Through him the soil of labor shines henceforth,
   High o'er the silken broideries of kings.

The mechanism of external forms —
   The shifts that courtiers put their bodies through —
Were alien ways to him : his brawny arms
   Had other work than posturing to do!

Born of the people, well he knew to grasp
   The wants and wishes of the weak and small;
Therefore we hold him with no shadowy clasp, —
   Therefore his name is household to us all.

18

Therefore we love him with a love apart
  From any fawning love of pedigree :
His was the royal soul and mind and heart, —
  Not the poor outward shows of royalty.

Forgive us, then, O friends, if we are slow
  To meet your recognition of his worth :
We 're jealous of the very tears that flow
  From eyes that never loved a humble hearth.

———◆———

IN STATE.

BENEATH the vast and vaulted dome
That copes the Capitol, he lies ;
It is a dreary, dreary night :
    The stars in their eternal home
    Seem like the sad ethereal eyes
    Of seraphs, filled with tender light.

The Capitol is wrapt in mist ;
Strangely the shadows come and go :
The dome seems floating into air,
    Upborne by unseen hands, I wist :
    In solemn state he lies below,
    His pure hands folded as in prayer.

He lies in solemn state, alone, —
Alone, with only silence there, —
Alone with lofty lamps that rim
    Almost the very coping-stone ;
    Yet not alone, for all the air
    Is filled with tender thoughts of him.

And all night long the marble floors
Have echoed to the gentle tread

Of blessed and immortal feet;
  And through the open corridors
  The mighty and illustrious dead
  Have thronged all night his face to greet.

And they have bent, full-browed with pain,
And gazed through their celestial tears
Upon the face so dear to them, —
  Upon the man whose heart was fain
  Above all hearts these latter years
  To be like His of Bethlehem.

And so our heads are bowed with grief
Because we loved him, and because
But yesterday this great man stood
  Of many States the perfect chief,
  Dispensing justice and the laws,
  And mindful of the public good.

Alas ! it is a dreary night ;
For he we loved so much now lies
Beneath the vast and vaulted dome ;
  And in his eyes there is no light, —
  No light is in those loving eyes
  Which kindliness had made her home.

Harpers' Weekly.

---◆---

AN HORATIAN ODE.

BY RICHARD HENRY STODDARD.

NOT as when some great captain falls
In battle, where his country calls,
  Beyond the struggling lines
  That push his dread designs

To doom, by some stray ball struck dead :
Or, in the last charge, at the head
    Of his determined men,
    Who must be victors then !

Nor as when sink the civic great,
The safer pillars of the State,
    Whose calm, mature, wise words
    Suppress the need of swords ! —

With no such tears as e'er were shed
Above the noblest of our dead
    Do we to-day deplore
    The man that is no more !

Our sorrow hath a wider scope,
Too strange for fear, too vast for hope, —
    A wonder, blind and dumb,
    That waits — what is to come !

Not more astounded had we been
If madness, that dark night, unseen,
    Had in our chambers crept,
    And murdered while we slept !

We woke to find a mourning earth —
Our Lares shivered on the hearth, —
    The roof-tree fallen, — all
    That could affright, appall !

Such thunderbolts, in other lands,
Have smitten the rod from royal hands,
    But spared, with us, till now,
    Each laurelled Cæsar's brow !

No Cæsar he, whom we lament,
A man without a precedent,

Sent it would seem, to do
His work — and perish too !

Not by the weary cares of state,
The endless tasks, which will not wait,
　　Which, often done in vain,
　　Must yet be done again :

Not in the dark, wild tide of war,
Which rose so high, and rolled so far,
　　Sweeping from sea to sea
　　In awful anarchy ; —

Four fateful years of mortal strife,
Which slowly drained the nation's life,
　　(Yet, for each drop that ran
　　There sprang an armed man !)

Not then ; — but when by measures meet, —
By victory, and by defeat, —
　　By courage, patience, skill,
　　The people's fixed " We will ! "

Had pierced, had crushed rebellion dead, —
Without a hand, without a head : —
　　At last, when all was well,
　　He fell, — O how he fell !

The time, — the place, — the stealing shape, —
The coward shot, — the swift escape, —
　　The wife — the widow's scream, —
　　It is a hideous dream !

A dream ? — what means this pageant, then ?
These multitudes of solemn men,
　　Who speak not when they meet,
　　But throng the silent street ?

The flags half-mast, that late so high
Flaunted at each new victory ?
  (The stars no brightness shed,
  But bloody looks the red !)

The black festoons that stretch for miles,
And turn the streets to funeral aisles ?
  (No house too poor to show
  The nation's badge of woe !)

The cannon's sudden, sullen boom, —
The bells that toll of death and doom, —
  The rolling of the drums, —
  The dreadful car that comes ?

Cursed be the hand that fired the shot !
The frenzied brain that hatched the plot !
  Thy country's father slain
  By thee, thou worse than Cain !

Tyrants have fallen by such as thou,
And good hath followed, — may it now !
  (God lets bad instruments
  Produce the best events.)

But he, the man we mourn to-day,
No tyrant was : so mild a sway
  In one such weight who bore
  Was never known before !

Cool should he be, of balanced powers,
The ruler of a race like ours, —
  Impatient, headstrong, wild, —
  The man to guide the child !

And this he was, who most unfit
(So hard the sense of God to hit !)

Did seem to fill his place.
With such a homely face, —

Such rustic manners, — speech uncouth, —
(That somehow blundered out the truth!)
Untried, untrained to bear
The more than kingly care!

Ay! And his genius put to scorn
The proudest in the purple born,
Whose wisdom never grew
To what, untaught, he knew, —

The people, of whom he was one.
No gentleman like Washington, —
(Whose bones, methinks, make room,
To have him in their tomb!)

A laboring man, with horny hands,
Who swung the axe, who tilled his lands,
Who shrank from nothing new,
But did as poor men do!

One of the people! Born to be
Their curious epitome;
To share, yet rise above
Their shifting hate and love.

Common his mind (it seemed so then),
His thoughts the thoughts of other men:
Plain were his words, and poor, —
But now they will endure!

No hasty fool, of stubborn will,
But prudent, cautious, pliant, still;
Who, since his work was good,
Would do it, as he could.

Doubting, was not ashamed to doubt,
And, lacking prescience, went without :
    Often appeared to halt,
    And was, of course, at fault :

Heard all opinions, nothing loth,
And loving both sides, angered both :
    Was — not like Justice, blind,
    But watchful, clement, kind.

No hero this, of Roman mould ;
Nor like our stately sires of old :
    Perhaps he was not great, —
    But he preserved the State !

O honest face, which all men knew !
O tender heart, but known to few !
    O wonder of the age,
    Cut off by tragic rage !

Peace !   Let the long procession come,
For hark ! — the mournful, muffled drum, —
    The trumpet's wail afar, —
    And see ! the awful car !

Peace !   Let the sad procession go,
While cannon boom, and bells toll slow :
    And go, thou sacred car,
    Bearing our woe afar !

Go, darkly borne, from State to State,
Whose loyal, sorrowing cities wait
    To honor all they can
    The dust of that good man !

Go, grandly borne, with such a train
As greatest kings might die to gain :

The just, the wise, the brave
Attend thee to the grave !

And you, the soldiers of our wars,
Bronzed veterans, grim with noble scars,
      Salute him once again, —
      Your late commander — slain !

Yes, let your tears, indignant, fall,
But leave your muskets on the wall :
      Your country needs you now
      Beside the forge, the plough !

(When Justice shall unsheathe her brand, —
If Mercy may not stay her hand, —
      Nor would we have it so, —
      She must direct the blow !)

And you, amid the master-race,
Who seem so strangely out of place,
      Know ye who cometh ?   He
      Who hath declared you free !

Bow while the body passes, — nay,
Fall on your knees, and weep, and pray —
      Weep, weep — I would ye might —
      Your poor, black faces white !

And, children, you must come in bands,
With garlands in your little hands,
      Of blue, and white, and red,
      To strew before the dead !

So, sweetly, sadly, sternly goes
The fallen to his last repose :
      Beneath no mighty dome,
      But in his modest home :

The churchyard where his children rest,
The quiet spot that suits him best :
 There shall his grave be made,
 And there his bones be laid !

And there his countrymen shall come,
With memory proud, with pity dumb,
 And strangers far and near,
 For many and many a year !

For many a year, and many an age,
While history on her ample page
 The virtues shall enroll
 Of that paternal soul !

————◆————

SOUTH CAROLINA. — 1865.

BEHOLD her now, with restless, flashing eyes,
 Crouching, a thing forlorn, beside the way !
 Behold her ruined altars heaped to-day
With ashes of her costly sacrifice !

How changed the once proud State that led the strife,
 And flung the war-cry first throughout the land !
 See helpless now the parricidal hand
Which aimed the first blow at the nation's life !

The grass is growing in the city's street,
 Where stand the shattered spires, the broken walls ;
 And through the solemn noonday silence falls
The sentry's footstep as he treads his beat.

Behold once more the old flag proudly wave
 Above the ruined fortress by the sea !
 No longer shall that glorious banner be
The ensign of a land where dwells the slave.

Hark! on the air what swelling anthems rise:
  A ransomed people, by the sword set free,
  Are chanting now a song of liberty;
Hear how their voices echo to the skies!

Oh righteous retribution, great and just!
  Behold the palm-tree fallen to the earth,
  Where Freedom, rising from a second birth,
No more shall trail her garments in the dust!
                                    Harpers' Weekly.

———◆———

IO TRIUMPHE!

BY LIEUTENANT RICHARD REALF.

NOT ever, in all human time,
    Did any man or nation
Plant foot upon the peaks sublime
    Of Mount Transfiguration,
But first in long preceding hours
    Of dread and solemn being,
Clashed battle 'gainst Satanic powers,
    Alone with the All-seeing.

God's glory lights no mortal brows
    Which sorrow hath not wasted;
No wine hath He for lips of those
    His lees who never tasted.
Nor ever, till in bloodiest stress
    The heart is well appróved,
Does the All-brooding Tenderness
    Cry, " This is my belovéd! "

O land, through years of shrouded nights
    In triple blackness groping,
Toward the far prophetic lights
    That beacon the world's hoping, —

Behold! no tittle shalt thou miss
  Of that transforming given
To all who, dragged through hell's abyss,
  Hold fast their grip on heaven.

The Lord God's purpose throbs along
  Our stormy turbulences;
He keeps the sap of nations strong
  By hidden recompenses.
The Lord God sows his righteous grain
  In battle-blasted furrows,
And draws from present days of pain
  Large peace for calm to-morrows.

From strokes of unseen cimitars
  A million hearts are bleeding;
A cry runs tingling to the stars
  Of babes' and widows' pleading:
While at hell's altars sacrificed, —
  God's martyred son forever, —
Lies the clear life that crystallized
  Our kingliest endeavor.

And yet beneath our brimming tears
  Lies nobler cause for singing
Than ever in the shining years,
  When all our vales were ringing
With happy sounds of mellow peace;
  And all our cities thundered
With lusty echoes, and our seas
  By freighted keels were sundered.

For lo! the branding flails that drave
  Our husks of foul self from us
Show all the watching heavens we have
  Immortal grain of promise.

And lo! the dreadful blasts that blew
   In gusts of fire amid us
Have scorched and winnowed from the true
   The falseness which undid us.

No floundering more, for mind or heart,
   Among the lower levels;
No welcome more for moods that sort
   With satyrs and with devils;
But over all our fruitful slopes,
   On all our plains of beauty,
Fair temples for fair human hopes,
   And altar-thrones for duty.

Wherefore, O ransomed people, shout!
   O banners, wave in glory!
O bugles, blow the triumph out!
   O drums, strike up the story!
Clang, broken fetters, idle swords!
   Clap hands, O States, together!
And let all praises be the Lord's,
   Our Saviour and our Father.
                          Harpers' Weekly.

APPENDIX.

REBEL POETRY.

APPENDIX.

FAREWELL TO BROTHER JONATHAN.*

BY CAROLINE.

FAREWELL! we must part; we have turned from the land
Of our cold-hearted brother, with tyrannous hand,
Who assumed all our rights as a favor to grant,
And whose smile ever covered the sting of a taunt;

Who breathed on the fame he was bound to defend, —
Still the craftiest foe, 'neath the guise of a friend;
Who believed that our bosoms would bleed at a touch,
Yet could never believe he could goad them too much;

Whose conscience affects to be seared with our sin,
Yet is plastic to take all its benefits in;
The mote in our eye so enormous has grown,
That he never perceives there's a beam in his own.

O Jonathan, Jonathan! vassal of pelf,
Self-righteous, self-glorious, — yes, every inch self, —
Your loyalty now is all bluster and boast,
But was dumb when the foemen invaded our coast.

In vain did your country appeal to you then,
You coldly refused her your money and men;

* A reply to "Brother Jonathan's Farewell to Sister Caroline,'
p. 1.

19

Your trade interrupted, you slunk from her wars,
And preferred British gold to the Stripes and the Stars!

Then our generous blood was as water poured forth,
And the sons of the South were the shields of the North;
Nor our patriot ardor one moment gave o'er,
Till the foe you had fed we had driven from the shore!

Long years we have suffered opprobrium and wrong,
But we clung to your side with affection so strong,
That at last, in mere wanton aggression, you broke
All the ties of our hearts with one murderous stroke.

We are tired of contest for what is our own,
We are sick of a strife that could never be done;
Thus our love has died out, and its altars are dark,
Not Prometheus's self could rekindle the spark.

O Jonathan, Jonathan! deadly the sin
Of your tigerish thirst for the blood of your kin;
And shameful the spirit that gloats over wives
And maidens despoiled of their honor and lives!

Your palaces rise from the fruits of our toil,
Your millions are fed from the wealth of our soil;
The balm of our air brings the health to your cheek,
And our hearts are aglow with the welcome we speak.

O brother! beware how you seek us again,
Lest you brand on your forehead the signet of Cain;
That blood and that crime on your conscience must sit:
We may fall — we may perish — but never submit!

The pathway that leads to the Pharisee's door
We remember, indeed, but we tread it no more;
Preferring to turn, with the Publican's faith,
To the path through the valley and shadow of death!

"CALL ALL! CALL ALL!"

BY " GEORGIA."

Whoop! the Doodles have broken loose,
Roaring round like the very deuce
Lice of Egypt, a hungry pack, —
After 'em boys, and drive 'em back, —

Bull-dog, terrier, cur, and fice,
Back to the beggarly land of ice;
Worry 'em, bite 'em, scratch and tear
Everybody and everywhere.

Old Kentucky is caved from under,
Tennessee is split asunder,
Alabama awaits attack,
And Georgia bristles up her back.

Old John Brown is dead and gone!
Still his spirit is marching on, —
Lantern-jawed, and legs, my boys,
Long as an ape's from Illinois!

Want a weapon?   Gather a brick,
Club or cudgel, or stone or stick;
Anything with a blade or butt, —
Anything that can cleave or cut.

Anything heavy, or hard, or keen!
Any sort of slaying machine!
Anything with a willing mind,
And the steady arm of a man behind.

Want a weapon?   Why, capture one!
Every Doodle has got a gun,
Belt, and bayonet, bright and new;
Kill a Doodle, and capture *two!*

Shoulder to shoulder, son and sire!
All, call all! to the feast of fire!
Mother and maiden, and child and slave,
A common triumph or a single grave.
                        Rockingham Register.

———◆———

MARYLAND.*

BY JAMES R. RANDALL.

THE despot's heel is on thy shore,
        Maryland!
His torch is at thy temple door,
        Maryland!
Avenge the patriotic gore
That flecked the streets of Baltimore,
And be the battle-queen of yore,
        Maryland!   My Maryland!

Hark to wand'ring son's appeal,
        Maryland!
My mother State! to thee I kneel,
        Maryland!
For life and death, for woe and weal,
Thy peerless chivalry reveal,
And gird thy beauteous limbs with steel,
        Maryland!   My Maryland!

Thou wilt not cower in the dust,
        Maryland!

* No song was such a favorite as this among Rebels at the South
and "Copperheads" at the North. Officers have told me that they
have heard it in the small hours of the night sung in undertones
but with fierce enthusiasm in Baltimore, by people professing
"Union sentiments," and who supposed that their secret and pre-
tended social gatherings were unobserved.

Thy beaming sword shall never rust,
    Maryland!
Remember Carroll's sacred trust;
Remember Howard's warlike thrust;
And all thy slumberers with the just,
    Maryland! My Maryland!

Come! 't is the red dawn of the day,
    Maryland!
Come! with thy panoplied array,
    Maryland!
With Ringgold's spirit for the fray,
With Watson's blood, at Monterey,
With fearless Lowe, and dashing May,
    Maryland! My Maryland!

Come! for thy shield is bright and strong,
    Maryland!
Come! for thy dalliance does thee wrong,
    Maryland!
Come! to thine own heroic throng,
That stalks with Liberty along,
And give a new Key to thy song,*
    Maryland! My Maryland!

Dear Mother! burst the tyrant's chain,
    Maryland!
Virginia should not call in vain,
    Maryland!
She meets her sisters on the plain:
" *Sic semper*," 't is the proud refrain,
That baffles minions back amain,
    Maryland!
Arise in majesty again,
    Maryland! My Maryland!

* "The Star Spangled Banner" was written during the war of 1812 by Francis Key of Maryland.

I see the blush upon thy cheek,
     Maryland!
But thou wast ever bravely meek,
     Maryland!
But lo! there surges forth a shriek
From hill to hill, from creek to creek, —
Potomac calls to Chesapeake,
     Maryland!   My Maryland!

Thou wilt not yield the Vandal toll,
     Maryland!
Thou will not crook to his control,
     Maryland!
Better the fire upon thee roll,
Better the blade, the shot, the bowl,
Than crucifixion of the soul,
     Maryland!   My Maryland!

I hear the distant thunder hum,
     Maryland!
The Old Line's bugle, fife and drum,
     Maryland!
She is not dead, nor deaf, nor dumb:
Huzza! she spurns the Northern scum!
She breathes — she burns! she 'll come! she 'll come!
     Maryland!   My Maryland!

POINTE COUPEE, April 26, 1861.

THE DESPOT'S SONG.

BY "OLE SECESH."

WITH a beard that was filthy and red,
His mouth with tobacco bespread,
Abe Lincoln sat in the gay White House,
A-wishing that he was dead:

Swear! swear! swear!
Till his tongue was blistered o'er;
Then, in a voice not very strong,
He slowly whined the Despot's Song: —

Lie! lie! lie!
I 've lied like the very deuce!
Lie! lie! lie!
As long as lies were of use;
But now that lies no longer pay,
  I know not where to turn;
For when I the truth would say,
  My tongue with lies will burn!

Drink! drink! drink!
Till my head feels very queer!
Drink! drink! drink!
Till I get rid of all fear!
Brandy and whiskey and gin,
  Sherry and champagne and pop;
I tipple, I guzzle, I suck 'em all in,
  Till down dead-drunk I drop.

Think! think! think!
Till my head is very sore!
Think! think! think!
Till I could n't think any more!
And it 's oh! to be splitting of rails,
  Back in my Illinois hut;
For now that everything fails,
  I would of my office be " shut!"

Jeff! Jeff! Jeff!
To you as a suppliant I kneel!
Jeff! Jeff! Jeff!
If you could my horrors feel,

You 'd submit at discretion,
    And kindly give in
To all my oppression,
    My weakness and sin !

———◆———

REBELS.

[' General Beauregard, now in command of the Rebel forces in
Charleston, has much fame as a tactician." — *Harpers' Weekly.*]

YES, call them Rebels! 't is the name
    Their patriot fathers bore ;
And by such deeds they 'll hallow it,
    As they have done before.
At Lexington and Baltimore
    Was poured the holy chrism,
For freedom marks her sons with blood,
    In sign of their baptism.

Rebels, in proud and bold protest,
    Against a power unreal, —
A unity which every quest
    Proves false as 't is ideal.
A brotherhood, whose ties are chains,
    Which crushes what it holds,
Like the old marble Laocoon,
    Beneath its serpent folds.

Rebels against the malice vast, —
    Malice that naught disarms, —
Which fills the quiet of their homes
    With vague and dread alarms.
Against the invader's daring feet,
    Against the tide of wrong,
Which has been borne, — in silence borne, —
    But borne perchance too long.

They would be cowards, did they crouch
    Beneath the lifted hand,
Whose very wave, ye seem to think,
    Will chill them where they stand.
Yes, call them Rebels! 't is a name
    Which speaks of other days,
Of gallant deeds and gallant men,
    And wins them to their ways.

Fair was the edifice they raised,
    Uplifting to the skies;
A mighty Samson 'neath its dome
    In grand quiescence lies.
Dare not to touch his noble limb,
    With thong or chain to bind,
Lest ruin crush both you and him, —
    This Samson is not blind!

FLIGHT OF DOODLES.

I COME from old Manassas, with a pocket full of fun;
I killed forty Yankees with a single-barrelled gun:
It don't make a niff-a-stifference to neither you nor I,
Big Yankee, Little Yankee, all run or die.

I saw all the Yankees at Bull Run;
They fought like the devil when the battle first begun:
But it don't make a niff-a-stifference to neither you nor I,
They took to their heels, boys, and you ought to see 'em fly.

I saw old Fuss-and-Feathers Scott, twenty miles away;
His horses stuck up their ears, and you ought to hear 'em
    neigh:
But it don't make a niff-a-stifference to neither you nor I,
Old Scott fled like the devil, boys; root, hog, or die.

I then saw a " Tiger," from the old Crescent City;
He cut down the Yankees without any pity:
Oh! it don't make a diff-a-bitterence to neither you
  nor I,
We whipped the Yankee boys, and made the boobies cry.

I saw South Carolina, the first in the cause,
Shake the dirty Yankees till she broke all their jaws:
Oh! it don't make a niff-a-stifference to neither you
  nor I,
South Carolina give 'em ———, boys; root, hog, or die.

I saw old Virginia, standing firm and true;
She fought mighty hard to whip the dirty crew:
Oh! it don't make a niff-a-stifference to neither you
  nor I,
Old Virginia's blood and thunder, boys; root, hog, or
  die.

I saw old Georgia, the next in the van;
She cut down the Yankees almost to a man:
Oh! it don't make a niff-a-stifference to neither you
  nor I,
Georgia's sum in a fight, boys; root, hog, or die.

I saw Alabama in the midst of the storm;
She stood like a giant in the contest so warm:
Oh! it don't make a niff-a-stifference to neither you
  nor I,
Alabama fought the Yankees, boys, till the last one did
  fly.

I saw Texas go in with a smile,
But, I tell you what it is, she made the Yankees bile:
Oh! it don't make a niff-a-stifference to neither you
  nor I,
Texas is the devil, boys; root, hog, or die.

I saw North Carolina in the deepest of the battle;
She knocked down the Yankees and made their bones
    rattle:
Oh! it don't make a niff-a-stifference to neither you
    nor I,
North Carolina's got the grit, boys; root, hog, or die.

Old Florida came in with a terrible shout;
She frightened all the Yankees till their eyes stuck out:
Oh! it don't make a niff-a-stifference to neither you
    nor I,
Florida's death on Yankees; root, hog, or die.

———◆———

ANOTHER YANKEE DOODLE.

YANKEE Doodle had a mind
    To whip the Southern traitors,
Because they did n't choose to live
    On codfish and potatoes.
        Yankee Doodle, doodle-doo,
          Yankee Doodle dandy;
        And so, to keep his courage up,
          He took a drink of brandy.

Yankee Doodle said he found
    By all the census figures,
That he could starve the Rebels out
    If he could steal their niggers.
        Yankee Doodle, doodle-doo,
          Yankee Doodle dandy;
        And then he took another drink
          Of gunpowder and brandy.

Yankee Doodle made a speech;
    'T was very full of feeling:

" I fear," says he, " I cannot fight,
　But I am good at stealing."
　　　　Yankee Doodle, doodle-doo,
　　　　　Yankee Doodle dandy;
　　　　　Hurrah for Lincoln! he's the boy
　　　　　To take a drop of brandy.

Yankee Doodle drew his sword,
　And practised all the passes:
Come, boys, we'll take another drink
　When we get to Manassas.
　　　　Yankee Doodle, doodle-doo,
　　　　　Yankee Doodle dandy;
　　　　　They never reached Manassas plain,
　　　　　And never got the brandy.

Yankee Doodle soon found out
　That Bull Run was no trifle;
For if the North knew how to steal,
　The South knew how to rifle.
　　　　Yankee Doodle, doodle-doo,
　　　　　Yankee Doodle dandy;
　　　　　'Tis very clear I took too much
　　　　　Of that infernal brandy.

Yankee Doodle wheeled about,
　And scampered off at full run;
And such a race was never seen
　As that he made at Bull Run.
　　　　Yankee Doodle, doodle-doo,
　　　　　Yankee Doodle dandy;
　　　　　I haven't time to stop just now
　　　　　To take a drop of brandy.

Yankee Doodle, oh, for shame!
　You're always intermeddling;
Let guns alone, they're dangerous things, —
　You'd better stick to peddling.

Yankee Doodle, doodle-doo,
Yankee Doodle dandy;
When next I go to Bully Run
I ll throw away the brandy.

Yankee Doodle, you had ought
To be a little smarter;
Instead of catching woolly heads,
I vow you 've caught a tartar.
Yankee Doodle, doodle-doo,
Yankee Doodle dandy;
Go to hum, you 've had enough
Of Rebels and of brandy.

———◆———

JUSTICE IS OUR PANOPLY.

BY DE G.

[Copy of verses found in a pocket-book picked up by a private of the Fifth Regiment Zouaves, U. S. A. There was no date attached to them.]

WE 'RE free from Yankee despots,
We 've left the foul mudsills;
Declared fore'er our freedom, —
We 'll keep it, spite of ills.

Bring forth your scum and rowdies,
Thieves, vagabonds, and all;
March down your Seventh regiment,
Battalions great and small.

We 'll meet you in Virginia, —
A Southern battle-field, —
Where Southern men will never
To Yankee foemen yield.

Equip your Lincoln cavalry,
   Your NEGRO *light*-brigade,
Your hodmen, boot-blacks, tinkers,
   And scum of every grade.

Pretended love for negroes
   Incites you to the strife;
Well, come each Yankee white man
   And take a negro wife.

You 'd make fit black companions, —
   Black heart joined to black skin;
Such *unions* would be glorious, —
   They 'd make the devil grin.

Our freedom is our panoply:
   Come on, you base *black*-guards,
We 'll snuff you like wax-candles,
   Led by our Beauregards.

P. G. T. B. is not alone, —
   Men like him with him fight;
God's providence is o'er us,
   He will protect the right.

THE STARS AND BARS.

BY A. J. REQUIER.

FLING wide the dauntless banner
   To every Southern breeze,
Baptized in flame with Sumter's name, —
A patriot and a hero's fame, —
   From Moultrie to the seas!
That it may cleave the morning sun,
   And, streaming, sweep the night,

The emblem of a battle won
  With Yankee ships in sight.

Come, hucksters, from your markets;
  Come, bigots, from your caves;
Come, venal spies, with brazen lies
Bewildering your deluded eyes,
  That we may dig your graves;
Come, creatures of a sordid clown
  And drivelling traitor's breath,
A single blast shall blow you down
  Upon the fields of Death.

The very flag you carry
  Caught its reflected grace,
In fierce alarms, from Southern arms,
When foemen threatened all your farms,
  And never saw your face;
Ho! braggarts of New-England's shore,
  Back to your hills, and delve
The soil whose craven sons forswore
  The flag in eighteen-twelve!

We wreathed around the roses
  It wears before the world,
And made it bright with storied light,
In every scene of bloody fight
  Where it has been unfurled;
And think ye now the dastard hands
  That never yet could hold
Its staff, shall wave it o'er our lands,
  To glut the greed of gold?

No! by the truth of Heaven
  And its eternal Sun,
By every sire whose altar-fire
Burns on to beckon and inspire,

It never shall be done ;
Before that day the kites shall wheel
  Hail-thick on Northern heights,
And there our bared aggressive steel
  Shall countersign our rights !

Then, spread the flaming banner
  O'er mountain, lake, and plain ;
Before its bars degraded Mars
Has kissed the dust with all his stars,
  And will be struck again ;
For, could its triumph now be stayed
  By Hell's prevailing gates,
A sceptred Union would be made
  The grave of sovereign States.

—◆—

THE IRISH BATTALION.*

WHEN Old Virginia took the field,
  And wanted men to rally on, —
To be at once her sword and shield, —
  She formed her First Battalion.

Although her sons were Volunteers,
  And brave as ever bore a brand,
The good old lady had her fears
  That they might prove but weak of hand.

---

  * It is worthy of remark, that while Rebel organs made great
and constant boast of that poor inheritance, Cavalier and Jacobite
blood, and reviled the Union armies on account of the number of
Irishmen in their ranks, the proportion of which was in reality very
small, there was yet occasion for such verses as these, and the
" Song of the Irish Brigade," which follows. It seems, after all
rather a sorry confession that " Old Virginia " took three hundred
Irishmen to form her First Battalion.

She therefore wisely cast about
  For men of mettle and of mould,
With nerve of steel and muscle stout,
  Like those that lived in days of old.

She wanted men of pluck and might,
  Of fiery heart and horny hand,
To wield a pick as well as fight,
  Or build a breastwork out of sand.

Or should she march to meet the foe
  That threatened on her western border,
She wanted willing men to go,
  When told, to put her roads in order.

Or should the Volunteers retreat,
  With baggage that might make them tarry,
'T would blunt the edge of their defeat
  To bear a hand and help them carry.

Or should some die of fell disease, —
  The surgeons having failed to save, —
Sure men who work with so much ease,
  Would volunteer to dig a grave!

For these, and reasons quite as sound,
  When Old Virginia went to war,
She circumspectly viewed the ground
  And plumped the middle man from taw!

In other words, to change the figure,
  When she stood up and took her rifle,
And put her finger on the trigger,
  She meant to work, and not to trifle.

And standing thus, yet wanting then
  Some regulars to rally on,
  20

She took three hundred Irishmen
    And formed her First Battalion.

And when the storm of battle sweeps,
    Where fiercest foemen sally on,
There, hard at work, or piled in heaps,
    She'll find her bold Battalion.

———◆———

BOMBARDMENT OF VICKSBURG.

DEDICATED WITH RESPECT AND ADMIRATION TO MAJOR-GENERAL EARL VAN DORN.

FOR sixty days and upwards
    A storm of shell and shot
Rained round us in a flaming shower,
    But still we faltered not!
" If the noble city perish,"
    Our grand young leader said,
" Let the only walls the foe shall scale
    Be ramparts of the dead ! "

For sixty days and upwards
    The eye of heaven waxed dim ;
And even throughout God's holy morn,
    O'er Christian's prayer and hymn,
Arose a hissing tumult,
    As if the fiends of air
Strove to engulf the voice of faith
    In the shrieks of their despair.

There was wailing in the houses,
    There was trembling on the marts,
While the tempest raged and thundered,
    'Mid the silent thrill of hearts :

But the Lord, our shield, was with us;
    And ere a month had sped,
Our very women walked the streets
    With scarce one throb of dread.

And the little children gambolled, —
    Their faces purely raised,
Just for a wondering moment,
    As the huge bombs whirled and blazed!
Then turning with silvery laughter
    To the sports which children love,
Thrice mailed in the sweet, instinctive thought,
    That the good God watched above.*

Yet the hailing bolts fell faster
    From scores of flame-clad ships,
And above us denser, darker,
    Grew the conflict's wild eclipse;
Till a solid cloud closed o'er us,
    Like a type of doom and ire,
Whence shot a thousand quivering tongues
    Of forked and vengeful fire.

But the unseen hands of angels
    These death-shafts warned aside,
And the dove of heavenly mercy
    Ruled o'er the battle-tide;
In the houses ceased the wailing,
    And through the war-scarred marts
The people strode with the step of hope
    To the music in their hearts.

COLUMBIA, S. C., August 6, 1862.

---

* It has been stated by one professing to have witnessed the fact, that some weeks after the beginning of this terrific bombardment, not only were ladies seen coolly walking the streets, but that in some parts of the town children were observed at play, only interrupting their sports to gaze and listen at the bursting shells.

A SOUTHERN SCENE.

" O MAMMY ! have you heard the news ? "
   Thus spake a Southern child,
As in the nurse's aged face
   She upward glanced and smiled.

" What news you mean, my little one ?
   It must be mighty fine
To make my darling's face so red,
   Her sunny blue eyes shine."

" Why, Abram Lincoln, don't you know,
   The Yankee President,
Whose ugly picture once we saw,
   When up to town we went, —

" Well, he is going to free you all,
   And make you rich and grand,
And you 'll be dressed in silk and gold,
   Like the proudest in the land.

" A gilded coach shall carry you
   Where'er you wish to ride ;
And, mammy, all your work shall be
   Forever laid aside."

The eager speaker paused for breath,
   And then the old nurse said,
While closer to her swarthy cheek
   She pressed the golden head :

" My little missus, stop and res', —
   You' talking mighty fas' ;
Jes' look up dere, and tell me what
   You see in yonder glass ?

" You sees old mammy's wrinkly face,
　　As black as any coal,
And underneath her handkerchief
　　Whole heaps of knotty wool.

" My darlin's face is red and white,
　　Her skin is soff and fine,
And on her pretty little head
　　De yallar ringlets shine.

" My chile, who made dis difference
　　'Twixt mammy and 'twixt you ?
You reads the dear Lord's blessed book,
　　And you can tell me true.

" De dear Lord said it must be so ;
　　And, honey, I for one,
Wid tankful heart will always say, —
　　His holy will be done.

" I tanks mas' Linkum all de same,
　　But when I wants for free,
I 'll ask de Lord of glory,
　　Not poor buckra man like he.

" And as for gilded carriages,
　　Dey 's notin' 't all to see ;
My massa's coach, what carries him,
　　Is good enough for me.

" And, honey, when your mammy wants
　　To change her homespun dress,
She 'll pray like dear old missus,
　　To be clothed with righteousness.

" My work 's been done dis many a day,
　　And now I takes my ease,

A waitin' for the Master's call,
   Jes' when the Master please.

" And when at las' de time 's done come,
   And poor old mammy dies,
Your own dear mother's soff white hand
   Shall close dese tired old eyes.

" De dear Lord Jesus soon will call
   Old mammy home to Him,
And He can wash my guilty soul
   From ebery spot of sin.

" And at His feet I shall lie down,
   Who died and rose for me ;
And den, and not till den, my chile,
   Your mammy will be free.

" Come, little missus, say your prayers ;
   Let old mas' Linkum 'lone,
The debil knows who b'longs to him,
   And he 'll take care of his own."

BEYOND THE POTOMAC.

BY PAUL H. HAYNE.*

THEY slept on the fields which their valor had won !
But arose with the first early blush of the sun,
For they knew that a great deed remained to be done,
     When they passed o'er the River.

---

  * This piece was originally published in the *Richmond Whig* at
the time of " Stonewall " Jackson's last raid into Maryland.

They rose with the sun, and caught life from his light, —
Those giants of courage, those Anaks in fight, —
And they laughed out aloud in the joy of their might,
   Marching swift for the River.

On! on! like the rushing of storms through the hills, —
On! on! with a tramp that is firm as their wills, —
And the one heart of thousands grows buoyant and thrills
   At the thought of the River.

On! the sheen of their swords! the fierce gleam of their
  eyes
It seemed as on earth a new sunlight would rise,
And king-like, flash up to the sun in the skies,
   O'er the path to the River.

But their banners, shot-scarred, and all darkened with
  gore,
On a strong wind of morning streamed wildly before,
Like the wings of Death-angels swept fast to the shore, —
   The green shore of the River.

As they march, — from the hill-side, the hamlet, the
  stream, —
Gaunt throngs whom the Foeman had manacled, teem,
Like men just roused from some terrible dream,
   To pass o'er the River.

They behold the broad banners, blood-darkened, yet fair
And a moment dissolves the last spell of despair,
While a peal as of victory swells on the air,
   Rolling out to the River.

And that cry, with a thousand strange echoings spread,
Till the ashes of heroes seemed stirred in their bed,
And the deep voice of passion surged up from the dead, —
   Ay! press on to the River.

On! on! like the rushing of storms through the hills,
On! on! with a tramp that is firm as their wills,
And the one heart of thousands grows buoyant, **and**
    thrills,
        As they pause by the River.

Then the wan face of Maryland, haggard and worn,
At that sight, lost the touch of its aspect forlorn,
And she turned on the Foeman full statured in scorn,
        Pointing stern to the River.

And Potomac flowed calm, scarcely heaving her breast,
With her low-lying billows all bright in the west,
For the hand of the Lord lulled the waters to rest
        Of the fair rolling River.

Passed! passed! the glad thousands march safe through
    the tide.
(Hark, Despot! and hear the wild knell of your pride,
Ringing weird-like and wild, pealing up from the side
        Of the calm-flowing River.)

'Neath a blow swift and mighty the Tyrant shall fall:
Vain! vain! to his God swells a desolate call,
For his grave has been hollowed, and woven his pall,
        Since they passed o'er the River.

---◆---

THE OLD RIFLEMAN.

BY FRANK TICKNOR, M. D.

Now, bring me out my buckskin suit!
    My pouch and powder, too!
We'll see if seventy-six can shoot
    As sixteen used to do.

Old Bess ! we 've kept our barrels bright !
 Our triggers quick and true !
As far, if not as *fine* a sight,
 As long ago we drew !

And pick me out a trusty flint !
 A real white and blue ;
Perhaps 't will win the *other* tint
 Before the hunt is through !

Give boys your brass percussion-caps !
 Old " shut-pan " suits as well !
There 's something in the *sparks ;* perhaps
 There 's something in the smell !

We 've seen the red-coat Briton bleed !
 The red-skin Indian too !
We never thought to draw a bead
 On Yankee-doodle-doo !

But, Bessie ! bless your dear old heart !
 Those days are mostly done ;
And now we must revive the art
 Of shooting on the run !

If Doodle must be meddling, why,
 There 's only this to do, —
Select the black spot in his eye
 And let the daylight through !

And if he does n't like the way
 That Bess presents the view,
He 'll, maybe, change his mind and stay
 Where the good Doodles do !

Where Lincoln lives. The man, you know,
 Who kissed the Testament ;

To keep the Constitution ?   No !
To keep the Government !

We 'll hunt for Lincoln, Bess ! old tool,
   And take him half and half ;
We 'll aim to *hit* him, if a fool,
   And *miss* him, if a calf !

We 'll teach these shot-gun boys the tricks
   By which a war is won ;
Especially how seventy-six
   Took Tories on the run.

" SOUTHRONS. "

You can never win them back —
    Never ! never !
Though they perish on the track
    Of your endeavor ;
Though their corses strew the earth
That SMILED upon their birth,
And blood pollutes each hearth-
    Stone forever !

They have risen to a man,
    Stern and fearless ;
Of your curses and your ban
    They are careless.
Every hand is on its knife,
Every gun is primed for strife,
Every PALM contains a life,
    High and peerless !

You have no such blood as theirs
    For the shedding :

In the veins of Cavaliers
      Was its heading !
You have no such stately men
In your " abolition den,"
To march through foe and fen,
      Nothing dreading !

They may fall before the fire
     Of your legions,
Paid with gold for murderous hire, —
     Bought allegiance ;
But for every drop you shed
You shall have a mound of dead,
So that vultures may be fed
      In our regions !

But the battle to the strong
     Is not given,
When the Judge of Right and Wrong
     Sits in heaven ;
And the God of David still
Guides the pebble with *His will*, —
There are giants yet to kill, —
      Wrongs unshriven !

———◆———

THE GUERILLAS.*

Awake and to horse, my brothers !
   For the dawn is glimmering gray ;
And hark ! in the crackling brushwood
   There are feet that tread this way.

* These stirring verses, which we copy from a Southern ex-
change, are from the patriotic pen of a lady of Kentucky, who has
achieved a national reputation as a poetess and authoress. — *Louis-
ville Courier.*

"Who cometh?"   "A friend."   "What tidings?"
    "O God! I sicken to tell;
For the earth seems earth no longer,
    And its sights are sights of hell!

"From the far-off conquered cities
    Comes a voice of stifled wail,
And the shrieks and moans of the houseless
    Ring out, like a dirge on the gale.

"I've seen from the smoking village
    Our mothers and daughters fly;
I've seen where the little children
    Sank down in the furrows to die.

"On the banks of the battle-stained river
    I stood as the moonlight shone,
And it glared on the face of my brother,
    As the sad wave swept him on.

"Where my home was glad, are ashes,
    And horrors and shame had been there,
For I found on the fallen lintel
    This tress of my wife's torn hair.

"They are turning the slaves upon us;
    And, with more than the fiend's worst art,
Have uncovered the fire of the savage
    That slept in his untaught heart! *

"The ties to our hearths that bound him
    They have rent with curses away,
And maddened him, with their madness,
    To be almost as brutal as they.

"With halter and torch and Bible,
    And hymns to the sound of the drum,

* It need hardly be said that this charge is unfounded.

They preach the gospel of murder,
   And pray for lust's kingdom to come.

" To saddle! to saddle! my brothers!
   Look up to the rising sun,
And ask of the God who shines there
   Whether deeds like these shall be done!

" Wherever the vandal cometh,
   Press home to his heart with your steel;
And when at his bosom you cannot,
   Like the serpent, go strike at his heel!

" Through thicket and wood, go hunt him;
   Creep up to his camp-fire side;
And let ten of his corpses blacken
   Where one of our brothers hath died.

" In his fainting, foot-sore marches,
   In his flight from the stricken fray,
In the snare of the lonely ambush,
   The debts we owe him pay.

" In God's hand alone is vengeance,
   But he strikes with the hands of men;
And his blight would wither our manhood,
   If we smite not the smiter again.

" By the graves where our fathers slumber,
   By the shrines where our mothers prayed,
By our homes and hopes and freedom,
   Let every man swear on his blade,

" That he will not sheathe nor stay it,
   Till from point to hilt it glow
With the flush of Almighty vengeance,
   In the blood of the felon foe."

They swore: and the answering sunlight
  Leaped red from their lifted swords;
And the hate in their hearts made echo
  To the wrath in their burning words.

There's weeping in all New England,
  And by Schuylkill's banks a knell;
And the widows there and the orphans
  How the oath was kept, can tell.*

———◆———

THERE'S LIFE IN THE OLD LAND YET!

BY JAMES R. RANDALL.

BY the blue Patapsco's billowy dash
  The tyrant's war-shout comes,
Along with the cymbals' fitful clash,
  And the growl of his sullen drums.
We hear it! we heed it with vengeful thrills,
  And we shall not forgive or forget;
There's faith in the streams, there's hope in the hills,
  There's life in the old land yet!

Minions! we sleep, but we are not dead;
  We are crushed, we are scourged, we are scarred;
We crouch — 't is to welcome the triumph tread
  Of the peerless BEAUREGARD.
Then woe to your vile, polluting horde,
  When the Southern braves are met;
There's faith in the victor's stainless sword,
  There's life in the old land yet!

---

* It may add something to the interest with which these stirring
lines will be read, to know that they were composed within the
walls of a Yankee Bastile.   They reach us in manuscript, through
the courtesy of a returned prisoner. — *Richmond Examiner.*

Bigots! ye quell not the valiant mind
  With the clank of an iron chain;
The spirit of Freedom sings in the wind,
  O'er *Merryman, Thomas,* and *Kane;*
And we, though we smite not, are not thralls, —
  Are piling a gory debt;
While down by McHenry's dungeon-walls
  There's life in the old land yet!

Our women have hung their harps away,
  And they scowl on your brutal bands,
While the nimble poinard dares the day,
  In their dear defiant hands.
They will strip their tresses to string our bows,
  Ere the Northern sun is set;
There's faith in their unrelenting woes,
  There's life in the old land yet!

There's life, though it throbbeth in silent veins, —
  'T is vocal without noise;
It gushed o'er Manassas's solemn plains,
  From the blood of the MARYLAND BOYS!
That blood shall cry aloud, and rise
  With an everlasting threat;
By the death of the brave, by the God in the skies,
  There's life in the old land yet!

---◆---

EPIGRAM.

WHILST Butler plays his silly pranks,
And closes up New-Orleans' banks,
Our Stonewall Jackson, with more cunning,
Keeps Yankee Banks forever running.

Charleston Mercury.

THINKING OF THE SOLDIERS.

WE were sitting around the table,
   Just a night or two ago,
In the little cosy parlor,
   With the lamp-light burning low ;
And the window-blinds half opened,
   For the summer air to come,
And the painted curtains moving
   Like a busy pendulum.

Oh ! the cushions on the sofa,
   And the pictures on the wall,
And the gathering of comforts,
   In the old familiar hall ;
And the wagging of the pointer,
   Lounging idly by the door,
And the flitting of the shadows
   From the ceiling to the floor.

Oh ! they wakened in my spirit,
   Like the beautiful in art,
Such a busy, busy thinking, —
   Such a dreaminess of heart, —
That I sat among the shadows,
   With my spirit all astray ;
Thinking only — thinking only
   Of the soldiers far away :

Of the tents beneath the moonlight,
   Of the stirring tattoo's sound,
Of the soldier in his blanket, —
   In his blanket on the ground ;
Of the icy winter coming,
   Of the cold, bleak winds that blow,
And the soldier in his blanket,
   In his blanket on the snow.

Of the blight upon the heather,
   And the frost upon the hill,
And the whistling, whistling ever,
   And the never, never still;
Of the little leaflets falling,
   With the sweetest, saddest sound, —
And the soldier — oh! the soldier,
   In his blanket on the ground.

Thus I lingered in my dreaming, —
   In my dreaming far away, —
Till the spirit's picture-painting
   Seemed as vivid as the day;
And the moonlight faded softly
   From the window opened wide,
And the faithful, faithful pointer
   Nestled closer by my side.

And I knew that 'neath the starlight,
   Though the chilly frosts may fall,
That the soldier will be dreaming,
   Dreaming often of us all.
So I gave my spirit's painting
   Just the breathing of a sound,
For the dreaming, dreaming soldier,
   In his slumber on the ground.

   November 24, 1861.

——◆——

" STONEWALL JACKSON'S WAY."

COME, stack arms, men! Pile on the rails,
   Stir up the camp-fire bright;
No matter if the canteen fails,
   We 'll make a roaring night.
Here Shenandoah brawls along,
There burly Blue Ridge echoes strong,
   21

To swell the brigade's rousing song
  Of " Stonewall Jackson's way."

We see him now, — the old slouched hat
  Cocked o'er his eye askew ;
The shrewd, dry smile, the speech so pat,
  So calm, so blunt, so true.
The " Blue-Light Elder " knows 'em well ;
Says he, " That 's Banks — he 's fond of shell ;
Lord save his soul ! we 'll give him —— ; " well,
  That 's Stonewall Jackson's way."

Silence ! ground arms ! kneel all ! caps off !
  Old Blue-Light 's going to pray.
Strangle the fool that dares to scoff !
  Attention ! it 's his way.
Appealing from his native sod,
In *forma pauperis* to God :
" Lay bare Thine arm ; stretch forth Thy rod !
  Amen ! " That 's " Stonéwall's way."

He 's in the saddle now.   Fall in !
  Steady ! the whole brigade !
Hill 's at the ford, cut off ; we 'll win
  His way out, ball and blade !
What matter if our shoes are worn ?
What matter if our feet are torn ?
" Quick-step ! we 're with him before dawn ! "
  That 's " Stonewall Jackson' way."

The sun 's bright lances rout the mists
  Of morning, and by George !
Here 's Longstreet struggling in the lists,
  Hemmed in an ugly gorge.
Pope and his Yankees, whipped before ;
" Bay'nets and grape ! " near Stonewall roar ;
" Charge, Stuart ! Pay off Ashby's score ! "
  Is " Stonewall Jackson's way."

Ah ! maiden, wait and watch and yearn
   For news of Stonewall's band !
Ah ! widow, read with eyes that burn
   That ring upon thy hand.
Ah ! wife, sew on, pray on, hope on,
Thy life shall not be all forlorn.
The foe had better ne'er been born
   That gets in " Stonewall's way."

SONG FOR THE IRISH BRIGADE.

BY "SHAMROCK" OF THE SUMPTER RIFLES.

NOT now for the songs of a nation's wrongs,
   Nor the groans of starving labor ;
Let the rifle ring and the bullet sing
   To the clash of the flashing sabre !
There are Irish ranks on the tented banks
   Of Columbia's guarded ocean,
And an iron clank, from flank to flank,
   Tells of armèd men in motion.

And the frank souls there, clear, true, and bare
   To all, as the steel beside them.
Can love or hate, with the strength of Fate,
   Till the grave of the valiant hide them,
Each seems to be mailed *Ard Righ*,
   Whose sword's avenging glory
Might light the fight and smite for Right,
   Like Brian's in olden story !

With pale affright and panic flight
   Shall dastard Yankees, base and hollow,
Hear a Celtic race, from their battle-place,
   Charge to the shout of " *Faugh-a-ballagh !* "

By the souls above, by the land we love,
 Her tears and bleeding patience,
The sledge is wrought that shall smash to naught
 The brazen liar of nations.

The Irish green shall again be seen
 As our Irish fathers bore it, —
A burning wind from the South behind,
 And the Yankee rout before it! —
O'Neil's red hand shall purge the land, —
 Rain fire on men and cattle, —
Till the Lincoln snakes in their own cold lakes
 Plunge from the blaze of battle.

The knaves that rest on Columbia's breast,
 And the voice of true men stifle,
We 'll exorcise from the rescued prize, —
 Our talisman, the rifle;
For a tyrant's life a bowie-knife!
 Of Union-knot dissolvers,
The best we ken are stalworth men,
 Columbiads and revolvers!

Whoe'er shall march by triumphal arch,
 Whoe'er may swell the slaughter,
Our drums shall roll from the Capitol
 O'er Potomac's fateful water!
Rise, bleeding ghosts, to the Lord of Hosts,
 For judgment final and solemn;
Your fanatic horde to the edge of the sword
 Is doomed, — line, square, and column.

THE CONFEDERATE FLAG.

I.

TAKE that banner down, 't is weary;
Round its staff 't is drooping dreary;
Furl it, fold it, let it rest;
For there 's not a man to wave it,
For there 's not a sword to save it,
In the blood that heroes gave it;
And its foes now scorn and brave it:
Furl it, hide it, let it rest.

II.

Take that banner down, 't is tattered, —
Broken is its staff and shattered;
And the valiant hosts are scattered,
Over whom it floated high.
Oh, 't is hard for us to fold it!
Hard to think there 's none to hold it;
Hard, for those who once unrolled it,
Now must furl it with a sigh.

III.

Furl that banner, furl it sadly;
Once six millions hailed it gladly,
And ten thousand wildly, madly
Swore it should forever wave;
Swore that foeman's sword should never
Hearts like theirs entwined dissever;
And that flag should float forever
O'er their freedom or their grave.

IV.

Furl it, for the hands that grasped it,
And the hearts that fondly clasped it,
Cold and dead are lying low;

And that banner, it is trailing,
While around it sounds the wailing
Of its people in their woe.

v.

For, though conquered, they adore it, —
Love the cold, dead hands that bore it;
Weep for those who fell before it:
Pardon those who trail and tore it:
Oh, how wildly they deplore it,
Now to furl and fold it so!

vi.

Furl that banner!   True, 't is gory;
But 't is wreathed around with glory,
And 't will live in song and story,
Though its folds are in the dust;
For its fame on brightest pages,
Penned by poets and by sages,
Shall go sounding down the ages:
Furl its folds, for now we must.

vii.

Furl that banner softly, slowly;
Furl it gently, — it is holy, —
For it droops above the dead:
Touch it not, — unfurl it never, —
Let it droop there, furled forever,
For its people's hopes are fled.

New York Freeman's Journal.

INDEX OF AUTHORS.

INDEX OF FIRST LINES.

THE END.

The Romantic Tradition in American Literature

An Arno Press Collection

Alcott, A. Bronson, editor. **Conversations with Children on the Gospels.** Boston, 1836/1837. Two volumes in one.

Bartol, C[yrus] A. **Discourses on the Christian Spirit and Life.** 2nd edition. Boston, 1850.

Boker, George H[enry]. **Poems of the War.** Boston, 1864.

Brooks, Charles T. **Poems, Original and Translated.** Selected and edited by W. P. Andrews. Boston, 1885.

Brownell, Henry Howard. **War-Lyrics** and Other Poems. Boston, 1866.

Brownson, O[restes] A. **Essays and Reviews Chiefly on Theology, Politics, and Socialism.** New York, 1852.

Channing, [William] Ellery (The Younger). **Poems.** Boston, 1843.

Channing, [William] Ellery (The Younger). **Poems of Sixty-Five Years.** Edited by F. B. Sanborn. Philadelphia and Concord, 1902.

Chivers, Thomas Holley. **Eonchs of Ruby:** A Gift of Love. New York, 1851.

Chivers, Thomas Holley. **Virginalia;** or, Songs of My Summer Nights. (Reprinted from *Research Classics,* No. 2, 1942). Philadelphia, 1853.

Cooke, Philip Pendleton. **Froissart Ballads,** and Other Poems. Philadelphia, 1847.

Cranch, Christopher Pearse. **The Bird and the Bell,** with Other Poems. Boston, 1875.

[Dall], Caroline W. Healey, editor. **Margaret and Her Friends.** Boston, 1895.

[D'Arusmont], Frances Wright. **A Few Days in Athens.** Boston, 1850.

Everett, Edward. **Orations and Speeches,** on Various Occasions. Boston, 1836.

Holland, J[osiah] G[ilbert]. **The Marble Prophecy,** and Other Poems. New York, 1872.

Huntington, William Reed. **Sonnets and a Dream.** Jamaica, N. Y., 1899.

Jackson, Helen [Hunt]. **Poems.** Boston, 1892.

Miller, Joaquin (Cincinnatus Hiner Miller). **The Complete Poetical Works of Joaquin Miller.** San Francisco, 1897.

Parker, Theodore. **A Discourse of Matters Pertaining to Religion.** Boston, 1842.

Pinkney, Edward C. **Poems.** Baltimore, 1838.

Reed, Sampson. **Observations on the Growth of the Mind.** *Including,* **Genius** (Reprinted from *Aesthetic Papers,* Boston, 1849). 5th edition. Boston, 1859.

Sill, Edward Rowland. **The Poetical Works of Edward Rowland Sill.** Boston and New York, 1906.

Simms, William Gilmore. **Poems:** Descriptive, Dramatic, Legendary and Contemplative. New York, 1853. Two volumes in one.

Simms, William Gilmore, editor. **War Poetry of the South.** New York, 1866.

Stickney, Trumbull. **The Poems of Trumbull Stickney.** Boston and New York, 1905.

Timrod, Henry. **The Poems of Henry Timrod.** Edited by Paul H. Hayne. New York, 1873.

Trowbridge, John Townsend. **The Poetical Works of John Townsend Trowbridge.** Boston and New York, 1903.

Very, Jones. **Essays and Poems.** [Edited by R. W. Emerson]. Boston, 1839.

Very, Jones. **Poems and Essays.** Boston and New York, 1886.

White, Richard Grant, editor. **Poetry:** Lyrical, Narrative, and Satirical of the Civil War. New York, 1866.

Wilde, Richard Henry. **Hesperia:** A Poem. Edited by His Son (William Wilde). Boston, 1867.

Willis, Nathaniel Parker. **The Poems, Sacred, Passionate, and Humorous, of Nathaniel Parker Willis.** New York, 1868.